Why America Is
Such a Hard Sell

Why America Is Such a Hard Sell

Beyond Pride and Prejudice

Juliana Geran Pilon

ROWMAN & LITTLEFIELD PUBLISHERS, INC.
Lanham • Boulder • New York • Toronto • Plymouth, UK

ROWMAN & LITTLEFIELD PUBLISHERS, INC.

Published in the United States of America
by Rowman & Littlefield Publishers, Inc.
A wholly owned subsidiary of The Rowman & Littlefield Publishing Group, Inc.
4501 Forbes Boulevard, Suite 200, Lanham, Maryland 20706
www.rowmanlittlefield.com

Estover Road
Plymouth PL6 7PY
United Kingdom

British Library Cataloguing in Publication Information Available

Library of Congress Cataloging-in-Publication Data

Pilon, Juliana Geran.
 Why America is such a hard sell : beyond pride and prejudice / Juliana Geran Pilon.
   p. cm.
 Includes index.
 ISBN-13: 978-0-7425-5148-0 (cloth : alk. paper)
 ISBN-10: 0-7425-5148-2 (cloth : alk. paper)
 ISBN-13: 978-0-7425-5149-7 (paper : alk. paper)
 ISBN-10: 0-7425-5149-0 (paper : alk. paper)
 1. Anti-Americanism. 2. National characteristics, American. 3. Pride and
vanity—Political aspects—United States. 4. Prejudices—Political aspects—United
States. 5. United States—Foreign relations—Philosophy. 6. Diplomacy. 7. United
States—Foreign relations—2001- 8. Globalization—Political aspects—United
States. 9. Multiculturalism—United States. I. Title.

E895.P55 2007
 303.48'273009045—dc22   2006028327

Printed in the United States of America

One of the most wonderful things about *Pride and Prejudice* is the variety of voices it embodies. . . . All tensions are created and resolved through dialogue. . . . In Austen's novels, there are spaces for oppositions that do not need to eliminate each other in order to exist. There is also space—not just space but a necessity—for self-reflection and self-criticism. Such reflection is the cause of change. . . . All we needed was to read and appreciate the cacophony of voices to understand its democratic imperative.

—Azar Nafisi

We must meet our duty and convince the world that we are just friends and brave enemies.

—Thomas Jefferson

Contents

Preface: On a Personal Note

A group of elderly, retired men gathers each morning at a café. They drink their coffee and sit for hours discussing the world situation. Given the state of the world, their talks usually are depressing. One day, one of the men startles the others by announcing, "You know what? I am an optimist." The others are shocked, but then one of them notices something fishy: "Wait a minute! If you're an optimist, why do you look so worried?"

"You think it's easy to be an optimist?"

—Rabbi Joseph Telushkin, *Jewish Humor*

Me too, I'm an optimist—albeit a worried one. I worry about the fact that America is disliked by people who don't understand it; that Americans don't understand that others don't understand them; that Americans themselves don't understand others and often have no clue how to go about it—worse yet, don't even care. I worry that others do not appreciate Americans, but even more that Americans often do not appreciate themselves. Obviously, the puzzled reader has every right to wonder, like the old men from the Jewish joke, how I can still call myself an optimist. It's actually quite simple; as my grandmother would have said: "So why you should ask? Isn't America the greatest country?"

My grandmother practically always answered a question with a question, which rendered her as wise as Socrates, and thus taught me that no statement is final. I can assure the readers who are willing to worry with me, or who are at least curious about the deplorable history of U.S. public diplomacy, that by the end of these xxx pages they will at least have a better idea of what the question of the title actually means: So why *is* America such a hard sell, anyway? If it makes you all feel any better, and it certainly does me, let me tell you from the outset that America does not have to be such a hard sell, **IF**, I hasten to add—and it's a big, bold **IF**—enough of us put our minds to it and figure out what it takes.

So, now you know why I'm worried. But, I ask you: after 9/11, how could I not have written such a book?

Leo Rosten, the Jewish Ambrose Bierce, could well add another illustration to clarify the meaning of *chutzpah* in his unique dictionary, *The Joys of Yiddish*: chutzpah is when an immigrant comes to this country and, before you know it, starts telling Americans what they should do. Worse, it's when such an immigrant presumes to criticize Americans for their chutzpah. You guessed it: that's just what I am about to do in this book. But please have patience, and bear with me—at least I've done some homework. In fact, I have been preparing to write this book for roughly a lifetime, even before my family arrived in this land of milk and honey nearly half a century ago, although I didn't know it as yet. In my family, you're never too young for homework.

I grew up in postwar Romania, which means I was a Communist by default, like the other toddlers. As I grew older, I paraded on May Day along with the rest of my fellow Pioneers, enthusiastic about equality, selflessness, peace, and a day off from homework. However, as the masquerade lost its panache, the pancake makeup of Communist propaganda gradually wore off, revealing the hideous grimace of the Big Lie. Fortunately, our family left soon after I turned fourteen.

I had no way of knowing that my parents had started the process of trying to leave the country immediately after the fall of Hitler. The state soon retaliated against their act of treason, the implicit refusal to declare eternal devotion to the Workers' Paradise: my father was barred from running some kind of big office in the Ministry of Foreign Trade. Instead, he was named "planning economist" in the Ministry of Construction—an absurd position that, despite the fancy title, involved neither planning nor economics. But that did not bother him one bit, as he was able to find time to supplement the tiny salary with scientific translations from German and Hungarian. In fact, we had been extremely lucky, since besides requesting to emigrate, my father also refused to join the Communist Party, on the blatantly unproletarian grounds that he didn't want to join any parties. Talk about chutzpah! We could have all landed in jail. Then one fair day in October, the jail door opened.

I will never forget the thunderstruck look on my mother's face when the coveted little postcard arrived, requesting that we all show up at the passport office. Wow! We were going to America! I knew very little about the Cursed Capital of Capitalism, but that didn't make any difference. America was more than a country: it was a kind of forbidden dream. It was, above all, where the other half of our family resided. My mother's father and three of her siblings, who had left forty years earlier, had sent us photographs from New York and Detroit, which invariably showed them smiling, as well as, it so happens, dressed to kill. From their letters, we gathered with some astonishment that no one was telling them what to say and especially what not to say. As far as we were concerned, no way could America be a "hard" sell.

After the initial shock that nearly electrocuted us all, the news of our imminent departure filled me with exhilaration. I was ready for the adventure: capitalism, here we come! We left penniless, like all the other emigrants, forbidden to take anything besides a few personal items, and definitely no money. The abolition of property was strictly enforced, less out of ideological purity than as one last gasp of sadism and greed. It only made us more eager to start breathing the pure ether of freedom. I couldn't wait to hit the ground running.

It proved not to be quite so simple. Little did I know that soon after our arrival the Vietnam War would start heating up. Preoccupied by my new language, each new word bringing me just a little closer to the friendly folks who were now my compatriots, it took me a good while to notice the cultural spasms of my own generation. Everyone seemed to be rooting for me, apparently charmed by my Romance "accent" and exotic birthplace they didn't know existed, let alone know how to locate on a map. But no sooner had I started feeling that I was beginning to connect than I found myself speechless again.

With a posttraumatic sense of déjà vu, I watched, astonished, my geographically challenged friends screaming obscenities against their malevolent "military-industrial complex" and heard the familiar, strident denunciations of American imperialism. What was I to say to those who defended the Vietnamese people's alleged right to choose Communism? How was I to explain that no one "chooses" Communism, at least no one who knows what it means in the real world? On occasion, I tried to describe what it was like to grow up with lies, hypocrisy, and fear, but polite uncomprehending blank stares convinced me to save my breath. My greatly improved grammar notwithstanding, the audience had no idea what I was talking about, nor did they seem to wish to find out.

With time, I came to appreciate that my friends were not entirely to blame for failing to comprehend my stories. I reached a better appreciation for the reasons why they opposed the war in Vietnam. It was becoming increasingly clear that the war had not been adequately explained to them—or, for that matter, to the rest of the world. It was also obvious that American education— indeed, the culture at large—was keeping the public very much in the dark about the true nature of life beyond the Berlin Wall. I mustered the courage to talk about this to Mr. Siegel, my high school history teacher, who handed me a book by Richard Hofstadter entitled *Anti-Intellectualism in America*. It was decided then and there that I would become a teacher of philosophy. With typical youthful hubris (measurably exacerbated by a mother for whom adoring one's children was not merely a commandment but a job description), I was determined to do what I could to inspire my countrymen to appreciate ideas and their potential for good and ill.

When I emerged a decade later, after spending countless self-indulgent hours in the library, interrupted only by the receipt of an almost anticlimactic doctorate from the University of Chicago, it began to dawn on me that I had lived in a parallel world from most of my peers. As the adage has it, "If you remember the sixties, you haven't been there." With that decade uncommonly intact in my sheltered memory, I was ready to join the world once again, but I wasn't quite sure how. Just in the nick of time, my parents serendipitously suggested that the three of us return for a visit to our former home, to Romania. It was during the course of that trip, which I sought to capture in my book *Notes from the Other Side of Night*, that I saw, in stark contrast, the muzzled despair of my childhood friends juxtaposed against the comfortable ignorance of my beloved America. From that perspective, my genial giant new homeland seemed particularly oblivious both to its greatness and to its clumsiness. There just had to be some way for me to help, by putting to good use the education earned by growing up under Communism, complementing the esoteric learning acquired at my neo-Gothic Midwestern university, where I had sought the keys to the kingdom. The kingdom turned out to be a dugout in a protracted war against elusive enemies, but as far as I was concerned, fake slogans and staged May Day parades, along with the *Federalist Papers* and Aristotle's *Nicomachean Ethics*, were my boot camp. In any case, I wanted to enlist.

Life gave me more than one chance to do just that, sometimes in curiously circuitous ways, which I will divulge later in this book, when relevant. In 1980, after a couple of years of teaching followed by postgraduate studies in international affairs at the Hoover Institution on War, Revolution, and Peace, I joined the Heritage Foundation to start up the United Nations Assessment Project. My philosophical background allowed me to appreciate the ways that savvy Communist language twisters manipulated General Assembly resolutions by standing truth on its head, by creating a political culture to suit their nefarious intentions. At the same time, I was able to uncover the tactics used by Soviet agents to corrupt Third World diplomats and use the tax-exempt edifice on Turtle Bay as a massive espionage base. But what I found most astonishing and outrageous was the monumental stupidity of the United States, which allowed itself to be outmaneuvered, outwitted, and outvoted by representatives of illegitimate and unscrupulous regimes almost from the outset. It was my first exposure to the sorry state of American public diplomacy.

As the political ground began to shake in Poland in 1989 in what would soon become the earthquake that leveled the ideological foundations of the Soviet Empire, I joined the National Forum Foundation (NFF, now part of Freedom House) as executive director to help design and administer a program for Eastern European young leaders to come to the United States for three-month internships in either media, business, or government. With each magical new crack within the Iron Curtain, new waves of visiting fellows would join the initial group of Poles and Hungarians: from Czechoslovakia, Slovenia, Croatia, and, by the end of that extraordinary year, even—who would have thought it the previous Christmas?—my poor beloved Romania.

Three years later, NFF had become the largest such program in the United States, having trained more leaders from the former Soviet Bloc than any other nongovernmental organization. Not all were elected to office, or became press secretaries, or senior staff members to newly elected presidents, or members of parliament, but most did. Others started their own businesses. We lost track of a few. A handful didn't amount to very much. But the program as a whole was a resounding success, and I could see what a huge impact even a very brief encounter with America would mean to people who needed only a nudge to appreciate the power of freedom. At least in this instance, American public diplomacy was not an oxymoron after all.

My destiny's next stop was the International Foundation for Election Systems, now known as IFES, whose motto was "Making Democracy Work." During the decade I spent at IFES as director of programs, I came to appreciate the far-reaching potential of well-designed democracy projects, the effect of genuine dialogue between our local partners and the "expats"—Americans and other Westerners we employed, who learned as much as they taught. Most importantly, we witnessed the enormous amount of goodwill that such programs can generate.

But who else knew about this type of work? Certainly not the bulk of the American public, who was footing the bill; not the journalists we were talking to, in the United States and in the field; why, not even members of Congress who appropriated much of the money for such activities. In fact, we were lucky if anyone besides our own program officers in the U.S. Agency for International Development (USAID), the agency that administered most of the funds we received, read our detailed, lengthy reports, complete with "impact indicators."

It amazed me how Americans could be doing so much to help the rest of the world without the message getting out, either in this country or abroad. Wouldn't everyone be better off if it were known how well we can work together with people from other nations, how much goodwill can be—and often actually is—generated by people-to-people interactions? When such high-profile disasters as the tsunami elicit American assistance, the media sometimes do notice, and then, predictably, what follows is often well-deserved gratitude for the people of the United States. But does it have to take a tsunami?

It seems that way. Meanwhile, for a variety of complex reasons, anti-Americanism is on the rise. Admittedly, America is a particularly hard sell nowadays, as everyone is focusing on the bungled postwar reconstruction of Iraq. But this is no reason for our global activities designed to strengthen democracy, self-government, and self-reliance to go virtually unreported and unnoticed. It's not just the media's fault; the blame extends much farther. For starters, it must be appreciated that public diplomacy has to be, above all else, public.

I had already decided to write about the appalling ineptness with which we conduct this sort of communication when the president told the country that he too was beginning to think about "getting the message out." Something is definitely wrong when even the Bush administration—not known for its propensity to self-criticism—admits that nothing short of radical has to happen in the way the nation conducts public diplomacy. On March 14, 2005, the president stressed that his appointment of Karen Hughes, a trusted old friend, as head of the State Department's global communication activities, with rank of "ambassador," reflected his strongest "personal commitment to the international diplomacy that is needed in historic times." Historic times demand historic measures; Press Secretary Scott McClellan explained, "We need to look for new ways to improve our public diplomacy." To that end, nothing short of finding unprecedented "ways to revamp and reform"[1] our public diplomacy will do. *Revamp* is not a wimpy word, and these aren't wimpy times. It is high time to stop getting it wrong.

That presidential boost came none too soon, for I was still smarting from my father's reaction when I told him what I was up to. "I see. A *chachem* with a PhD in philosophy is going to give America selling tips." (Parenthetical illustrative joke: "Max was awakened from a deep sleep by his wife with this plea: 'Please close the window, Max—it's cold outside!' '*Chachem*!' sighed Max. 'And if I close the window, will it be warm outside?'")[2] "OK," said my father, "good luck to you. Or I should say, good luck to America. But tell me: why would anybody want to sell America?" At ninety-two, he still doesn't miss a beat. I had to admit, he had a point. Don't worry about "selling" America—it's the policies, stupid: just do the right thing and hope for the best. The pundits were writing a book a day about what the United States "should do," about what policies would save the world—or rather, what policies were bound not to save the world. Was it or was it not a good idea to go to war against Iraq? Is it or is it not good policy to send money to a democratically elected group in the Palestinian territories that nevertheless refuses to acknowledge the right of a neighboring UN member to exist?

You don't have to read the British empiricists, or know any Latin, to agree that *esse es percipi*—which, in rough translation, means "to be is to be perceived." Doing the right thing is just doing what is perceived to be right—politically speaking, at least. Which, of course, brings me back to public diplomacy. Why, I kept asking myself, after all the ink spilled elucidating America's role in the world, are we still so clumsy? I felt that something very obvious had been missing. Maybe we weren't closing the window because it wasn't going to make the outside any warmer.

The evidence is impossible to deny: anti-Americanism is pervasive and growing, with deadlier effects now than ever, as the technology of terror has improved along with all the tools of greater knowledge and miraculous healing. Admittedly, far too often we do resort to "hard sell" tactics with debatable wisdom. But that does not explain either the magnitude or the intensity of the rage. How can this be when America so often acts altruistically, or at worst to protect its interests, but never out of sheer greed as did the kings of old, or with sadism like the fanatical dictators of Germany, Russia, Iraq, and Iran?

Let's have it, then: what's the charge? Bottom line: Americans are invariably accused of being arrogant, whence the label "the ugly American." Americans are also thought ignorant of everything, from languages and world history to gourmet cooking. We'll gloss over the fact that McDonald's is attracting more non-American palates than you can shake a proverbial stick at. Still, there is more than a grain of truth in the charge that Americans, unwittingly or not, exude unnecessarily excessive pride and prejudice.[3]

So, I turned to—whom else?—Jane Austen, the certified ultimate authority on the subject. She was my favorite kind of pundit, both insightful and witty. Above all, however, she suffered no hypocrites. It had been Austen, after all, who had written, "Nothing is more deceitful than the appearance of humility. It is often only carelessness of opinion, and sometimes an indirect boast." Touché. Is it not the most ardent proponents of American humility, the virulent critics of American arrogance, who turn out themselves to be the most arrogant?

Ironically, I owe it to an Iranian writer and teacher of Anglo-American comparative literature, the rightfully acclaimed Azar Nafisi, whose brilliance is matched only by her warmth and compassion, for making me realize the full extent of Jane Austen's profound contemporary relevance. In my estimation, Nafisi has understood better than anyone the essence of the democratic spirit that Jane Austen presciently glorified, which also happens to be the true message of America. Writes Nafisi, "One of the most wonderful things about *Pride and Prejudice* is the variety of voices it embodies. There are so many different forms of dialogue: between several people, between two people, internal dialogue and dialogue through letters. All tensions are created and resolved through dialogue."[4]

Nafisi's luscious word "multivocality," which refers to the blend of diverse personalities and inflexions, disparate emotional and cognitive reactions to the world, and the harmonious "cacophony of voices," graphically captures that delightfully wise novel's "democratic imperative." The very same democratic imperative is what America was meant to nurture, and what it has sought to implement over the course of its history, though not always successfully—not even to itself. I am convinced that America is able to do better, but not without transcending the pride and prejudice that sabotage its intrinsic greatness. This is much harder than it may seem, for the twin worm gnawing at America's soul comes camouflaged in a variety of comely disguises that mask the self-righteousness, impatience, and miseducation that may prove our nemesis. But it must be done so that we may recapture the sublime humility of America's pure dream, not only for ourselves, but for all of God's children.

NOTES

1. Press briefing by Scott McClellan, Office of the Press Secretary, March 14, 2005, www.whitehouse.gov.

2. See Leo Rosten, *The Joys of Yiddish* (New York: Pocket Books, 1970), 62–65, for a fuller explanation of the word, with more illustrations.

3. And let's bite the bullet, folks, and admit it: boorishness. Just listen to David Sedaris—no Francophile himself—describing the experience of running into a Texan couple on a bus in Paris in *Me Talk Pretty One Day*, CD 2-32865 (New York: Time Warner Audiobooks, 2001).

4. Azar Nafisi, *Reading Lolita in Tehran: A Memoir in Books* (New York: Random House, 2003), 268.

Acknowledgments

I owe the idea for this book, and its somewhat eclectic style, to Azar Nafisi's refreshing appreciation of the contemporary relevance of Jane Austen complemented by a profound sympathy for American idealism, tempered by an understanding of its limits. While we came from opposite corners of the world, we both experienced and then fled totalitarian ideologies that deny human beings the right to dream. As I got to know Azar better, I was won over by her warmth, as is everyone whom she touches. If I needed any convincing for the proposition that civilizations need not clash, she provided it in spades.

I also wish to thank the Institute of World Politics, the unique graduate school devoted to the study of statecraft and national security where I have taught for over a decade, from the time when I was still engaged in full-time democracy-building. While "strategic" is a term woefully misused and misunderstood, both in the academy and government, IWP has never wavered from a clear grasp of its true meaning. Some of my fine colleagues offered invaluable comments; many have even taken the time to read my manuscript. Military tactician General Walter Jajko; World War II historian Marek Chodakiewicz; political warfare analyst Michael J. Waller; comparative intelligence expert Jack Dziak; American warfare specialist Jack Tierney; and our common inspiration, Institute founder and president, former national security official John Lenczowski, have all contributed critical ideas to my book.

Indispensable funding for my project was provided once again by the Earhart Foundation, which had supported my earlier book on the topic of postcommunist nationalism in Eastern Europe, more than a decade ago. I thank warmly foundation president Ingrid Gregg, and the board of directors, for their trust in my interdisciplinary approach to all issues of a humanist nature, as we were taught by our learned mentors at the University of Chicago. A special hug goes to Professor Joseph Cropsey, whose lectures on John Locke and Adam Smith inspired me as a freshman at that hallowed institution, and whom I have recently rediscovered. I only wish my first philosophy teacher and later dissertation advisor, Professor Manley Thompson, a scholar of American pragmatism, were still alive, so I might thank him in person for patiently guiding me as I tried to devour the classics, and slowing me down.

Next, I wish to thank IFES (the International Foundation for Election Systems), and especially its president, Richard Soudriette, who afforded me the opportunity, as Vice President for Programs, to help emerging democracies run elections and strengthen democratic institutions. The invaluable lessons learned at IFES made me realize not only how vastly difficult it is to try to affect other cultures, but also how exhilarating the attempt can be, as both sides emerge changed, with a better appreciation of one another and themselves.

Finally, some friends took time from their busy lives to comment on my manuscript as it evolved, among them: the ever-sunny Kevin F. F. Quigley, president of the National Peace Corps Association; humanist scientist David Greer, Assistant Dean of the Elliott School for International Affairs at George Washington University; naval security expert Larry Cosgriff, one of my best students; Sheila Weidenfeld, author of the delightful account of her stint as Betty Ford's press secretary, *First Lady's Lady*; and Lee Edwards, Heritage Foundation Senior Fellow, who despite devoting more energy than is humanly possible to raising funds for the historic Victims of Communism Memorial, still found time to encourage me to write this book, offered advice, and introduced me to Chris Anzalone, my trusted and compassionate editor at Rowman & Littlefield publishing company. Chris understood immediately the message of this book, and provided much-needed perspective through the thicket of my research. All authors should be so lucky.

Families are usually thanked at the very end because they come first, having to put up with the author on a daily basis. I am grateful to my feisty life partner, Roger Pilon, whose eloquent prose and crisp logic have always been an inspiration; to my father, Peter Geran, whose sense of humor has been a life-saver; and to my sister, Veronica Gerber, whose common sense has seen me through some tough times. My children, Danielle and Alexander, needless to say, are my special beacon. This book is written for them, as I hope and trust that they will see the American Dream inspire the rest of the world long into this century.

Why America Is Such a Hard Sell: An Overview

The verdict seems to be that America is currently a "hard sell"—meaning both hard to sell and sold too hard. The ambiguity is deliberate on my part. For, on the one hand, we are finding increasingly that our promised land looks less promising to others, at least to those not clamoring to cash in on the promise themselves. We are reportedly misunderstood, disliked, distrusted, and even hated—an ill will that appears to be affecting even some of our products, especially those identified most obtrusively as "Made in the USA." On the other hand, an antagonistic reaction to the United States is itself allegedly caused by a hard-sell approach, a Madison-Avenue-style, in-your-face public diplomacy qua marketing, which predictably misfires when local sensitivities and customs are ignored, either out of ignorance or insensitivity or both.

On occasion, the hard sell is all too conscious and flauntingly deliberate: we resort to it in frustration, overreacting to what we consider to be infuriatingly unwarranted, vicious, and even murderous anti-Americanism, which 9/11 only confirmed in spades. Arguably the hardest sell of all comes at the point of a gun, but that aspect is not within the purview of this book. By the time the United States resorts to bullets, selling, as such, is over, the marketplace of goods and ideas having closed not just for the Sabbath but for good. The whole point of any form of diplomacy, whether private or public, is to keep the store lit around the clock, both metaphorically and literally, particularly considering that it is, after all, always daytime—and another day—somewhere on the globe.

A wide variety of reasons have been offered for America's less-than-felicitous public image, such as "It's not us—it's *them*"; "We can do whatever we wish—we are the strongest," or, in another version, "Someone's gotta do it"; "We may look like an empire, but we are not—and anyway, we refuse to admit it"; "Consumerism *über alles*"; and "We have a duty to the world," to name but a few.

America in particular, and Western civilization in general, will always have enemies, but the reasons are usually far from obvious. Observed from within, one's perceptions are inevitably distorted, if only by the motion of the personal camera. Dispassionate reflection usually requires both spatial and temporal distance. Whatever America's "true" (rather than imperfectly reported or perceived) image, neither excessive self-flagellation nor complacent—let alone pugnacious—repudiation of what may well be false or distorted facsimiles constitutes a rational response to unpopularity.

To be sure, image alone must never dictate action; we should not be slaves to alleged public opinion. At the same time, action and image are by no means mutually exclusive: correct action, at least in principle, carries its own justification, assuming effective communication. Wrongheaded policies, by contrast, can be spruced up by the pancake-and-rouge of public relations only up to a point. America's leadership should obviously strive to pursue the right policies, wisely implemented after serious reflection, relying on the most accurate possible information, mindful of mirror imaging and wishful thinking. Our motives should be worthy in our own eyes, while the national interest remains uncompromised. But this is not enough; we should also, as best we can manage, strive to make our intentions understood by others. That, in a nutshell, is the ultimate goal of what some call "public diplomacy," and others "public affairs"—a predicament that the State Department, ever the champion of compromise (and, some would snicker, "obfuscation"), has papered over by creating the Bureau for Public Diplomacy and (or?) Public Affairs. Meanwhile, knee-jerk anti-Americans dismiss it as "propaganda," proceeding to mind read both the public and its leaders—all assumed guilty until proven innocent, which somehow never happens.

Spelling out official policy, even in our "tell it like it is" transparent culture, does not call for a naive truth-at-all-costs-in-all-circumstances commandment designed for scouts and saints. Sun Tzu, who wrote the first and best treatise on the art of war more than two thousand years ago, is reported to have said, "To subdue the enemy without fighting is the acme of skill."[1] But preemptive victories are not only rare; they happen to be the most difficult, especially if the enemy's morally challenged resourcefulness is underestimated. Nor is it a good idea to ignore relevant facts, notably cultural and political ones, and display arrogant impatience when things don't turn out as anticipated. In the war of perceptions, half-baked ideas never even get a chance, and clumsiness loses every time.

Self-described nation branders Simon Anholt and Jeremy Hildreth observe that "insufficient understanding of the different ways that foreign publics interpret American ideas has often bedeviled American policy and commerce overseas."[2] In spite of, or perhaps because of, our nation's multicultural pedigree, which can provide a false sense of anthropological omniscience, we have done an amazingly poor job of communicating with other peoples. It's as if we expected, whether in fact or on principle, to induce the world's cultural "pot" to emulate us by melting national peculiarities to a common pulp. We imagine to have done so successfully within our borders, in conformity with the imperative of progress. Politically speaking, the world's "flatness," hailed by Thomas Friedman in his sanguine new best seller,[3] cannot fail to inspire with its promise of impending global equality of opportunity. But a parallel premonition, if not outright endorsement, of eventual cultural leveling is rather more chilling. A flat human geography, devoid of the mountains and valleys of varied rituals, myths, and histories, is bound to be a sad place. Difference is obviously far, far harder to handle, especially in public diplomacy. Foreign publics require a different vocabulary and different lines of reasoning to present our message than does the home audience. But the challenge is not insuperable.

A challenge it is, nevertheless, proving too much for some who react excessively, either genuflecting or else capitulating before such perceptual differences. The "we are right, they are wrong" school seems to assume that cross-cultural communication is either impossible or very nearly so. At the other end of the spectrum, the reverential "we are wrong, they are right" school of public diplomacy holds that communication may only take place if one goes native. Deceptively magnanimous, based on the premise that one should believe another's eyes sooner than one's own, the latter seems more perverse than its seeming antithesis, yet both assume that one of the two parties engaging in the dialogue must be wrong.

By contrast, it is possible to hold that two parties with distinctly different perceptions can engage in dialogue while simultaneously retaining their separate identities. Even conflicting opinions may emerge unscathed in the aftermath of a seemingly insurmountable disagreement. Many divergent opinions are simply that: different. (Far from self-evident, this idea is rare even in the most tolerant of cultures, as the epidemic of political correctness glaringly testifies.) But disagreements are one thing, murderous intent another. Where do we draw the line between hostility to particular American policies, cultural artifacts, and cuisine, on the one hand, and commitment to the eradication of all American values on the other?

We Americans have traditionally put up with a great deal of verbal abuse just short of credible threats to our survival. We have a high degree of tolerance for calumny and even hate, which we supplant with quite a bit of homegrown mea culpa. We don't like the word *propaganda*, we don't feel comfortable with "political warfare," we hate to wage "psychological offensives," and for the most part we have gotten away with it, except for the fact that we've been accused of engaging in it. It seems all too plausible that America would deploy weapons of mass deception with impunity, and yet, counterintuitive as it may seem, Americans seem more comfortable defending the right to kill an enemy in self-defense than engaging in preemptive political warfare, even against sworn adversaries. As my colleague at the Institute of World Politics, Professor J. Michael Waller, is wont to say, "We'd sooner kill a man than persuade him."[4]

Even more puzzling is the inept way we present ourselves to the world, blithely assuming that familiarity breeds understanding. On the contrary, not only does it often breed contempt, but it also undermines our own self-image, to the point that we start believing the caricature that others draw of us. It is high time that we finally rose to the new challenge of rediscovering the truth about ourselves, as if our life, liberty, and even property were at stake—for indeed they are. Dubbed by some as the Fourth World War (presumably following the third—albeit undeclared—cold one), by others as the War for the Free World, and by still others as the Long (ambiguously connoting No-Near-End-in-Sight, Stay-the-Course, Certainly-No-Slam-Dunk-Operation, Too-Long, and even—dare we say it?—Endless) War,[5] we don't need to wait for Congress to declare it officially in order to know that it is as real as the national shrine at Ground Zero in central Manhattan.

The time has come for introspection: following a dose of healthy self-criticism, along with a sober, rather than merely self-congratulatory, reassessment of our formidable strengths, we must take stock of what the necessary ingredients are of a more effective global outreach strategy tailored for the twenty-first century. We can do it; we have what it takes. But we must engage in a calculated effort not to repeat at least some of the more obvious and preventable of our previous mistakes.

The first culprit on the list is pride, the most redolent and insidious of vices, so easily mistaken for daring, confidence, and optimism, as these admittedly coexist alongside the egotism and imagined grandeur that have invariably caused the downfall of the high and mighty. Since any effective remedy requires an accurate assessment of the disease, the reader who is too busy to plod through the preliminary literary and historical background and would rather just go straight to the quick-fixing "next steps" would be well advised, and humbly importuned, to bear with the rest of us. This applies equally to pride's other half, prejudice, a trait no less lacking in modesty, both intellectual and emotional, and no less dangerous. The two-faced Janus reflects ignorance and egocentrism, no matter what fancy garb they may vainly use for camouflage.

In contemporary terms, the twin handicap goes a long way to explain why America is so misunderstood, disliked, and even hated, often not for what it is but for what it is perceived to be. Our plummeting popularity is partly the result of what we ourselves have projected. The history of American self-styled "public diplomacy," which in reality seldom reached the right "publics" and even less often managed to be particularly "diplomatic," deserves no great accolades. The inauspicious demise of the United States Information Agency (USIA), absorbed near the end of the Clinton administration by the Department of State, provides ample proof of our reluctance to engage in what might be perceived as self-serving propaganda. In the final analysis, it seems that we either cannot or do not want to decide how to communicate with the world beyond our borders, at least not through an agency explicitly devoted to the task. It isn't even clear whether we have the patience it requires, let alone the tools. A plethora of commissions and councils are advising reinstating the moribund agency, seemingly more out of desperation than a conviction that much would change sufficiently to make a difference.

Meanwhile, USAID shows signs of being headed in the same direction as USIA, its current administrator, Randall Tobias, spending most of his time in Foggy Bottom after Secretary of State Condoleezza Rice appointed him undersecretary of state in charge of foreign aid. Since most of his senior policy and management staff have already schlepped their files and *tsatskes* into their new offices at State (or, rather, old ones, USAID having migrated into the Reagan Building from State less than a decade before), the handwriting on the wall seems to spell absorption by some other name. Experts, real and self-styled, inside and outside the administration, are understandably wringing their hands, blogging, and writing reports, op-eds, and even books.

The latest and most comprehensive study, released in August 2006, is the product of a high-powered task force, a coproduction of the Brookings Institute and the Center for Strategic and International Studies (CSIS). The study explores the panoply of foreign aid programs conducted by the United States, urging the creation of a new cabinet-level department based on the British model to address the current lack of coordination that characterizes U.S. development assistance. The report, unfortunately, fails to take into consideration the public diplomacy aspect of foreign aid. Moreover, it focuses exclusively on coordinating public projects without addressing the mammoth contribution of private individuals, foundations, and corporations. While no one could object to coordination as such, consolidation is not necessarily a panacea. On the contrary, it may even exacerbate problems if it results in overregulation and discontinuing different approaches to problems under the guise of avoiding duplication, and it could amount to little more than an expensive, clumsy, and overbureaucratic reorganization of the deck furniture on the tottering *Titanic* that is U.S. public diplomacy today. It certainly wouldn't hurt to learn from the private sector, and to find a more effective way of interacting with it.

That sector, of course, includes the so-called nonprofits (I urge the reader to check out the latest CEO salaries among the tax exempts to consider whether the term is not a misnomer) and also the commercial sector. Most people believe, and with good if not sufficient reason, that the main business of America is now, and has always been, business. We like to think we're really good at selling. But are we, when it comes to selling—or, more precisely, explaining—ourselves? Notwithstanding our Olympian economic performance, the answer is not particularly comforting. The verdict is in: we have trouble selling not only "Brand America" but also some of America's brands. This book will explore some of the reasons for this difficulty, and also some measures being taken by the business community to mitigate the problem with very encouraging results.

Solutions are also being sought for government-conducted public diplomacy, and are duly being offered. The recommendations that politicians like best, of course, are the kind that can be implemented within the current or, at the latest, the next fiscal year, and that make you look like you are doing something, whether or not you are indeed. Within these parameters, a report by the bipartisan Defense Science Board, released in October 2004, concluded that the Pentagon should take charge of coordinating U.S. self-promotion. Less than a year later, some parts of the plan were more or less in place, and the Pentagon is engaged in rather more public-diplomacy-type activities than it cares to admit.

The plan comes at a steep price, however, in both quality and credibility (or lack thereof), thus demonstrating once again that when the military gets into the public relations and media business, the news is mixed. Excelling at its main job of winning wars, the defense establishment should not be expected to show more finesse in public communication than do other government agencies, whether directly or through outsourcing. For a number of good reasons, notably the expectation that it should confine itself to war zones, it may show less. The resulting fallout should have surprised no one; unfriendly fire, both inside and outside the United States, has been hitting its five-sided, ill-starred target next door to Crystal City, causing unnecessary (if predictable) embarrassment of the administration.

Whatever the relative value of arguments pro and con regarding the wisdom of public relations being in any way subsidized, produced, or even coordinated by either the United States military or the State Department, global communication is now and always will be in the purview of other agencies, as well as the private sector. Therefore, if our diplomats, both official and unofficial, aren't taught how to navigate their way out of the proverbial paper bag, won't we keep missing the political (proverbial) boat? And if even our intelligence analysts are better at talking to satellites than to human beings, it should come as no surprise that we occasionally miss the low-tech indicators figuratively, and even literally, staring us in the face. The greatest power on earth should be able to do better.

It can, and in fact it does. I cite numerous examples of remarkable acts of courage, ingenuity, and generosity that ordinary Americans, whether government-sponsored, privately assisted, or on a voluntary basis, are now performing daily throughout the world. American beauty—decidedly not as portrayed by Hollywood—at once spiritual and human, is everywhere, too often left unsung and even unnoticed. Unself-conscious and genuine, the true, if generally anonymous, celebrities of our vast, multifaceted, and often exasperatingly ornery United States prove that we are what we had always been meant to be: a beacon for all mankind. This may or may not translate into high ratings in popularity contests, but it will unquestionably prove worthwhile. Indeed, it is far more likely to do so if we stop obsessing about those ratings.

The spectrum of interactions between Americans and the rest of the world is wide beyond description. Some seem more unilateral than others. When we inform, train, sell, educate, perform, or indeed liberate, in each case we seem to deliver, while others are on the receiving end. But, on closer examination, each of these activities is reciprocal. To inform, we must first be heard, and then we must be understood, but finally, we must be believed: our message has to be received both intellectually and emotionally. Our audience must be engaged, and for that, it must be both willing and able. Much the same goes for training, educating, performing, and even selling. In turn, we cannot engage in any of these activities without a strong preexisting connection. The recipient of information must matter to us, whether as a friend or as an adversary. If the latter, the information will be designed to prevent harm to ourselves in any way possible or to harm the enemy. In the absence of threat, however, we must care to know our interlocutors well enough to understand what they want and what they think, and to speak their language both literally and figuratively.

Communication is not the ideal term to describe these interactions, because of its generally verbal connotation. *Public diplomacy* is the expression that comes closest, with *public affairs* a distant second, and *marketing* the most infelicitous because of its connotation of selling a product. *Strategic diplomacy*, and even *political warfare*, a close relative of *psychological warfare*, and the less ominous *psychological operations*, are generally assumed to target primarily hostile "interlocutors." To be sure, each of these expressions has a purpose and plays a particular role, having acquired its own peculiar connotations over time. Semantic, no less than bureaucratic, overhauls, therefore, should be approached with caution: change may not only create a false sense of security, but it can prove destructive, ignoring the evolution of thought and speech patterns that have adapted in an otherwise dysfunctional political ecosystem. Nevertheless, for reasons that will become clearer through the course of this book, I propose to introduce a new term to underscore the importance of a whole new way of looking at interrelated activities currently sequestered in separate categories. That term is *strategic outreach*. Its denotation embraces not only foreign aid, educational and academic exchanges, and democracy building, but also most of what passes for public diplomacy, short of public affairs narrowly understood. Strategic outreach can be done well or badly, with or without coordination, and with or without much knowledge of those we seek to reach. "Engage in Random Acts of Kindness" is fine for a bumper sticker; it should not constitute the guiding principle of U.S. foreign assistance. Strategic outreach, specifically, differs from the ordinary kind in being deliberate and targeted. But all outreach, whether strategic or not, can miss its mark, fail in its objectives, and create more harm than good. Convinced that experience has provided some useful lessons, I offer five basic rules of strategic outreach (six, if you count the "rule" admonishing to resist inertia and actively "think out of the box").

The rules capture the need to assess the context, evaluate the challenges, and face our peculiar handicaps. For what is true of the dysfunctional intelligence apparatus applies in spades to the cacophony of official outreach efforts: each bureaucracy guards its domain jealously, fails to communicate with related agencies and bureaus, seldom cooperates with the private sector effectively, and generally misses the big picture. This is partly because that picture is never adequately articulated, as the background research required for an informed strategic vision is either untapped or unavailable, and partly because the current incentive mechanisms tend to reward caution, hesitancy, lack of imagination, and conformity.

If I were hard pressed to make so-called structural recommendations, the kind that bureaucrats prefer, I might come up with the idea of creating something like an independent entity called the American Global Outreach and Research Agency. Its task would be to promote synchronicity between the State Department's Bureau of Public Diplomacy, including the Bureau of Public Affairs and the Bureau for Educational and Cultural Affairs, and the U.S. Agency for International Development, the Peace Corps, and a wide variety of activities currently under the supervision of some fifty other government entities, notably the departments of Justice, Treasury, Labor, Interior, Energy, and, above all, Defense. But the independence of such an agency would have to be scrupulously guaranteed, as would close cooperation with the private sector.

It must be stressed that the private sector in fact provides by far the lion's share of support for foreign outreach. This is amply demonstrated in a new report by Carol C. Adelman, director of the Center for Global Prosperity at the Hudson Institute, entitled *Global Philanthropy Index 2006*. This report, the first comprehensive estimate in dollar figures of all the aid directed at the developing world, offers a glimpse into the stunning quantity and breathtaking variety of assistance. "In 2004," for example, writes Adelman, "American private giving through foundations, corporations, voluntary organizations, universities, colleges, religious organizations, and immigrants sending money to families and villages back home, totaled at least $71 billion dollars—over three and a half times U.S. government development aid."[6] America's official aid packages—little over one-half provided through USAID—in the amount of nearly $20 billion, is by far the largest in the world, with Japan ranking a distant second at $8.9 billion. U.S. government overseas development assistance, known as ODA, constitutes no less than one-fourth of the total global aid.

The putative strategic outreach agency's acronym, AGORA, would be most apt: in ancient Greece, the word literally meant "public marketplace" and referred primarily to the popular political assembly that met there. Today, our agora is surely the whole world, whether we care to admit it or not. As the saying goes, it is the worst of times, and the best of times. But I, for one, will make no such recommendation, in the expectation that an illusion of cure will only exacerbate the disease. After all, isn't this what happened with the intelligence reorganization? No one person can perform miracles, not even Ambassador John Negroponte, however well inclined he may be. The miracle required must involve many people working toward the same end. In an important sense, it involves us all; it takes nothing less than the adoption of a new paradigm, a new weltanschauung—new, at least, by contrast with the current mode of thinking, but actually deeply rooted in our history.

NOTES

1. Sun Tzu, *The Art of War* (London: Oxford University Press, 1982), 3:3.

2. Simon Anholt and Jeremy Hildreth, *Brand America: The Mother of All Brands* (London: Cyan Books, 2004), 82.

3. Thomas Friedman, *The World Is Flat: A Brief History of the Twenty-first Century* (New York: Farrar, Strauss & Giroux, 2005).

4. One exception was the period of America's Revolutionary War—understandably, since we were then in greatest danger. See J. Michael Waller, "Propaganda: The American Way," *Internationalist—a Journal of Culture and Currents* 3, no. 4 (Summer 2006).

5. For a serious assessment of this new state of alert, see Frank J. Gaffney and colleagues, eds., *War Footing: 10 Steps America Must Take to Prevail in the War for the Free World* (Annapolis, MD: Naval Institute Press, 2006).

6. Carol C. Adelman, *The Index of Global Philanthropy 2006* (Washington, DC: Hudson Institute, 2006), 14.

Introduction: America's Mixed Legacy

> I have been a selfish being all my life, in practice, though not in principle. As a child I was taught what was *right*, but I was not taught to correct my temper. I was given good principles, but left to follow them in pride and conceit. . . . I was spoilt by my parents, who though good themselves, almost taught me to be selfish and overbearing, . . . to think meanly of all the rest of the world, to *wish* at least to think meanly of their sense and worth compared with my own. Such . . . I might still have been but for you, dearest, loveliest Elizabeth! . . . By you, I was properly humbled.

So does dashing Fitzwilliam Darcy gallantly propose marriage, with heartfelt passion just short of pathos, to the clever and witty Elizabeth Bennett in the deliciously satisfying resolution to Jane Austen's jewel of a novel, which enjoyed immediate success upon publication in 1813. It barely merits mentioning that any resemblance between the romances then hugely popular with English ladies and Austen's stellar opus was purely coincidental. Her carefully crafted prose survives to this day, its delightful dialogue no less enduring than its subtle wisdom. The merciless irony of her pen deftly condemns all sycophancy, materialism, ignorance, arrogance, and betrayal with a coy and amusing lightness whose seeming effortlessness renders it that much more devastating.

Her touch is manifestly light as literary genre; it is also elusive to facile categorization. While evidently a social critic with a sense of morality (however unself-righteous), Jane Austen can hardly be called a dialectical revolutionary: the "contradictions" of her society, which she so cunningly exposes and almost imperceptibly ridicules, defy dualism. The rich may be pompous, frivolous, haughty, and, yes, prejudiced, but then again, so may the impecunious. Darcy's self-criticism, while entirely deserved, could and should have been reciprocated by Elizabeth, whose meager means do not exempt her from blame for her own pride which had blinded her with prejudice against the young man who, in proposing to her, so effusively thanks her for chastening him. Jane Austen is no more partial to the one than she is to the other, and neither is quite spared the prickle of her wry satire.

After all, the two protagonists in fact mirror one another. So does Austen scholar Mark Schorer describe the peculiarly oxymoronic symmetrical asymmetry of Darcy and Elizabeth: "By Darcy's pride, she is prejudiced. [But] it should be observed that for Americans these distinctions do not exist and for most of us they are reversed: it is Darcy who is prejudiced against a lower social order, and Elizabeth who is poor but proud in the face of his prejudice; Jane Austen did not consciously hold, even though she observed, this prejudice."[1] In other words, Darcy and Elizabeth are both proud *and* both clearly prejudiced.

And while the distinction is real, these evils are Siamese twins: prejudice presupposes the pride of assumed knowledge as against the humility of skepticism; pride, meanwhile, implies the prejudice of self-importance, of one's superiority and even infallibility. This dual malady is better known as hubris—the source of tragedy according to the ancient Greeks, the root cause of man's original sin in the Judeo-Christian tradition. Far from mere oversight or simple foible, the presumption of possessing incontrovertible—which is to say, quasi-divine—knowledge comes perilously close to irreverence, indeed blasphemy. But, for pretending to know even more than the gods by defying their decree, madness itself provides no alibi. No fire-breathing preacher she, Jane Austen's witty admonitions against hasty judgment that lacks sufficient evidence, against vanity and excessive self-regard, succeed no less effectively for the seemingly mundane themes and their bucolic setting.

However strong-minded, Darcy and Elizabeth are all too ready to admit they are wrong the moment they realize it, which makes them so singularly appealing—far more so for being flawed human beings like the rest of us. Although nothing escapes Austen's sharp eye and even sharper pen, even her most self-absorbed, pseudoeducated, and hypocritical characters possess an endearing quality, which reminds the reader of his (and no less often, her) own occasional lapses. But there is no mistaking what Austen abhors. Writes Azar Nafisi, "It is not accidental that the most unsympathetic characters in Austen's novels are those who are incapable of genuine dialogue with others. They rant. They lecture. They scold. This incapacity for true dialogue implies an incapacity for tolerance, self-reflection and empathy."[2] An insidious lack of empathy is the virulent effect of pride exacerbated by prejudice; an incapacity for true dialogue, its most dangerous curse. And no one has expressed this more elegantly than Miss Austen.

Unfortunately, many, if not most, Americans know Austen's charming novels only through their film versions, which lack the subtle narrative turns of phrase whose elegance is impossible to convey, no matter how brilliantly acted the dialogue. The literal image, moreover, undermines symbolism even more effectively than does the written word. Therefore, the idea that America itself may be afflicted with a sort of "pride" and "prejudice," much like Austen's protagonists, might seem peculiar at best. Is this a mere conceit?

Not so. The "pride" that brought so many of us here, that made our European ancestors leave their homes convinced of the need—and their own ability—to start anew, to reject the apparently immutable trajectory that life had offered them thus far, persists to this day. So does the "prejudice" that we've got it right. What is more, we are convinced—and with ample reason—that we are the future, the promise, the answer. Or, at any rate, we tacitly assume that the future will have to be conceived here, its promise not only our responsibility but our right. America is the lovely bride, her groom the world—whether the cantankerous, commitment-phobic planet knows it or not—if not now, eventually.

Granted, humor emerges from Jane Austen's satire as it never will from the inscrutable somber script of actual history. The tragicomedy of our many errors—both America's and the world's—do not qualify as funny even to the most relentlessly undaunted comic. How can we hope for a happy ending in the aftermath of September 11, given the embroilments in Iraq and Afghanistan, the interminable incendiary conflicts between Israelis and Palestinians, and the borderless crusade, sometimes translated with dubious regard for etymology as "jihad," against modernity and secularism, spelled "U-S-A"? Under these circumstances, can we realistically expect to survive another century, let alone another millennium or two? Or is the liberal-universalist dream marriage between the United States and the rest of the world, resulting in one happy globalist family, a mere mirage, while reality becomes the nightmare modestly previewed on September 11? The world may refuse to join us in blissful harmony, but it cannot bring us down in flames. We won't stand for it.

We refuse to give in to despair, and we certainly won't just stand there and take it; such an attitude would be entirely un-American. Talk-show host John Gibson of Fox Television has captured the nation's feisty mood after the cataclysmic event and the ensuing war against the regime of Saddam Hussein: "The war in Iraq put the world on notice. America will fight."[3] The sitting president seemed ideally suited to take the legendary "Don't Mess with Texas" to its logical next step. If the world decided this was a case of a cocky superpower overreaching, so be it.

Gibson captures a critical aspect of the aftershock that followed all too soon after 9/11, which surprised Americans almost as much as the event itself: "a garish parade of hatred for America, open-throttle and full steam ahead. . . . The international press decided, in virtual lockstep, that the question was not merely to hate America and Americans, but how strongly, how violently—how much."[4] America suddenly found itself not only terrorized but far more isolated than she felt she deserved. How could we not strike back? George W. Bush rose to the podium to speak for a wounded, uncomprehending nation that welcomed his feisty resolve.

By contrast, after a very short-lived outpouring of sympathy, the subsequent international response only confirmed Americans' sense of undeserved isolation, exhibiting, observes Gibson, an "off-the-charts level of venom, a scandalous parade of mistaken assumptions of Americans" due to what could only be a "purposeful refusal to understand Americans . . . incongruously coupled with a nearly constant repetition of the utter falsehood that the world knows America better than it knows itself."[5] The bottom line was that Americans simply "could not understand what was being said about them," but, whatever it was, they didn't like it one bit. All that hostility only fueled the fire of their determination to "win the war on terror" and—as they might put it in Texas—"show 'em who's boss."

It's true that the war on terror is no ordinary battle. For such a "war" to be eventually "won" depends, in the first place, on how we define "winning" in this context. It is certainly impossible to eliminate all murderous action randomly directed at civilians—Western, American, or any other nationality for that matter—for the sole purpose of sowing fear. It is also impossible to prevent people from seeking publicity for whatever reasons, whether lofty, leftist, rightist, or just plain loony. Whether we "win" what may be defined as an inchoate "war" on terror depends, too, on how we understand ourselves and the world around us, with a minimum of wishful thinking, so as to avoid threats caused by misinformation, self-deception, ignorance, and, even more often, by incompetence.

Without denying destiny its proper due, I suggest that we emulate clever Jane Austen by opting for optimism. She herself had found her inspiration in an otherwise forgettable five-volume novel entitled *Camilla*, written by the very briefly famous Fanny Burney in 1792, whose only passage worthy of survival contains the novel's clever underlying moral. It is concisely articulated by a Dr. Lyster, duly mindful of the underlying paradox: "The whole of this unfortunate business . . . has been the result of PRIDE and PREJUDICE. . . . Yet this, however, remember: if to PRIDE and PREJUDICE you owe your miseries, so wonderfully is good and evil balanced, that to PRIDE and PREJUDICE you will also owe their termination."[6]

And so it must be. In our damnation is our salvation. A hopeful conclusion, since humans are slated to inherit the handicap (divinely ordained, we must know) that doomed our first parents. Austen believed that we may yet redeem ourselves. But she knew the caveat: we have to learn how. No reminder *ex machina* is needed to convince us that it won't happen automatically. Nor is it possible to provide a simple handbook with a catchy title designed for the bestseller list—something like "Seven Steps to World Peace," published by, say, the United Nations Press.

I submit instead that to build a world that is reasonably safe for American-style freedom, for free enterprise and creativity, for both enthusiasm and spiritual reflection, we'll need to revise our strategies. Americans will have to admit that Karl von Clausewitz' pithy (if nearly always misunderstood) admonition that war is political intercourse by other means implies not only that the "other means" must both precede and follow war, but that global engagement is hard work rather than just hard sell. Peace, in a sense, is war by other means. Although read mainly by students of national security and military strategy, usually at such specialized schools as the Naval War College or the Institute of World Politics, Clausewitz had considered war as the last resort, the option that remained when all else had failed. He wisely warned, "War is the province of chance. In no other sphere of human activity must such a margin be left for this intruder. It increases the uncertainty of every circumstance and deranges the course of events."[7] Even a war that one may consider to have "won" will have unanticipated consequences that may lead to even greater harm. And given today's cataclysmic weaponry, avoiding war is obviously more critical than ever.

It is also more difficult. As Henry Kissinger has noted, unlike the situation in Europe during the nineteenth and twentieth centuries when the two most stable adversaries consisted of international systems that had the advantage of relatively uniform perceptions, "the order that is now emerging will have to be built by statesmen who represent vastly different cultures."[8] This requires an altogether new level of sophistication and knowledge. It also requires a strong commitment to diplomacy at all levels, both private and public.

And, more to the point, the job is not only never ending, but the end product is no product at all, but a state of mind. One reason why "branding America" has become exponentially harder is that we are no longer quite sure why we are failing, and even less sure of what kind of enterprise this is in the first place. Americans may well ask themselves: We know how to sell everything else, so why not our dream? Maybe the easiest answer is also the most obvious: it's because dreams cannot be sold.

Nothing less will do than a radical change in our modus operandi and way of thinking, which to many in the public diplomacy business, methinks however much they may protest otherwise, is likely to sound a little like telling Falstaff to go on a diet. But so they must; otherwise, the chances of success fall in the sorry range of slim to none.

Even recognizing that no circumstances are ever as "ordinary" as they appear in the omniscient, or at least post-scient, hindsight of history, these are particularly extraordinary circumstances. The threat of physical annihilation aside, mankind (all right, humankind) today is facing a crisis of monumental proportions. As technology races at intellectually and, even more important, emotionally astronomical speeds, human beings are ill equipped to catch their spiritual breath. Sensually overstimulated but spiritually undernourished, we are no longer convinced that we are on the right path, let alone able to convince everyone else to follow. It is true that a record number of Americans attend religious services. But how many find the inner peace that modernity is unwittingly sabotaging with escalating, neosatanic effectiveness? As the search for the Holy Grail that we each choose to pursue becomes harder to define as we rush to program ourselves out of magic and mystery, we are overcome with doubt. Is it truly holy, and if so, why does it seem increasingly more elusive?

In the United States, the grail is sometimes known as "the American Dream." It is the archetypal dream we have all pursued, in one way or another. In America, most of us like to tout that dream as quintessentially modern, defining it as the embodiment of liberty, its crowning glory, whose very desirability yet precarious attainability, perhaps as often as its perceived decadence and moral insufficiency, leads some to murderous rage. That phenomenon, known as "transnational terrorism," is now the tradecraft of choice for Islamist extremists whose reach is global, elusive, and apocalyptic. Ignoring it is not an option, but neither is capitulation. We obviously cannot cease dreaming, or continuing to seek others to join us. What, then, is to be done? If there is any silver lining to the ongoing, unanticipated, undeclared Fourth World War, which pits civilization against chaos, it is the fact that Americans have to realize that they can no longer put off growing up and learning how to communicate with the rest of the world more effectively. We cannot afford to be either clumsy, rosy eyed, or disingenuous.

Without doubt, America will never persuade its hardcore enemies to abandon their fury. Accordingly, the well-meaning but hopelessly naive advisors, some academically anointed, or inclined, who recommend a calm, rational, compassionate, or diplomatic "outreach" to the unconvertible are at best kidding themselves. At worst, they are endangering us all, insofar as they minimize the need for hard-nosed and effective statecraft that includes not only military preparedness but—indeed, especially—political warfare. Survival aside, we must also rearticulate, at the risk of sounding somewhat oxymoronic, the *ideals* of the United States of America in *realistic* terms, devoid of feel-good pathos, but we must also not succumb to self-defeating, pre-emptively capitulating cynicism.

Freedom is too ambiguous, and is therefore too vacuous a word, although it comes closest. But even if words are critical—and minimizing their impact is no proof of skill—they are never sufficient. It will take nothing less than setting education back on track, starting in kindergarten and on to the highest level of graduate training, reversing the downward trend that alarmed University of Chicago professor Allan Bloom two decades ago when he warned that the American mind was fast closing, before that mind is shut tight. It will take a serious foreign policy that somehow finds a way to transcend the hopelessly self-defeating partisanship exacerbated by America's majoritarian, FPTP (first-past-the-post) electoral system, a foreign policy based on a far more accurate appreciation of international public opinion and guided by long-term strategic planning that takes into account the challenges of a global economy and transnational communication. In a word, the United States must stop watching the world with eyes wide shut. It must defend itself against attack while at the same time embracing the historic opportunity to help others join us on the plodding, rocky road to "self-determination," a goal to which the United Nations has paid lots of lip service but precious little heed.

America will not, however, prevail through the hard sell, call it "branding" or "strategic marketing" (the terms most en vogue lately), or, emulating Lenin and his successors, "propaganda." Nor will we succeed in converting the world to our way of thinking at the point of a gun—recognizing, of course, that guns must remain the weapon of choice in most life-and-death situations.[9] Conversely, "soft power" is misleading insofar as it suggests any sort of conciliation or appeasement, or if it naively assumes that we can triumph over mortal threats simply by "playing nice," by seeking to "win hearts and minds" as if the international stage were a popularity contest. Any approach that would require compromising our very essence as a people in order to please our enemies, one that would put the world's "consumers" in charge of the "brand," is doomed from the start.

Diplomacy, information dissemination, intelligence activities, dialogue, and cooperation need not imply lack of resolve or a diminished commitment to truth. We must continue our engagement through strategic foreign assistance and pursue mutually beneficial educational, cultural, commercial, and other types of exchanges with other countries. Understanding others does not imply moral relativism any more than helping others requires harming ourselves.

The good news is that we are already doing a great deal that is right, though it's a rather well-kept secret. The reasons vary widely: in many cases it is due to genuine modesty and a sense that tooting our own horn would be unseemly; sometimes it's because we proudly—all right, arrogantly—presume that everybody already knows what we do, or because we don't seem to care enough whether others like us or not. On the flip side, we do a lot of things wrong, either unwittingly or carelessly, for all to see: our headline-grabbing media are happy to oblige, ready to expose whomever, at the drop of a leak.

Among the more embarrassing reasons for our occasional Inspector Clouseau–style operational mishaps is, unhappily, sheer incompetence. Even our best, most elaborately trained professionals tend to enroll in quasi-technocratic graduate programs that do little to instill the kind of broad-based, wisdom-enhancing learning that has traditionally produced the worldliness demanded of statesmanship and may promote effective communication across cultures. Ignorance thus leads to prejudice: we judge either by what we think we know or, absent genuine knowledge, by taking at face value the opinions of those who somehow manage to convince us that they know better.

At the start of the twenty-first century, however, America is powerful enough to be able to afford a little less ignorance and prejudice toward the rest of the world, to dispense with unwarranted pride, and to believe in the possibility of long-term strategic thinking. As Simon Anholt and Jeremy Hildreth state in their clever, eye-catching little book, *Brand America*, "Americans have a habit of mistaking America for the world, and so lose out on many opportunities to present their case to important overseas audiences far faster, more simply, more accurately and more successfully, just because they haven't appreciated the need to *translate*"[10] (by which they don't mean merely finding foreign words to replace the American English).

At the same time, no country, not even America, is sufficiently powerful and PR sensitive to imagine that it can engage in hard sell without either figuring out what exactly it is selling, or why. We should stop thinking of it as "selling" in the first place. It makes it look like once it's done, the job is over—no refunds, no returns. Don't we wish it were that easy.

NOTES

1. Jane Austen, *Pride and Prejudice*, with an introduction by Mark Schorer (Boston: Houghton Mifflin Company, 1956), xii.

2. Azar Nafisi, *Reading Lolita in Tehran* (New York: Random House, 2003), 268.

3. John Gibson, *Hating America: The New World Sport* (New York: HarperCollins, 2004), 13.

4. Gibson, *Hating America*, 13.

5. Gibson, *Hating America*, 12.

6. Fanny Burney, *Camilla* (Oxford: Oxford University Press, 1999).

7. See Karl von Clausewitz, *War, Politics and Power*, trans. Edward M. Collins (Washington, DC: Regnery, 1962), part 3.

8. Henry Kissinger, *Diplomacy* (New York: Simon & Schuster, 1994), 27.

9. "Pacifism" is either the euphemism of the coward, the wishful thinking of the isolationist, or the dreamy delusion of the naive. For an excellent discussion of the need for appreciating the value of being feared first and loved later, see Michael A. Ledeen, *Machiavelli on Modern Leadership: Why Machiavelli's Iron Rules Are as Timely and Important Today as Five Centuries Ago* (New York: St. Martin's Press, 1999).

10. Simon Anholt and Jeremy Hildreth, *Brand America: The Mother of All Brands* (London: Cyan Books, 2004), 82.

Part I

WHY AMERICA IS
SUCH A HARD SELL

Chapter One

How Can You Tell?

I am willing to love all mankind, except an American.

—Samuel Johnson

Why even "sell" America at all, when it really should sell itself? Isn't it obvious that we are living comfortably nestled between two enormous oceans in the best of all possible worlds? Were it not for selfish tyrants who prevent their peoples from living like us, wouldn't everyone follow readily in our footsteps? Once freed, doesn't everyone with half a brain catch the same train to progress, whistling Yankee-Doodle all the way to the bank, pursuing happiness, and fulfilling the dream? George W. Bush, speaking for the electoral majority that returned him to office in 2004, along with Republican senators, congressmen, and governors, in what amounted to a national mandate, seems to echo this widespread sentiment. People everywhere want "freedom," President George W. Bush has been repeatedly telling the world, with genuine sincerity.

Both Vice President Dick Cheney and former Defense Secretary Donald Rumsfeld, to mention but the principal architects of the Iraq war of 2003, evidently agreed. This may have been the main reason for the unanticipated complications (arguably, morass) that followed the rapid military victory. Council on Foreign Relations fellow David Phillips is undoubtedly correct when he credits Ahmad Chalabi's success in persuading some of the brightest members of this administration that "Iraqis were practically begging to be invaded," and that "after liberation, the country could be run on the cheap." The coincidence between what they were predisposed to believe and what Chalabi was telling them evidently doomed them to gullibility.[1]

Americans seem to assume that enslaved people need only look to us to find out what freedom means. We are convinced that most of them would tell us, if they were free to do so, how much they wish we could help them share in that freedom. This president has pledged his support, in keeping with an enlightened national interest, which assumes that what's good for the world is also good for America. However much ridiculed by the more supercilious of his opponents, George W. Bush is only the latest president to articulate this common American perception. After all, the tautologically manifest merits of American-style democracy have enjoyed axiomatic status among the nation's most distinguished, academically anointed foreign policy experts.

Consider, for example, the reaction after the fall of the Soviet Bloc. When Francis Fukuyama announced in 1989 that "the End of History" had arrived at last, for reasons he attributed to Hegel-disciple-turned-Eurobureaucrat Alexander Kojeve, the conservative journal *The National Interest* could barely print enough extra copies of his bold prophecy fast enough. Undaunted by the little-known Frenchman's premature announcement of that momentous event more than half a century too soon, the economic determinists who hailed Fukuyama's "Mission Accomplished" victory cry couldn't contain their joy. It all seemed like the proper climax for the Reagan Era, even more exhilarating than a Hollywood ending, if slightly more improbable.

The success inspired Fukuyama's highly popular subsequent book, published in 1992, even more boldly titled *The End of History and the Last Man*. While *New York Times* columnist Thomas Friedman gallantly blames the catchy title for implying more finality to this triumph than does the book itself, he commends Fukuyama for the accurate insight that liberalism and free-market capitalism had proved to be "the most effective way to organize society."[2] It is certainly true that Fukuyama cannot be faulted for capitalizing on the need of the American public—sound-bite conditioned, optimism addicted, and pundit parroting—to latch on to "a single catchy thought, 'The One Big Thing,' the central moving part, the essential motor that would drive international affairs in the post-Cold War world."[3] To paraphrase T. S. Elliott, modern man cannot bear too much reality—or, at any rate, he certainly has little tolerance for complexity.

To the profound disappointment of Americans looking for a new excuse to continue basking in blissful ignorance of history, the latter's vaunted demise resembled the original announcement of Mark Twain's death: vastly exaggerated. The Cold War–era Manichean view of the world, so simple in its dialectical symmetry, which had stood us well for half a century or more, now lay dismally shattered, with no similarly facile yin-yang-like model to replace it.

Figuring it all out was left to a crew of ill-suited experts: amiable ambassadors, some of whose credentials consisted of little more than handsome political contributions that purchased their pivotal posts, usually barricaded behind terrorist- and information-proof citadels; underpaid and overworked staffers of almost-constantly campaigning members of the House and Senate foreign affairs committees, whose constituencies were far more likely to read the sports than the world affairs section of their skimpy home newspapers; and presidents whose cabinet members were no less baffled by the rapid implosion of Communism than was everybody else. No wonder America's foreign policy floundered.

The public had hoped for a New World Order, a quick fix, a ready answer. Alas, all they got for their money was intellectual indigestion and a premonition of what Robert Kaplan dubbed "the Coming Anarchy."[4] The book's subtitle, "Shattering the Dreams of the Post Cold War," spoke volumes about the malaise that defined the 1990s: the dreams of normalcy, the expectation that we could all get back to business, never mind history or ideology or whatever, had been just plain shattered. So was the black-and-white canvas of international affairs, as difficult conflicts all over the darn map resisted being squeezed into catchy, headline-friendly antinomies. How to sort out military coups alternating with pseudoelections littering the African continent? What to do with the Russian-speaking post-Soviet Muslim "stans" led by cleverly or not-so-cleverly repackaged ex-Communists, busy carving out legitimizing national identities (out of whole cloth, if necessary) in Central Asia? Who were the good guys in Latin American militarist quasi-democracies oscillating among drug lords, Marxists, and assorted demagogues? This looked nothing like the kind of multiple-choice world favored by the foreign-affairs-challenged American consumer.

As Marxist-Leninism lay moribund throughout the former Soviet Bloc, the lame public diplomacy for which we had long been chastised, if not outright ridiculed, was already headed for what looked like a sure meltdown. Much as we had anxiously, and hopefully, awaited and prayed for the Evil Empire's day of reckoning, once it collapsed under the weight of its self-contradictions, we proved ill prepared to lead the world as the sole superpower. We thought that all we had to do was, well, be ourselves, which is to say we were caught tongue-tied, unaware that we were even supposed to untie it. In a way, it was just as well, since the inmates inside the Workers' "Paradise" had had it with words. But it wasn't about words. It was about "the vision thing," as our then-president so very aptly put it. We had underestimated the price of limelight. Man, did we ever.

ANTI-AMERICANISM ON THE RISE

> For some reason or other, the European has rarely been able to see America except in caricature.
>
> —J. R. Lowell

We call it "anti-Americanism," and while it is hardly new, it now seems to be everywhere. At first blush, it seems utterly paradoxical, though eminently explicable once the blush wears off. In parts of Western Europe, they never quite forgave us for helping them recover from World War II. Eastern Europe, with a little more justification, blames us for having sold them to the Soviets in the first place, and then failing to save them. Finally, after they removed their own shackles, they held us responsible for not delivering the prosperity that they assumed to be synonymous with capitalism. They felt more or less entitled to this prosperity after living quashed under the Soviet boot, like irksome insects, for some half a century—underestimating how entrenched their arthropodal legacy had become. Still, compared with its Western counterpart, Eastern Europe is a friend.

Things are a lot worse in Africa, where corrupt and mendacious officials conveniently blame us for everything from the poverty spawned by kleptocracy to HIV/AIDS, while their subjects blame us for propping up those officials with perpetually renewed loans from international banking institutions and "humanitarian assistance" that end up in precisely the wrong pockets. As for Asia, the post-Communist totalitarians in charge of the "People's" Republic of China position their agents throughout the United States to steal whatever technology they can get their hands on, while North Korea alternately threatens us with atomic obliteration and deigns to accept our food. Both continue to regard us with open suspicion, however divergent their tactics, as the only remaining "hegemon," a term the Chinese have done a great deal to turn into an unqualified pejorative, an accusation at least as scathing as "tyrant," if not more so.

It has not helped that Americans expected the demise of the Soviet Union to lead almost miraculously to a "perpetual peace" that even the ivory-towering theoretician Immanuel Kant, who wrote a pamphlet with that title in 1793, thought improbable at best. It took the chutzpah of a Jew named Marx to turn St. Augustine on his head by proclaiming not only that the Heavenly City of Absolute Peace is to be established on earth and only on earth, but that it would happen inevitably, and—yes—soon.[5] (It is impossible to resist imagining how differently history would have turned out had he been blessed with even an iota of his vaudevillian namesakes' sense of humor.)

With dialectically materialist certainty, according to Marx the Deadly Serious, Nirvana was scheduled to bless humanity after the international proletariat, guided by their historically anointed Communist vanguard, united to establish the dictatorship of the propertyless, exchanging their heavy chains for virtual infallibility and virtuous selflessness. Conflict was to evaporate along with law, statehood, and greed; so would history end, not with a whimper but with a class-obliterating bang, like a bad dream. A century and a half later, the free-market determinists, who eerily echoed Marx, similarly declared the globe essentially safe for our—the American—dream. Accordingly, ready or not, here we came, and we could see no reason why everyone else wouldn't be ready and set to go for it.

They weren't. Already in June 2003, a report by an Independent Task Force of the Council on Foreign Relations (CFR) sounded the diplomatic equivalent of alarm bells louder than ambulance sirens. The carefully understated conclusion was:

> The United States has a growing problem. Public opinion polls echo what is seen in foreign editorials and headlines, legislative debate, and reports of personal and professional meetings. Anti-Americanism is a regular feature of both mass and elite opinion around the world. A poll by the *Times* of London, taken just before the war in Iraq, found respondents split evenly over who posed a greater threat to world peace, U.S. president George W. Bush or then Iraqi leader Saddam Hussein. At the same time, European antiwar protests drew millions, and several national leaders ran successfully on anti-American platforms.[6]

The task force pressed the point with urgency bordering on alarm: "Americans at home and abroad face an increased risk of direct attack from individuals and from small groups that now wield more destructive power. The amount of discontent in the world bears a direct relationship to the amount of danger Americans face." CFR has since sponsored studies and lectures on anti-Americanism, hoping both to better understand the phenomenon and to come up with constructive recommendations. Other universities and private-sector research initiatives have followed suit.

But things have gotten, if anything, even worse. The fascinating new study by Andrew Kohut and Bruce Stokes of the Pew Research Center, ominously entitled *American against the World: How We Are Different and Why We Are Disliked*,[7] illustrates the growing, widespread hostility to the United States with solid survey results gathered from ninety-one thousand respondents in fifty nations—at any rate, as solid as survey results can be expected to get. Almost three-quarters of all non-Americans polled say that the world would be improved if America faced a rival military power. Far more disturbing, about half the citizens of Lebanon, Jordan, and Morocco think that suicide attacks on Americans in Iraq are justified.

It is not necessary to posit, as does Harvard professor Samuel Huntington in his stimulating, if simplistic, and much-celebrated book *The Clash of Civilizations and the Remaking of World Order*, "the ubiquity of conflict." It is not necessary to agree with his flat-out, absurdly apodictic declaration that "it is human to hate" because "for self-definition and motivation people need enemies."[8] Suffice it to note that humans are much more prone than any other carnivorous species to kill for self-preservation and food, in the absence of any provocation, and even for what appears to be the fun of it.[9]

The particular manifestations of human aggression, however, depend on many factors. And while some forms of hatred are seemingly unrelated, others come in identifiable clusters. It is impossible to understand anti-Americanism without relating it to another type of phobia, namely anti-Semitism, particularly since the establishment of the state of Israel in 1948. It is no accident that the most virulent, most dangerous anti-Americanism is found among radical Islamicists, mainly—though, to be sure, not exclusively—Arab ones. The villain is identified not only as the U.S. government but also the people, the society itself. For this reason, the fact that the radicals' weapon of choice, the suicide bomb, kills ordinary citizens bothers them not at all. The extremists' targets are not mere policies but human beings and their beliefs.

While many extremist Muslims agree with Iran's current president that the Holocaust was little more than a well-staged, if a bit outlandish, case of American/Zionist disinformation, others decry that Hitler didn't finish the job.[10] But, increasingly, anti-Semitism is becoming linked with anti-Americanism, and increasingly from the Left. Richard Reid, better known as "the shoe bomber," who attempted to blow up an Air France plane bound from Paris to Florida exactly one year after 9/11, told his interrogators that he had formed his plan after a visit to Jerusalem, where he claims to have seen Jews "with guns" inside the al-Aqsa Mosque. When asked why he did not attack Israel directly, he responded, "Without America, there would be no Israel."[11]

America and Israel have become so indelibly identified in the radical Muslim mind that it's as if the alliance were a case of quasi-Siamese twinship. For example, a survey conducted by the Pew Center for Public Opinion released in July 2005 found that anti-Semitism is stronger than ever throughout the Arab world. This finding is consistent with many earlier polls, leading some to conclude that anti-Americanism would diminish, if not outright evaporate, were the United States to just stop supporting Israel. The conviction that the American alliance with Israel is contrary to our interests is by no means limited to Arabs and assorted foes of Israel whose prejudices come in various shapes and sizes. But "anti-isms" in general have little to do with policies and everything to do with deep-seated hostilities, some directed at oneself.

Anti-Semitism and anti-Americanism may not seem entirely parallel, yet the two concepts share a great deal. Both involve hostility directed at a group of people characterized by certain beliefs within a political, cultural, and economic context that may be loosely identified as capitalism, mercantilism, or imperialism.[12] Brandeis University professor Earl Raab noted that soon after September 11, 2001, an old form of anti-Semitism was increasingly coupled with anti-Americanism, and he observes a similar internal logic of "prejudice against America [that] illuminates and promulgates a similar prejudice against Israel, with or without an initial anti-Semitism."[13] Speaking in 2004 in Jerusalem, former deputy prime minister of Sweden Per Ahlmark was also struck by the growing impression that "America wants to dominate the world, exactly the allegations made in traditional anti-Semitic rhetoric about the Jews. . . . And suddenly these ideas are reflected in dramatic and alarming European opinion polls claiming that Israel and the United States are the most dangerous threats to world peace." Going on to cite Hebrew University Professor Alvin Rosenfeld's pamphlet published by the American Jewish Committee, which confirmed how extreme anti-Americanism and anti-Israelism are merging, Ahlmark mentions the peace poster displayed in European antiwar rallies which reads, "Hitler Had Two Sons: Bush and Sharon."[14]

Indeed, in 1993, after the first World Trade Center bombing by the nascent al-Qaeda organization, one of the terrorists, Abdul Rahman Yasin, stated that the initial goal of the plotters was to blow up Jewish neighborhoods in Brooklyn, but later the final target was selected because the "majority of the people who work in the World Trade Center are Jews."[15] When the planning recommenced, five years later, Lawrence Wright disclosed in an article published by *The New Yorker* that Osama bin Laden's chief theoretician, Ayman al-Zawahiri, had commissioned a study on the Jewish influence in America, "which led the recently constituted International Islamic Front for Jihad against Jews and Crusaders to place the territory of the United States within its sights."[16]

More recently, Josef Joffe, publisher and editor of the German weekly *Die Zeit*, has diagnosed anti-Americanism as a "derivative" form of anti-Semitism, detecting both structural and psychological similarities. The linkage of America the Great Satan with Israel the Little Satan is nothing new in the Islamic world, where it has been condemned for at least three decades. The change following September 11, observes Joffe, is that "the pairing of the two 'Satans' is no longer just an Islamic affair."[17] In his brilliant new book, *Überpower: The Imperial Temptation of America*, he points out that a key aspect of anti-ism as such, besides demonization, is conspiracy: where anti-Americanism most obviously intersects and overlaps with anti-Semitism is in the obsessive belief that "the United States seeks domination over the rest of the world, which is also the theme of the anti-Jewish Protocols of the Elders of Zion, recently revived throughout the Arab world, as well as in Japan, among other countries."[18]

It should come as no surprise that the same Jew who predicted the end of history also penned the most potent anti-Semitic diatribe in the nineteenth century. Karl Marx[19] blasted Judaism for having secularized its own deity, transforming it into the god of exchange and commerce. In other words, he

accuses Judaism of having become Americanized. If "the imaginary nationality of the Jew is the nationality of the merchant, of the money man in general," as Marx put it, one can infer that the nationality of "America" is the embodiment of Judaic commercialism. For Marx, the melting pot beyond the
Atlantic represents the cauldron of hell that swallows the utopian Atlantis. By
the same token, Osama bin Laden's Satan-worshiping enemies bear an uncanny resemblance to Marx's capitalists. The servant of Allah and the champion of atheism make mighty strange but undeniable bedfellows.

SOME AMERICAN PRODUCTS
ARE GETTING HARDER TO SELL

Global consumers have spoken: They're not feeling any love for American
brands.

—New York (CNN/Money), August 12, 2005

Evidence is growing that American corporations are also facing serious challenges from an upsurge of anti-Americanism. Even *Forbes* seems worried: the
bottom line is that the bottom line of some American companies may not be
quite as profitable as it used to be. While in the short term there is probably
no reason to panic, caution is very much in order. Whether it's because America gives the impression that "it can throw its weight around at will" now that
it remains the sole world power, or because anti-Americanism is itself "an expression of hubris among the rest of the world" whose pride is hurt because
it "is now less important to America than America is to it," businesses are
well advised to watch out. Specifically, "consumer brands that portray themselves as slices of Americana may need to distance themselves"[20] from their
nation—a sad conclusion, but hard to dismiss and ignore.

Attuned to the challenge, particularly since the start of the Iraq war in March
2003 and the accompanying inaction by those putatively in charge of public
diplomacy, the business community created an organization designed to both
analyze and seek effective responses to the situation. Business for Diplomatic
Action (BDA) was deliberately set up to take the public diplomacy bull by its
horns before it did even more damage to the corporations' bottom line. Or, as
BDA president and chairman of the advertising group DDB Worldwide, Keith
Reinhart, told the *Financial Times* on August 2, 2005, "Right now the U.S.
government is not a credible messenger." The BDA had come to the conclusion, therefore, that the private sector itself has to take the initiative and "must
work to build bridges of understanding and co-operation and respect through
business-to-business activities."[21] The BDA's well-designed website offers

useful links to articles and other sites that focus on the problems of the public diplomacy dimension of America's commercial predicament.

In recognition of the elementary fact that conducting the proper research is the logical prerequisite for designing a winning strategy, BDA commissioned Zogby International to produce a "Report on Corporate and Foreign Policy," which it completed in October 2005. A set of expert interviews with a select group of heavy hitters—several senior executives from "some of the most iconic American brands," together with a few of the top "thought leaders" in the domain of public diplomacy—has since been published.[22]

The decision to produce this report was prompted by the fact that a (very) brief period of sympathy for America after 9/11 (note the banner "WE ARE ALL AMERICANS") was followed by quite a backlash—a fact that most Americans failed to realize. On November 21, 2004, Fox News aired a program called *Breaking Point: Hating America*, designed to underscore that very fact. Fairleigh Dickinson University professor Michael B. Goodman summarizes the four dominant features of global perception that translate into anti-Americanism. First, there is a feeling that American companies exploit other countries or "take more than they give." Second, American brands tend to "enhance thinking and behavior that clash with local customs or cultural or religious norms." This displays the third feature, "gross insensitivity and arrogance," demonstrated in the failure to use local language and "the belief that Americans want everyone to be like them." Most critical, the fourth feature is the perception that "for Americans money is more important than people," or "hyperconsumerism."[23]

The business community is not, and does not wish to be, in the business of arguing whether the perceptions are accurate or not, but it has to face the fact that brands, even more than almost everything else, are all about perceptions; hence, the marketer's job is to manage them as best he can. It is important, therefore, to assess the nature of the problem, the magnitude of its impact, and possible approaches to a solution. The Zogby Report concludes that rising anti-American sentiment is widespread: on a scale of one to five (with one representing "no" threat and five being "extreme"), the average ranking by corporate and thought leaders was about 3.5. Many reported experiencing it personally, in many regions of the world.

That threat is measured not only in declining sales but in the increased cost of security, described sometimes as "enormous." Nor is this true only or even primarily in Middle Eastern countries. Mike Eskew, chairman and CEO of United Parcel Service, told interviewer John Zogby that "security issues are pretty much paramount throughout the world." One way that UPS deals with the problem is to distance itself from its American origin: "We don't want to be viewed as an American company abroad," says Eskew. "We have approximately 40,000 global managers—39,996 of which [*sic*] are non-U.S. citizens."[24]

While most business leaders believe that the main (if not the only) culprit is U.S. foreign policy, one of the (unnamed) thought leaders interviewed by Zogby observes that "business can have an effect on anti-American sentiment," and this person categorically rejects Eskew's approach as feeding that very sentiment. On the contrary, "American companies should not avoid the connection with being American. People around the world are buying into a lifestyle and ideology that is American and to try to disassociate would be damaging."[25]

If hiding the American pedigree is reminiscent of a gorilla trying to look invisible behind a twig, the best advice is to reach out to the local communities. Says one corporation executive, "High profile American companies will always be seen as American, thus they may be sure to cooperate with the local government. They can be models for good Americans." Admittedly, that does assume that the local government is worthy of such cooperation—a tall assumption in far too many cases. But it's a start.

NOTES

1. David L. Phillips, *Losing Iraq: Inside the Postwar Reconstruction Fiasco* (New York: Westview Press, 2005), 72.

2. Thomas Friedman, *The Lexus and the Olive Tree* (New York: Anchor Books, 2000), xxi.

3. Friedman, *The Lexus*, xxi.

4. Robert D. Kaplan, *The Coming Anarchy: Shattering the Dreams of the Post Cold War* (New York: Vintage Books, 2000). The original article "The Coming Anarchy," which is included in this book, was published in 1994 by the *Atlantic Monthly*.

5. Karl Marx and Friedrich Engels urged workers throughout the world in 1848 to unite and overthrow the bourgeoisie. See "Manifesto of the Communist Party," in Lewis S. Feuer, ed., *Basic Writings on Politics and Philosophy: Karl Marx and Friedrich Engels* (Garden City, NY: Anchor Books, 1959), 1–41.

6. Council on Foreign Relations, *Finding America's Voice: A Strategy for Reinvigorating U.S. Public Diplomacy*, report of an Independent Task Force, June 2003, 1.

7. Andrew Kohut and Bruce Stokes, *America against the World: How We Are Different and Why We Are Disliked* (New York: Times Books, 2006).

8. Samuel Huntington, *The Clash of Civilizations and the Remaking of World Order* (New York: Simon & Schuster, 1997), 130.

9. One of the most brilliant anthropological analyses of the human propensity for violent conflict remains John Keegan's *A History of Warfare* (New York: Vintage Books, 1994).

10. See Gabriel Schoenfeld, *The Return of Anti-Semitism* (San Francisco: Encounter Books, 2004), chap. 2.

11. Associated Press, "Shoe Bomb Suspect Says He Was Targeting Enemies of Islam, Court Documents Say," September 12, 2002.

12. For an in-depth analysis of this phenomenon, see Martin Tolchin and Susan J. Tolchin, *A World Ignited: How Apostles of Ethnic, Religious, and Racial Hatred Torch the Globe* (Lanham, MD: Rowman & Littlefield, 2006).

13. Earl Raab, "Antisemitism, Anti-Israelism, Anti-Americanism," *Judaism*, Fall 2002, www.cinnibgriybdcinnibsebse.irg.firyns.kifuversuib/index.php/t16004.html.

14. Per Ahlmark, "Anti-Semitism and Anti-Americanism: Dangerous Links," speech delivered at the Third Plenary Session of the Global Forum against Anti-Semitism, October 27, 2004, Jerusalem, Israel.

15. Leslie Stahl interview with Ramzi Ahmed Yousef, on *60 Minutes*, June 2, 2002.

16. Schoenfeld, *The Return of Anti-Semitism*, 54; the article by Lawrence Wright, "The Man Behind Bin Laden," was published in *The New Yorker* on September 16, 2002.

17. Josef Joffe, "Nations We Love to Hate: Israel, America and the New Anti-semitism," article based on a lecture delivered at the Center for German Studies at Ben Gurion University, Spring 2004.

18. Josef Joffe, *Überpower: The Imperial Temptation of America* (New York: W. W. Norton, 2006), 76.

19. One thesis, propagated most famously by Karl Marx in one of his earliest essays entitled "On the Jewish Question," argues that capitalism and Judaism are identical in their quasi-religious worship of money. "Money is the jealous God of Israel before whom no other god may stand," declared the young German-Jewish revolutionary in 1843. "Money debases all the gods of many and turns them into commodities. Money is the universal, self-constituted value of all things. It has therefore robbed the whole world, human as well as natural, of its own values." See David McClellan, ed., *Karl Marx: Selected Writings* (Oxford: Oxford University Press, 1977), 60.

20. Paul Maidment, "Commentary—Is Brand America in Trouble?" *Forbesonline*, September 21, 2005, www.Forbes.com.

21. Kevin Allison, "World Turning Its Back on Brand America," *Financial Times/UK*, August 2, 2005.

22. "Report on Corporate and Foreign Policy: Expert Interviews," Zogby International, Fall 2005; www.businessfordiplomaticaction.org/learn/articles/zogbyglobal-listenining05.doc.

23. Michael B. Goodman, "Restoring Trust in American Business: The Struggle to Change Perception," *Journal of Business Strategy* 26, no. 4 (2005): 32.

24. Zogby International, "Report on Corporate and Foreign Policy: Expert Interviews," Fall 2005, 11.

25. Zogby International, "Report on Corporate and Foreign Policy," 11.

Chapter Two

It's Them, Not Us

Oh mother of a mighty race,
Yet lovely in thy youthful grace!
The elder dames, thy haughty peers,
Admire and hate thy blooming years,
With words of shame
And taunts of scorn they join thy name.

—William Jennings Bryan

We are not a homogeneous nation but a highly diverse society—and proud of it. Some people don't think our image has much to do with the way we communicate, but merely reflects our policies and our behavior. Others consider anti-Americanism to be as old as the nation, its latest upsurge no less inevitable, though perhaps more worrisome in light of the much greater danger of terrorism in the nuclear age. Liberals deplore America's post–Cold War preeminence in the economic and military spheres, while still others, both conservatives and liberals, for entirely divergent reasons, despair at the global appeal of a popular culture that keeps reaching increasingly higher (or is it lower?) levels of vulgarity, seemingly ad infinitum.

Some self-styled American intellectuals, afraid perhaps that being described by an apparent oxymoron may prove warranted, loudly lament their predicament as culturally disenfranchised subjects in the self-elected dictatorship of the booboisie (curmudgeon H. L. Mencken's pithy name for the would-be *snobes* among the nouveaux riches). Alongside are the not-so-nouveaux riches, and the not-so-riches whose (admittedly often tasteless) democracy this is. Meanwhile, conservatives decry the metastasis of evil, decadence, sloth, and global ingratitude.

So do such polar universes coexist, engaged for the most part in parallel monologues, some more histrionic than others. The "it's not us, it's *them*" crowd on the Right tends to be either ignored or misrepresented by the "blame-America-first" crowd on the Left. The result is—as they like to say in Washington—gridlock, with the obligatory demonization by the opponents in the American political soccer game, each team oblivious to the fact that when the ball is their own nation's reputation, a goal by either side is an automatic no-win.

I submit that a major reason for our inability to gauge what works in the global marketplace of images and ideas is the all-too-facile rejection of the "other side" as just plain wrong. In reality, each "side" chooses to focus on only one part of the complex picture, preaching to its own converted. And as our domestic battles take precedence over global dialogue, the squeaky wheel of anti-Americanism ends up with the bulk of the international media's greasy coverage. New York University (NYU) professors Andrew Ross and Kristin Ross, in a recent volume of essays based on a conference on anti-Americanism held at NYU, offer an exhaustive, relatively recent bibliography.[1] In the discussion that follows, I outline some of the principal analyses in sufficient detail to note where each contributes to the discussion and yet falls short of a solution.

WHAT PROBLEM?

Handsome, rich, magnanimous, and bold, it would seem that the United States has every reason to be proud of itself, if it so wishes. And yes, we Americans do wish it, though we aren't always certain *how* to show it, *when* to show it, and even *why*, exactly, since we don't really *have* to show it: America just is what it is, for all to see. Certain we are, too, that all do see; how could they not? And surely they must—or should, or had better—see what we see: the present and the future, or the present in terms of the future. Given half a chance, could the rest of the world not wish to join us in the best of all possible presents/futures? Surely they will, if they haven't already, if they know what's good for 'em.[2]

After all, the United States obviously has countless reasons, even if clearly not "every reason," to be proud. We are freer and less inhibited than most, more confident, and hence more self-critical and more optimistic that we will prevail over any enemy, given enough time and money. We are the mightiest nation both economically and militarily, especially compared with our comrades with whom we share Western Civilization (even though many continue to fight over the title of its original ownership). Conservatives rally around books such as Dinesh D'Souza's ostentatiously unapologetic *What's So Great About America?* The former White House domestic advisor, currently Rishwain research scholar at the Hoover Institution, buoys kindred patriotic spirits with superlatives such as "America is the greatest, freest, and most decent society in existence. It is an oasis of goodness in a desert of cynicism and barbarism."[3] It's hard not to get a little carried away when you find yourself embattled in the middle of a guerilla-style image attack in unfamiliar territory.

D'Souza reminds his readers of the plethora of usually unknown true American heroes: individual stories of personal courage demonstrated by countless ordinary Americans who are anything but ordinary, defying the odds, helping others around the globe; countless instances of unquestioning selflessness and ingenuity with no expectation of reward; and that inimitable starting-all-over-and-making-it spirit we find within when we least expect it—in brief, a seemingly bottomless reservoir of energy that defies statistics. And all because we know that as Americans we do not have to prove to ourselves that we are the future: we tacitly, unassumingly, assume it. We believe in the American Dream, convinced that we are not only imagining but, mirabile dictu, living it. We have thus become a beacon to the world; so quit the nay-saying.[4]

This nation has splendidly blended a variety of traditions, the "salad bowl" more nourishing as it became increasingly multihued. Secure in our predominance, we aren't reluctant to admire others: we delight in doling out praise where praise is warranted, and sometimes even where it is not. We generously (only seldom condescendingly) bow before the British (and most other) gentry for their well-honed manners, admire the patina and style (though decidedly not the plumbing) of the ancient world, marvel at Asian attention to exquisite detail in gardening and culinary garnish (while admittedly balking at the hefty price tags), and applaud the robust sensuality of African dance—a mere couple of centuries too late to repent for the initial contempt, most prevalent in the cotton-growing climates. We've adopted and borrowed from everyone, taking what suited us, and marketed the results with enviable—and amply envied—commercial success.

Comparing American and Japanese cultures, James Fallows praises America for being different, and in many ways—though certainly not all—superior to others, and chastises us for failing to fully appreciate the true source of our strength. "American society," writes Fallows, "is the world's purest expression of the individualist belief—the idea that a society can flourish if each person is freed to pursue happiness as he or she sees fit." Our job is basically "to show that a society based on them can continue to succeed."[5] Others may not always get the message—it may take time, and effort—but Fallows is convinced that in the end they will.

If the so-called war of ideas seems to be taking place between American society and others, between the New World and the Old, the West and "the rest," pitting "us" against "them," in reality the true war involves some of "them" against one other. Referring to Islamism, our main enemy, journalist David Frum and former assistant secretary of defense Richard Perle note that its future "will be decided by Muslims themselves, by reference to their own values and their own interests."[6] While we certainly have it in our power "to encourage a reassessment of those interests," ultimately they will have to do it themselves.

Each of these approaches that defends America's basic nature, that resists changing with the winds of popular opinion, clearly contains a large element of truth. D'Souza, for example, is right that we are the most successful nation on earth, indeed the most successful in all of human history. But surely he goes too far as he swoons over the "confident, self-reliant, tolerant, generous, future-oriented" *homo Americanus* whose less flattering traits may be found in all too many of its actual specimens. I could not agree more with D'Souza that the United States is better than any nation on earth in all of human history. But that misses the point. It is where we fall short that care must be taken. Born to an immortal mother and favored by two goddesses, Achilles was invincible but for his heel. Our metaphorical heel is potentially no less lethal, which is why we have to take pains to locate and face the danger, and then do everything in our power to confront it.

Evidently, America is otherwise no Achilles but the product of fallible, if brilliant, Founders who set up a superb system of checks and balances that allows for enormous freedom of commerce and creativity. We need not be omnipotent and sinless to thrive and seduce. Well-meaning, patriotic Americans do us no favors when they overstate our virtues for fear that criticism will be used against us. In fact, it is not so much our alleged superior traits but our ability to handle our foibles that particularly endears us to the rest of the world.

I distinctly recall, in November 2000, the reaction of election officials from some two dozen emerging democracies to the controversy surrounding ballot counting in Florida and the ensuing dispute over who won the presidency. It was not, "See, you too make lots of mistakes, so who are you to tell everyone else how to conduct elections?" Rather, what we heard most often was, "This is most remarkable; at home, we would settle it with guns." The foremost historian of U.S. public diplomacy, Wilson P. Dizard, has amply documented the prevalence of this attitude. For instance, what impressed Polish audiences during the Cold War years who watched *The Grapes of Wrath*, which deliberately focuses on the miserable lives of the bottom rung in the United States, "over and above the play's artistry, was that unemployed Americans looked for jobs in their own automobiles."[7] So did the magnificent musical *Porgy and Bess*, which tackled America's struggle with racism, astonish many, not only because of the political and social sophistication implicit in its candor, but the mature talent and evident prominence of its cast. We need not be "perfect" to be respected. On the contrary, if our accomplishments speak for themselves, so do the stumbles and falls: it's the way we pick ourselves up that really impresses folks.

In a similar vein, the "More Like Us" attitude that James Fallows taunts with feisty self-confidence misses at least one important point: whether we like it or not, or more precisely, whether we think that others should like it—for their own good—the fact is that different cultures have a wide variety of approaches to human interaction which we ignore at our peril. Worse, we risk sending the wrong signal: some non-American readers may actually believe that Fallows' infelicitous title reflects an American crusade to make others be more like us, seeking to homogenize the world with a kind of cultural imperialism. Far better is a more open approach that underscores what we can—and do—learn from others and manage to incorporate without squelching, embracing without stifling. "The melting pot" is arguably a metaphor inferior to "salad bowl." To be fair, Fallows' main theme is that Americans should not feel they have to be more like the Japanese in order to emulate the latter's successes. In other words, we should be "more like ourselves" and mainly reconsider our priorities. Isn't it strange how saying it differently makes all the difference.

Finally, deflecting attention from America's conflict with the Muslim world—more specifically, with Muslim fundamentalist fanaticism—while legitimate and important in many respects, does not render the challenge any less daunting. We have a problem, and the best way to solve it is not necessarily by appointing young American Muslims to be sent abroad on behalf of the State Department to demonstrate how well we treat such folks, let alone by spending taxpayer dollars on Soviet-style documentaries in standard propagandese, depicting happy Muslims who have adapted successfully to the American way of life. Yet this is just the sort of naive stuff our professional public diplomats have come up with in the recent past. Fortunately, the amateurs were using their common sense as they hosted students in schools and colleges across the United States, visited the students' countries throughout the Middle East, and everyone kept in touch, as civil societies invariably do. This is not to claim that normal personal contact for mutual benefit is the best answer to the cultural divide. But it is certainly one of them.

An excessive propensity to deflect criticism away from the United States, the presumption that even the mildest criticism must reflect something wrong with the critics themselves, may well reflect nothing more than patriotic pride. However, it may belie insecurity and intolerance, or worse, prejudice against anyone who dares question this nation's preeminence. It's not always "them"; it is us far too often. And yes, we do have a problem.

WHY CAN'T THEY SPEAK AMERICAN?

The French are especially offended. After all, it was not until the mellifluous, vowel-rich Gallic vocabulary was adopted by the Saxons during the Middle Ages to supplement their own, rather more limited, gruff Anglican tongue, that English became rich and pliable enough—particularly after Shakespeare was done codifying the felicitous Romance adoption—to accommodate the many nuances of human thought and feeling. For this and a few other reasons, English—indeed, American—has become the main language of economic and political intercourse, to say nothing of its preeminence in the global popular culture. Microsoft has single-handedly extended computer- and, more generally, business-English into the living rooms and Internet cafés of every country, an imperial intrusion no less insidious for being inadvertent.

If ordinary Americans struggling with their phrase books will continue to be met with stony, hostile incomprehension in Paris or Moscow, so will the fluent Russian and French speakers. We Americans are beyond dialogue to their sworn enemies because of our alleged ostentation, insensitivity, arrogance, and affluence. Such is the caricature of "the ugly American" that we have done little to dispel, since we are often quite oblivious to its existence. Yet in countries where anti-Americanism is not de rigeur, a foreigner—even an American—making even the smallest attempt to learn the local dialect will be embraced with effusive, unguarded gratitude, as any Peace Corps volunteer fresh from the required preassignment boot-camp crash language training will gladly testify.

The problem is as old as America. A new beginning was eagerly sought by those who first landed, perhaps accompanied by success and prosperity, but above all affording the opportunity to be oneself. Although immigrants would continue to flood to America from all corners of the earth, for the most part they tried to learn English as quickly as possible. Even though many diligently taught their children and even their grandchildren to speak the language of their country of origin, it was usually an uphill battle to maintain a dual, let alone plural, linguistic and cultural literacy. And by the mid-1970s, faced with declining post–baby-boom student enrollments, many colleges and universities dropped the traditional foreign language requirements even for doctoral candidates. We were rapidly becoming among the most linguistically challenged people on the face of the planet.

By the year 2000, the Center for Applied Linguistics could state as an established fact, "It is well known in the United States that we have not kept up with the rest of the world in providing quality foreign language instruction to our students."[8] On September 19, 2000, then-secretary of education Richard Riley stated that strengthening foreign language instruction in the nation will build a better workforce, ensure national security, and improve other areas of education.

The testimony came a year almost to the day before the horrific blow to the twin citadels of the commercial capital of the world. The 2001 Hart-Rudman Report on National Security into the 21st Century (Phase III) determined that foreign language study and the "requisite knowledge" of foreign cultures was "vital" to America's national security and well-being. And still we lollygag, seemingly unfazed. In 2005, once again the Senate passed a resolution declaring it "the Year of Languages"[9]—an apt way to celebrate the fortieth anniversary of the Higher Education Act of 1965, which had declared foreign language study across the nation, let alone among diplomats and intelligence officials, as "vital" to the future welfare of the United States.

To be sure, learning foreign languages is difficult. Particularly daunting is the grammatically complex, two-version (one written or formal, and the other, quite different, spoken) Arabic, further differentiated into colloquial and classical, to say nothing of many specific dialects. Speaking with the compassion of someone who's had to survive in the field equipped primarily with a version of formal Arabic known as Modern Standard Arabic (MSA), intelligence analyst Jennifer Bremmer suggests that at least for our diplomats, who must be able to strike up a conversation, a reasonable compromise would be to teach the comparatively easy and relatively useful colloquial Arabic in addition to MSA. Otherwise, "try using MSA to strike up a conversation in a Cairo café or a Rabat taxi, and the reaction will range from polite bafflement to open hilarity."[10]

Potentially smoother cultural interaction and communication aside, recent calamities have underscored the national security implications of the alarming paucity of polyglot specialists in the fields of foreign intelligence and security. The findings of the 9/11 Commission and a slew of other evaluations are reflected in the National Intelligence Strategy released in October 2005, which states that the intelligence community will, among other things, "promote deeper cultural understanding [and] better language proficiency," as well as "recruit exceptional individuals from a diverse talent pool."[11] If genuine, this would imply a healthy departure from the hardly apocryphal "spook profiling" of yesteryear.

The post-9/11 committees' main concern was practical: understanding messages by criminals, terrorists who would threaten innocent lives, military, and other critical forms of communication is evidently indispensable. But concern for linguistic and cultural ignorance on a national scale is justified on broader grounds as well. America has become the center of modern civilization. Its leadership role may not have been sought, but abdication is impossible. Moreover, at this point the world is also undoubtedly dangerous; like it or not, if we don't protect mankind from self-annihilation, no one else is likely to be willing—let alone able—to do so. The rightly acclaimed advantages of globalization, of which we have been prime beneficiaries, and for which we have been alternately commended and blamed, come with built-in responsibilities with no expiration date in sight, and none anticipated.

Just a tad behind schedule, President Bush announced on January 5, 2006, before a gathering of U.S. university presidents at the State Department, that he will request $114 million in 2007 for programs designed to promote foreign languages as "part of a strategic goal, and that is to protect this country."[12] Secretary of State Condoleezza Rice, who introduced the president, added a commendable national mea culpa: "We have not, as a country, made the kind of intellectual investment that we need to make in the exchange of ideas, in languages and in cultures and our knowledge of them that we made in the Cold War." The president added that, in spreading democracy, it is very helpful to speak other people's languages. "You can't convince people unless you can talk to them."[13]

While hardly sufficient, this certainly does seem to be a prerequisite. But the president added that it would also be "a kind gesture," a way to combat the notion that the United States is bullying in imposing its concept of freedom. As he put it, "When Americans learn to speak a language, learn to speak Arabic, those in the Arabic region will say, 'Gosh, America's interested in us. They care enough to learn how we speak.'"[14] (I know what you're thinking. No, there probably isn't an exact equivalent for "gosh" in Arabic.) Speaking another person's language may still land you in lots of hot water—especially if you say the wrong thing at the wrong time—but it's a start. It's better than not landing in any water.

But "language" is far more than words; it encompasses an entire cultural context. Even more significant than teaching foreign languages to native Americans is the need to utilize more effectively the foreign-born speakers, many of whom are eager and eminently qualified to work not only in the obviously critical fields of intelligence and national security but in other capacities. A long-standing simplistic xenophobia[15] was only further exacerbated after 9/11, with self-defeating results. Arabic speakers are sometimes discriminated against for reasons that seem best described as naked prejudice.

Consider the case of Special Agent Bassem Youssef, who was blocked from a counterterrorism assignment in 2002 by his superiors in the FBI. Justice Department investigators have so far "provided no rationale" for this treatment. Dan Eggen of the *Washington Post* reports that "it represents another setback for the FBI as it struggles to attract Arabic speakers and informants in its fight against Islamic extremists," citing Senator Charles E. Grassley's (R-IA) assessment that "we have lost four years of expertise for the war on terror from a highly qualified Arab-American agent."[16] Youssef, a naturalized U.S. citizen who served as FBI legal attaché in Saudi Arabia for four years, had earned raves for his work on the Khobar Towers bombing and other investigations. But then-FBI director Louis J. Freeh's praise for Youssef's "very, very high performance" didn't deter his superiors from deciding, in February 2002, to waste his talents by transferring him to a unit that merely processed documents from Afghanistan and other overseas locations. That's when Youssef began making formal complaints; he will undoubtedly be vindicated, but who will compensate America and the world for the waste?

Learning languages in a school setting runs a distant second to native fluency. But second best is still better than the status quo. From a purely realistic strategic perspective, nothing can match a serious commitment to mastering the myriad languages and dialects of the world. No one was more determined in that endeavor from a strategic perspective than the Soviet KGB, second only to Great Britain whose imperial past provided ample incentive to learn about other peoples' cultures and habits. It never fails to astonish the international community how miserably unprepared in this regard our foreign policy community truly is. How can we possibly hope to win anything, even militarily, let alone hearts and minds, if we don't bother to figure out how to communicate? All the fancy talk of brotherhood is nothing but empty words if what others say is all (proverbial) Greek to us and vice versa. If we wait for everyone else to learn American first, we should not be surprised if it all gets lost in the translation even before we get a chance to say Hello.

By way of addendum, it may be said that at long last, at least the importance of Arabic is beginning to be better understood. It is now the "flavor of the month," linguistically speaking, leading National Defense University professor Daniel Kuehl to lament that other languages, and hence regions—notably Africa and Asia—are now being neglected.[17] This "what's in" and "what's out" approach to the world is surely better suited for *Vogue* or *People* magazines than it is for serious global outreach and intelligence.

NOTES

1. Andrew Ross and Kristin Ross, *Anti-Americanism* (New York: New York University Press, 2004), bibliographical notes, 315–19.

2. Fox Channel's John Gibson, the author of *Hating America: The New World Sport* (New York: HarperCollins, 2005), for example, entitles his concluding chapter "They're Wrong. We're Right. Get Used to It." He is specifically referring to the war in Iraq in the aftermath of 9/11, but the attitude is symptomatic of many Americans' frustration with knee-jerk hatred of us for reasons that seem unwarranted.

3. Dinesh D'Souza, *What's So Great about America* (Washington, DC: Regnery Publishing, 2004), 193.

4. Television talk-show host Christopher Matthews also summarized the idea crisply and succinctly in his recent popular book, *America: Beyond Our Grandest Notions* (New York: The Free Press, 2002). The mission had been defined at the outset in religious terms but would soon thereafter grow in scope: "By 1776, the notion of an American mission, as invoked by [Rev. John] Winthrop, had come to sound a more secular note" (195). Citing Thomas Paine's celebrated salvo from his revolutionary-era pamphlet *Common Sense*—"We have it in our power to begin the world over again"—Matthews concludes his book with bravado and optimism: "The same spirit that built this great country continues to rip across it today, the same destiny lures us, and the same optimistic, rebellious nature drives us that did even in those early, scary days when our country's body was small but its soul was large" (205).

5. James Fallows, *More Like Us: Putting America's Native Strengths and Traditional Values to Work to Overcome the Asian Challenge* (Boston, MA: Houghton Mifflin Company, 1989).

6. David Frum and Richard Perle, *An End to Evil: How to Win the War on Terror* (New York: Random House, 2003), 152.

7. Wilson P. Dizard Jr., *Inventing Public Diplomacy: The Story of the U.S. Information Agency* (Boulder, CO: Lynne Rienner Publishers, 2004), 192.

8. Ingrid Pufahl, Nancy C. Rhodes, and Donna Christian, *Foreign Language Teaching: What the United States Can Learn from Other Countries*, Center for Applied Linguistics, prepared for the U.S. Department of Education's Comparative Information on Improving Education Practice, December 2000.

9. S. Res. 28, February 17, 2005.

10. Jennifer Bremer, "Learning a Language of Dots and Differences," *Washington Post—Outlook*, October 16, 2005, B5.

11. *National Intelligence Strategy*, October 2005. George Friedman, founder and chairman of the intelligence company Stratfor, writes in *America's Secret War: Inside the Hidden Worldwide Struggle between America and Its Enemies* (New York: Doubleday, 2004), 73, "If there was a single weakness of the U.S. intelligence postures prior to September 11, . . . [it] was a profound lack of language skills and trained and sophisticated analysts to figure out what has been said."

12. Bradley Graham, "Foreign-Language Learning Promoted," *Washington Post*, January 6, 2006.

13. Graham, "Foreign-Language Learning Promoted."

14. Graham, "Foreign-Language Learning Promoted."

15. For an eminently readable account of the infamous Halloween Day Massacre, when President Jimmy Carter's CIA chief, Admiral Stansfield Turner, fired first- and

second-generation Americans, "the ones who didn't mind getting their hands dirty," see George Crile's *Charlie Wilson's War: The Extraordinary Story of the Largest Covert Operation in History* (New York: Atlantic Monthly Press, 2003), 56; "The criteria seemed to be to terminate the men who knew the language and the culture and who had served the longest in one spot."

16. Dan Eggen, "Retaliation Case of Arab Specialist at FBI Advances," *Washington Post*, July 18, 2006, A3.

17. "Winning the War of Ideas," panel discussion held at the Heritage Foundation, May 8, 2006.

Chapter Three

Consumerism Über Alles

The business of America is business.

—Calvin Coolidge

Some argue that America is merely bearing the brunt of the backlash against modernity; nevertheless, we've got it coming. Even the avowedly progressive, proglobalist *New York Times* columnist Thomas Friedman entitles a chapter from his turn-of-the-millennium best-seller *The Lexus and the Olive Tree* by paraphrasing the catchy name of megagiant Toys "Я" Us, "Revolution Is U.S." With almost stereotypical but undeniably justified self-confidence, Friedman summarizes the commercial preeminence of the United States as follows: "What is going on in the world today, in the very broadest sense, is that through the process of globalization everyone is being forced toward America's gas station," by which he means that "if you are not an American and don't know how to pump your own gas, I suggest you learn." Speaking like a political scientist, Friedman declares that "with the end of the Cold War, globalization is globalizing Anglo-American-style capitalism and the Golden Straightjacket. It is globalizing American culture and cultural icons."[1]

But, along with the good news, Friedman candidly informs the self-assured passengers of our high-flying machine, comes the bad news. For what this all means is that globalization is globalizing both "the best of America and the worst of America": "it is globalizing the American Revolution and it is globalizing the American gas station." And while you and I cannot easily imagine a world entirely without gas stations, even at the current astronomical prices courtesy of the Iraq war, OPEC, and the Chinese economic boom, still more indispensable to civilization as we know it is the revolution in expectations, which is quintessentially American.

47

The new, decadent version of the American Dream applies to both the best and the worst of America. The alloy consists of inextricably intertwined dualisms: the ethereal idealism of the Revolution, itself marred from the outset by shameful racism, alongside the noxious materialist fumes of gasoline, known also as the "black gold" of liberating, coveted prosperity. The contradictions of our dream capture the promise and the curse of our times. In subtle and not so subtle ways, we are convincing everyone that they, too, can join us.

Does this imply that everyone wishes, or is forced to wish, or wishes he (or, especially, she) might be in a position to wish, to be just like us? Not exactly, and yet, well, basically yes. Friedman struggles with the paradox: "Embedded in the Japanese, Western European and communist gas stations are social contracts very different from the American one, as well as very different attitudes about how markets should operate and be controlled."[2] He seems to imply that different ideologies accompany different expectations, different dreams (setting aside, for the moment, that "Communist social contract" is an oxymoron). Concretely, this would mean that stations outside U.S. borders presumably pay more attention to the distinctive traditions and value preferences of their respective cultural and ethnic communities (we'll take the much-traveled Friedman's word for it). By contrast, the American version is just, well, efficient. Friedman concludes that the main, if not in fact the only, purpose of the gas station in the United States is to provide the most gas at the cheapest price—whether the public likes it or not. In other words, "ready or not, this is the model that the rest of the world is increasingly being pressured to emulate."

"Being pressured" is tantamount to "hard sell"—if not in reality, at least in appearance. Writes Friedman, "America is blamed for this because, in so many ways, globalization is us—or is at least perceived that way by a lot of the world." "Globalization and modernity R us" is a catchy ad, with a catch: we aren't playing games. Friedman explains how the inference proceeds: "The most powerful agent pressuring other countries is Uncle Sam, and America's global armed forces keep these markets and sea lanes open for this era of globalization, just as the British navy did for the era of globalization in the nineteenth century."[3] His smooth journalistic style allows Friedman to gloss over "global armed forces," a phrase whose ambiguity becomes exponentially more important in the aftermath of the war in Iraq, making one wonder how literally he means it.

Literally enough, if one judges from the source of his assessment: the dean of Harvard's Kennedy School, Joseph A. Nye. The quote states that globalization can be traced in part back to American strategy after World War II when the United States was eager to create an open international economy presumably to forestall another depression while at the same time balancing

Soviet power and containing Communism. Nye, and, hence, Friedman, infer that the institutional framework and political pressures for opening markets were directly and (implicitly) exclusively "a product of American power and policy."[4] Given their "reinforcement" by technological developments in transportation and communication, America obviously "made it increasingly costly" for other countries to resist. To put an even finer point on it, Friedman takes this to mean that even during the Cold War, America was hard at work pushing for a global economy "for its own economic and strategic reasons."[5]

It was Thomas Friedman again who best described the passionate ambivalence toward the United States, which had already started to take on a sharper edge at the turn of the millennium. "For some people Americanization-globalization feels more than ever like a highly attractive, empowering, incredibly tempting pathway to rising living standards. For many others, though, this Americanization-globalization can breed a deep sense of envy and resentment toward the United States—envy because America seems so much better at riding this tiger and resentment because Americanization-globalization so often feels like the United States whipping everyone else to speed up."[6]

Friedman is American enough himself to assume that Ameriphiles outnumber its enemies, but he fully recognizes the deadly danger of resentment. And it doesn't even take a village. To paraphrase T. S. Elliott, the world may end just as easily with a whimper as with a bang. Repudiating history might be a fine way for a proud, brave nation to define its mission, but the risk of rallying everyone forward while seeming to ignore (or maybe just being oblivious of) the lessons of the past, along with the stubborn variety of human cultures, may render the United States dangerously, even lethally, vulnerable.

THE "COMMERCIALISM = AMERICANISM" EQUATION

The concept of "hard sell," of course, is quintessentially commercial; it refers to the kind of marketing technique that gives *c[k]apitalism* a bad name, at least in those circles where *profit* is similarly pejorative. Ideological biases aside, the traditional hard-line sales approach has received mixed reviews, on both tactical and strategic grounds. Its proponents have been accused of everything from sacrificing The Larger Picture in the name of the proverbial, and much-maligned, bottom line, to smearing the national reputation of the most God-fearing, or at least church-attending, nation on earth. To be sure, that deplored larger picture refers not only to the self-described lofty ideals of the militantly anti-business community but also to a company's profit in the longer run.

As businessmen realize, anti-Americanism is not only bad for diplomacy but bad for corporations. If we cannot "sell" America properly, our economy will suffer and, conversely, if advertisers don't recognize that selling a product entails selling the nation where it has been produced (or at least is perceived to have been produced), the nation may suffer as well. The latter point is predicated on the assumption that corporations, and especially the larger and hence even more sinister multinational c[k]orporations, are out to make a buck at any cost, prepared to say or do anything, legal or otherwise, to make a sale. Recent scandals implicating top executives cooking the books for personal profit have further rattled the already-frayed nerves of consumers. *Caveat emptor*, the decadent Roman equivalent of "buyer beware" (and we all know what happened to *them*), has taken on a whole new meaning in the age of double-booked digital accounting.

On some level, the frank, even ostentatious, commercialism of the global economic world that lives and dies by advertisement is as obvious as it seems inevitable. We are all accomplices, for how else to figure out what to purchase? Don't we just love ads? Especially the funniest: we rate them, praise their cleverness, and, more often than not, rush over to buy whatever it is they sell. How many of us bother to recall that *advertent* means "careful" or that *adverse* is a semantic cousin, and *advertise* itself used to mean ("Obs." in dictionary lingo) "to admonish; warn." And here we had imagined all along that commercials were just a form of entertainment. We prefer to be amused and don't much care for adversity. On second thought, we thrive on it. We amuse ourselves to death.

More to the point: we need information, and we need it fast. It does not take a degree in psychology to know that humans need far more than mere products. Even more, we all need the intangible, even subliminal, by-products: the dream, the illusion, the aura, worth no less money for being mostly the buyer's own placebo-style contribution. And yes, we need everyone else to participate in this complicated smoke-and-mirrors game of social and economic interaction that defines us, that gives definition to our inchoate efforts to harmonize the storms within our souls.

In brief, how else are we supposed to function and communicate if not by accumulating the instruments of modern life? We require both the necessary and the superfluous, which are in fact no less crucial. But that very imperative is what fuels the resentment—as if the lover blames the beloved for his yearning, for enticing him by her irresistible seduction. Equally entrapped, increasingly dissatisfied as one desire is satisfied only to give rise to another, the consumer may be expected to rage against the seemingly insatiable companies that feed on the blood of his wants and his never-sufficient bank credit.

How much worse when the companies are American and the profits pile up in the grubby little hands of ecologically insensitive members of the crassly entrepreneurial champions of conspicuous consumption. The engineers of the hard sell, so goes the antimaterialist wisdom, will sell us down the drain, all the way to hell, long before the coming of the Grim Reaper, fried in the global scorching to which our wasteful hedonism is destined. Consumers of the world, unite! Down with America's corporate caste, whose capital makes possible the things we so ardently wish we didn't want so very much to buy!

It may be worth remembering that free trade has been more popular in the United States than in most countries. Abundant evidence demonstrates the economic superiority of allowing market forces to operate unencumbered by regulations, onerous taxation, and short-sighted, politically motivated protectionism. Our financial success, therefore, is in large measure the result of giving people the products they seem to want. Ultimately, however, the question is not so much whether people think that we pursue globalization for our selfish little reasons, using hard-sell tactics honed inside the plush offices of Madison Avenue, as whether they understand—and value—advertising as such.

Among the more systematic efforts to understand why "they" say they hate our marketing techniques is a survey of international students from twenty-five different countries, enrolled at Regents College in London, England, conducted by journalism professor Jami A. Fullerton. Professor Fullerton reviews the literature that explores the effect of international perceptions on business, which lends some support among recent international advertising studies to the notion that America, once a brand asset, may now be "a negative strategy." Her own findings, which are consistent with international polls showing increasingly unfavorable feelings toward the United States, further showed that "attitudes towards America did seem to be related to attitudes towards advertising" as such: hence students who felt more positive about the former also did so about the latter, and vice versa. This "supports the idea that advertising is an international symbol of America and an icon of American culture. Advertising stands for capitalism, democracy and freedoms."[7] Admittedly, one cannot help but wish that it were not the main, let alone the only index of those ideals. We are a vastly complex people; alongside business moguls are Nobel Prize winners, dancers, sportsmen, violinists, astronauts, and philanthropists.

The subject under consideration, however, is how others perceive us, and Thomas Friedman has it about right when he observes that "in most societies, people cannot distinguish anymore among American power, American exports, American cultural assaults, American cultural exports and plain vanilla globalization."[8] Friedman argues that most people are unable to distinguish between the power and influence of the United States, on the one hand, and the mesmerizing seduction of the American Dream in its latest, materialist/consumerist metamorphosis.

In our self-confidence and the conviction that everyone would wish to be like us if they only knew it, we can fall all too easily into the potentially self-deluding—because self-serving—assumption that what's good for General Motors is good not only for America but also for the world. Quite aside from the fact that GM is now having to struggle alongside German and Japanese competitors, to say nothing of the fact that no automaker in the world market can afford not to have become transnational, American marketing experts are beginning to detect serious deleterious effects caused by the paradoxical love-hate relationship between American goods and their global customers on sales worldwide.

It is hardly accidental that hardest hit are goods with identifiably American names, such as the credit card American Express, while Visa and MasterCard are much less affected. The Edelman Trust Barometer for 2005, presented at the World Economic Forum in Davos in January 2005, indicated that for the second consecutive year, "opinion leaders are significantly less likely to trust individual U.S.-based global corporations operating in Europe and Canada, such as Coca-Cola (USA = 69 percent vs. Europe = 45 percent and Canada = 46 percent); McDonalds (58 percent vs. 25 percent and 27 percent); P&G (74 percent vs. 44 percent and 49 percent)."[9] An article published in the December 30, 2004, issue of the *Financial Times* by D. Roberts with the title "Tarnished Image: Is the World Falling out of Love with U.S. Brands?" was symptomatic of the concern among business leaders facing an increasingly dangerous backlash.

This ambivalent attitude, with only a slight touch of caricature, is basically what lies behind the sort of arguments being hurled at the business community, whose pursuit of the most "effective" marketing techniques seems somehow to have underestimated the zeal of those consumers whose product happens to be corporation bashing. Among the most recent books by the more articulate bashers are Alissa Quart's *Branded: The Buying and Selling of Teenagers*; John de Graaf, David Wann, and Thomas H. Naylor's *Affluenza: The All-Consuming Epidemic*; Kalle Lasn's *Culture Jam: How to Reverse America's Suicidal Consumer*; Naomi Klein's *No Logo*; and Eric Schlosser's *Fast Food Nation: The Dark Side of the All-American Meal*. These and lesser diatribes are part of a veritable cottage industry designed to provide ammunition for professional anticonsumerists, who are the ideological—and often actual—children of the sixties "make-love-not-war," also known by some as the "blame-America-first," generation.

The most recent book by Johny K. Johansson, the McCrane Shaker professor of International Business and Marketing at Georgetown University's McDonough School of Business, is among the more moderate, but still in the same mold. Claiming to reveal the one and only true "not-so-hidden cause of global anti-Americanism," the publisher's sales pitch reiterates his not-too-subtle title: *In Your Face: How American Marketing Excess Fuels Anti-Americanism.*[10] In a tough world, predict Johansson's publishers, hard sell inevitably spells "global rebellion." Speak of hard sell.

Given his stellar scholarly credentials, Johansson's unacademically impressionistic account of American corporate marketing practices is worth noting, not only for its tendentious arguments and the paucity of documentation, but for the fact that he seems oblivious to both. It's as if he considers the point of view he is advancing to be shared by most of his readers. In that, he is most likely correct, and that fact deserves attention in itself. His book is an elaborate *mea culpa* for having engaged in the grand conspiracy as management guru to student capitalists who grow up to exploit their unsuspecting buyer-victims.

A marketer himself, Johansson admits to having engaged in what he describes as scientific marketing experiments.[11] The deceptively impartial aura of science is just the sort of thing that can trap an otherwise respectable liberal academic. In search of some excuse, Johansson protests that he had been duped, as such research cannot but "help to shield us from the realization that we are in fact, evaluating means for manipulating people."[12]

He is especially pained by the realization that he has been teaching in, living in, and has implicitly become an accomplice of, the most cutthroat country of all: America. This, after all, is the country that invented marketing, that has glorified business, consumerism, and exploitation. Antiglobalism and anti-Americanism are virtually interchangeable. He commends sociologist George Ritzer's 1993 book on *The McDonaldization of Society* for having coined "a phrase that has become synonymous with the commercialization of societies everywhere," as well as Benjamin Barber's take on the same idea two years later in his widely popular *Jihad vs. McWorld.* The brunt of the world's ire against commercialization is directed against the United States.

It might be objected that since most of the world's multinationals are, of course, American, one may well expect them to be disproportionately targeted. Johansson admits this but dismisses it as hardly relevant. There are many other reasons. One is that "American brands are particularly bad" (defined as engaging in "sourcing and third-world exploitation"); another—more "likely"—is that "anti-globalizers tend to attack the biggest brands, partly because of their newsworthiness and lack of underdog sympathy." Johansson speculates that "there are a couple of reasons why it is more than a coincidence that

American brands are the only ones hit" in the pages of the aforementioned professional antiglobalists such as Naomi Klein.[13]

Mainly, these companies are accused of carrying "the in-your-face virus," which entails a tendency to "encourage an American lifestyle based on superficiality and fads, all engineered by profit-seeking marketers."[14] To justify this kind of inflammatory rhetoric, Johansson cites his own experience interviewing prospective job candidates for teaching positions in marketing, as well as generally accepted tactics among marketers, notably an increasing tendency to "compare marketing to warfare, with branding strategies conceived as an attack on a competitor's stronghold rather than simply satisfying customer needs."[15]

The upshot is that marketers seem to "use" people as tools in the never-ending search for profit. Given the global competitive climate, moreover, there is little choice but to resort to ruthless tactics, by using strong so-called promotional tools. By always being in a selling mode, so goes Johansson's argument, there is little sympathy for local businesses. He admits that American business schools have started to teach classes aimed at developing "cultural sensitivity." The problem, however, is that "many of the professors have little or no cultural knowledge or sensitivity themselves." This is not because they are all Americans—on the contrary: they have allegedly been "indoctrinated with mantras like 'Good marketing is good marketing everywhere,'" with the result that the typical graduate of an American business school, no matter what his country of origin, "emerges with a certain air of insolence" that is contributing to America's worsening name.[16]

Johansson aims to warn against companies, inebriated by success, unnecessarily alienating consumers—an occupational hazard of hard-nosed, hard-working salesmen. He notes that an obvious element of good global marketing is local adaptation, which is greatly simplified by advances in modular design and flexible manufacturing. The hard-hitting polemics see no hope whatever for reforming American corporate marketing behavior. French journalist Remi Kauffer can only compare this rapacious new breed of class enemies to the totalitarian USSR. "The Soviets benefited from people's fascination with an idealized picture of the world they were developing: the USSR, 'the workers' fatherland.' America had only to adapt this method on a different register, using an attraction that was not so much ideological as frankly material"[17]—take your pick. Immoral equivalence.

Kauffer deliberately chooses as a title the Soviet term of art, *Dezinformatsia*, which he defines as "techniques designed to mislead the enemy." Rather vaguely crediting "some American specialists" with the opinion that "it first occurred in the jargon of the intelligence services during the First World War" when German military staff allegedly applied it to certain fake radio communications, Kauffer glosses over the unique, monumentally expensive and sophisticated Soviet version. In fact, the more accurate technical term for the elaborate machinery run by the KGB is "active measures," in Russian, *aktivnyye meropriatia*. It is difficult to believe that Kauffer is unaware that *dezinformatsia* was used only in some circles, mainly before the 1960s, when the operations escalated by quantum leaps.[18]

But Kauffer prefers the Latinized version not only for its polemical superiority but for permitting a seamless transition to [Soviet-style, now subtler "Made in America"] disinformation campaigns conducted by American corporations used in what he describes as "a war that is carried out with an arsenal of myths and symbols." Still, a war it is, complete with casualties, and conducted by heartless, rapacious experts "in manipulating public opinion, brainwashing consumers, casting discredit upon competitors," and—most ominous—superb at covering up their traces. Heirs to the ruthless KGB, corporate gunslingers who now use the same "tried-and-true methods from the olden days" are nothing but "prudent wolves" whose footsteps are hard to trace, so "while one can often tell who benefits the crime, the tangible evidence is cruelly lacking."[19]

Which does not stop Kauffer from engaging in rhetoric redolent with purple (with a reddish tinge) prose that trembles with outrage at what he calls "American-dependence," the result of the absolute tyranny of "grammar and spelling rules imposed by Bill Gates," which insidiously ensures that "the language of Shakespeare reigns in the globalized universe."[20] The war of words is just the prelude, however, to "the ultimate goal of the offensive [which] is to 'sell' the American-style personality throughout the world."[21] And lest the quotation marks around the word "sell" are not sufficiently scary, consider the alleged "close bonds linking industrial development, commercial expansion, cultural penetration and modern forms of disinformation," reinforced by allegations (referred to only as "some sources") that behind it all is "technical support from the National Security Agency, which supervises and even controls a substantial share of the Internet traffic."[22] Marx himself could not have imagined that capitalism would reach such a high degree of sophistication. Pity the duped proletariat, whose conscience has been long obliterated, seemingly beyond redemption, by addiction to the opium of American-style consumerism.

The hand-wringing of some academics, worried that greedy Americans seek to impose upon the unsuspecting global consumer—by means of irresistibly seductive advertisements—products he doesn't want or need, conveniently omits the fact that American ingenuity is responsible for the vast majority of improvements in the lives of ordinary people: the sewing machine, the refrigerator, the washing machine, the vacuum cleaner, the radio and television set, electric combines, earthmovers, life-saving medicines and surgery techniques, to mention but a few of the more recent staples of modern life. If America were less oblivious to advertising the miracles that its freedom has spawned, it would demonstrate beyond any doubt that it has heralded the most explosive humanitarian revolution the world has ever known, footing the lion's share of the bill for R & D. As is often the case with Big Lies, those who charge the United States with capitalist dictatorship over the proletariat have got it exactly backward.

But corporate America is too timid to respond. On the contrary, it has consistently played right into the hands of its critics. The Capital Research Foundation has been studying patterns of corporate giving for nearly two decades. Its conclusion confirms the suspicion that big business has found it easier, or at least more effective, to bribe its enemies rather than to fight them. Since the bottom line is their bottom line, I will not condemn them, much as I deplore this form of ransom. Even less do I object to the volunteer work, donations to good causes, and other forms of thinly disguised penance for engaging in consensual profiteering. But liberal guilt has a way of obscuring the truth about America's genuine contribution to easing the plight of ordinary men and women everywhere.

At bottom, of course, what most bothers the self-styled elite is the aesthetics or, rather, the lack thereof. And in an important sense, the snobs among us are certainly correct: by appealing to the lower common denominator, American marketers manage to portray our society in a deplorably misleading way. Any resemblance between the beer-chugging American, who wolfs down those greasy McDonald hamburgers, and the sexy Paris Hilton, who lures him on screen to the nearest golden arches, is limited to their IQ, or lack thereof. Most of us are neither as vapid, nor as photogenic, let alone as wealthy as she. Most of us are real people, working and doing our best in real America. But we know: advertisements speak *to* us but not *for* us; they don't pretend to do so, and it is a mistake to expect them to do so.

The trouble is that the rest of the world doesn't and cannot be expected to understand. Still, we must not blame the advertisers. Their job is simply to sell their products as best they can. It behooves the rest of us to do something about our image. Specifically, it behooves us to let the rest of the world know who we really are: we must engage on many levels, and far more effectively than we have done so far. And no, we cannot do a "hard sell" on America's "brand" as if it were a Cadillac or a dishwasher.

THINLY DISGUISED ELITISM

Monopolizing the microphone, critics of American hard sell often resort to post-neo-Marxist solutions, variations on the theme that materialism must replace, or at least supplement, the dialectic of the marketplace with the monologue of state control, the subversive effects of consumerism assailed by modern-day inquisitors (some more grand than others) who endorse burning the greedy capitalist at the stake of public opinion. The contempt for the "bread-and-circuses" mentality of the masses has always been de rigeur among the arrogant intellectual elite. What the self-righteous anticonsumerists fail to admit is that most people want to live more satisfying, longer, richer lives. The products developed by American ingenuity, imagination, and hard work have made the lives of millions less difficult and more enjoyable. Writes Josef Joffe, "One need not resort to such sonorous terms as 'freedom,' 'the New Jerusalem,' or [other] . . . concepts that evoke religious transcendence and salvation. America's magnetism has very tangible roots."[23] The intangible ones need not evoke salvation to connote transcendence: we like to call it our dream, and we like to think that it may be shared by just about anyone.

Singapore's former ambassador to the United Nations, Kishore Mahbubani, reports having seen this everywhere, in Asia and in Africa; whenever he would speak to his guides or his drivers "and ask them what is their greatest aspiration, more often than not the answer would be 'I would love to go to America.' If I asked why, the answer inevitably would be something along the lines: "If I get to America, I will have a chance to succeed.'"[24] Mahbubani credits this sentiment to America's greatest contribution to the world—which, to paraphrase the advertisement, is "priceless"—in demonstrating "that a totally non-feudal order could be built. . . . With each passing generation, there were more and more success stories among the very poor."[25] Is it any wonder that elites throughout the globe have a stake in fueling resentment against the United States?

The obsession with the alleged negative aspects of America's consumerist image detracts from other problems in presenting our true face to the world, which run far deeper. In the end, what hurts us most is what people don't know about us rather than what they think they do. While economic power is certainly a critical factor in establishing America's preeminence as the world's premier nation, from the perspective of global understanding, it is, if certainly not irrelevant, a sideshow. The advantage we have enjoyed historically, our geographical and emotional distance from both East and West allowing us to embark upon a new experiment, has its downside. Not only do we know less about the world than we should; so does the world fail to know who Americans really are.

America has traditionally thrived on the little guy, who sometimes succeeds and sometimes does not, but is touched with beauty and courage in the quest. It is such little-known folk that James Agee sought to paint in the exquisite prose of *Let Us Now Praise Famous Men*, that Ralph Ellison conveyed in his daring portrait of a black *Invisible Man* who would not let others refuse to see him, and that Harriet Jacobs captured in the story of her own resurrection from slavery, *Incidents in the Life of a Slave Girl— Written by Herself*, to say nothing of the millions whose courage, talents, and beauty may have gone unnoticed but have left their mark in myriad ways, who have inspired, helped, and touched the hearts of kin and stranger, at home and far away, with no expectation of reward. It is the big-hearted, no-nonsense, remarkably ingenious and devoted troops in Iraq whose praises are sung by Robert Kaplan in his superb best seller *Imperial Grunts: The American Military on the Ground*.[26]

The difficulty lies in finding the language, the method that will convey the spirit of this nation through the mosaic of its complex reality. That reality must include not only the mistakes, which are sometimes monumentally stupid, and the inevitable squalor of vice found in all human dwellings, but also the golden treasure. No true picture of the American spirit can emerge without somehow salvaging at least a glimpse of the sacred shrine we have built here, the invisible cathedral to human hope and generosity, built on the harnessed virtues of ordinary people that define our Dream. Admittedly, it's far less a matter of sell than a matter of soul.

I suspect that each one of us knows at least one person who has demonstrated to someone in another country that profit is not all that matters to most people in the United States. Take my friend Paul DeGregorio, who has five daughters either in college or about to go and lives in a small house in the Midwest, bought a round-trip ticket for a young man he happened to meet while helping the young man's country of Moldova prepare for their first post-Communist elections. My friend and his family hosted him for six months and took him along everywhere, just to widen the young man's horizons. Another friend, Steve Bryen, paid for the upbringing and education of a dozen Vietnamese children. Still another, Seth Cropsey, opened an orphanage in Romania with start-up money from his academic salary. My own parents "adopted" an Oriental child whose parents could not afford even to feed him; for over a decade, they paid for his schooling and upkeep in return for grateful letters and photographs.

Such stories are multiplied by the millions, justifying the assessment by Ambassador Kishore Mahbubani that "Americans are by far the most philanthropic individuals in the world,"[27] a statement now amply demonstrated by the Hudson Institute Report on global philanthropy.[28] We also have the highest church attendance in the Western world.[29] But this story is harder to tell, or at least harder to disseminate electronically by television networks playing the ratings game, to justify the hefty price tag commanded by every second of advertisement. So other ways must be found. And found they are, but too few people know about them.

NOTES

1. Thomas Friedman, *The Lexus and the Olive Tree* (New York: Random House, 2000), 380.

2. Friedman, *The Lexus*, 381.

3. Friedman, *The Lexus*, 381.

4. Friedman, *The Lexus*, 382.

5. Friedman, *The Lexus*, 382.

6. Friedman, *The Lexus*, 383.

7. Jami A. Fullerton, "'Why Do They Hate Us?' International Attitudes toward America, American Brands and Advertising," in *Place Branding* 1, no. 2 (2005): 138.

8. The point is graphically illustrated by the Japanese newspaper *Nihon Keizai Shimbun*, in a story regarding a conference in Tokyo on globalization. An article published by the newspaper on June 4, 1999, carried the headline "The American-Instigated Globalization." A large portion of its readers undoubtedly considered such a headline redundant.

9. www.businessfordiplomaticaction.com/learn/research.html, cited in Michael B. Goodman, "Restoring Trust in American Business: The Struggle to Change Perception," *Journal of Business Strategy* 26, no. 4 (2005): 31.

10. Johny K. Johansson, *In Your Face: How American Marketing Excess Fuels Anti-Americanism* (Upper Saddle River, NJ: Financial Times Prentice Hall, 2004). This is the book's second printing.

11. Not everything is worth selling, he thinks: "My own solution has always been to believe in the product I am selling." Although he does admit that whether a product yields "positive benefits can of course be a tricky question, especially since in many advanced markets, the needs satisfied are typically not very basic," in Johansson, *In Your Face*, 42. Is a Corolla OK to peddle but not a Jaguar? Tough call.

12. Johansson, *In Your Face*, 49.

13. Johny Johansson, "Why Only American Brands?" in *In Your Face*.

14. Johansson, "Why Only American Brands?" 119.

15. Johansson, "Why Only American Brands?" 58.

16. Johansson, "Why Only American Brands?" 78.

17. Remi Kauffer, *Disinformation: American Multinationals at War against Europe* (New York: Algora Publishing, 2001), 101.

18. Richard H. Schultz and Roy Godson, *Dezinformatsia: Active Measures in Soviet Strategy* (McLean, VA: Pergamon-Brassey's International Defense Publishers, 1984), 2. This is the first and still one of the best short essays on this sophisticated web of deadly operations whose effects continue to be felt.

19. Kauffer, *Disinformation*, 6.

20. Kauffer, *Disinformation*, 98–99.

21. Kauffer, *Disinformation*, 218.

22. Kauffer, *Disinformation*, 222.

23. Josef Joffe, *Überpower: The Imperial Temptation of America* (New York: W. W. Norton, 2006), 108.

24. Kishore Mahbubani, *Beyond the Age of Innocence: Rebuilding Trust between America and the World* (New York: Public Affairs, 2005), 5.

25. Mahbubani, *Beyond the Age of Innocence*, 5.

26. Robert Kaplan, *Imperial Grunts: The American Military on the Ground* (New York: Random House, 2005).

27. Mahbubani, *Beyond the Age of Innocence*, 5.

28. Carol C. Adelman, *The Index of Global Philanthropy 2006* (Washington, DC: Hudson Institute, 2006).

29. George Weigel, *The Cube and the Cathedral: Politics without God* (New York: Basic Books, 2005).

Chapter Four

Empire Lite and Not-So-Lite

Our country is the world—our countrymen are all mankind.

—William Lloyd Garrison

While most conservatives have long believed that anti-Americanism is a communicable liberal disease, some of the most respected figures on the Right opposed to the war in Iraq have justified criticism of the United States as indicative of the world's resentment against America's self-appointment as the world's policeman. It is one thing to be the most preeminent global power, and quite another to overextend its reach, especially through military means. Instead of minding our own business, fighting our homegrown devils, so the argument goes, we venture abroad recklessly, seemingly in pursuit of empire.

This is dangerous and highly reprehensible, according to Catholic University political science professor Claes G. Ryn. In *America the Virtuous: The Crisis of Democracy and the Quest for Empire*, Ryn passionately denounces what he calls a form of neo-Jacobin "democratism—[which] puts great emphasis on democracy's superiority and missionary task."[1] He asks rhetorically, with barely veiled contempt, whether anti-American sentiment in the world "may be due to short-sighted, unsophisticated, arrogant, or heavy-handed conduct in combination with American and Western moral and cultural decline."[2] If America is indeed a superpower, it's because of its cancerous militarism, a disease that is bound to destroy not only the world but ultimately itself. Ryn speaks for many conservatives who lay the bulk of the blame for the war in Iraq on "neocons"—the likes of Paul Wolfowitz, Robert Kagan, Bill Kristol, Doug Feith, and Richard Perle—for the vicious "blending of democratism with the desire to turn the United States into a great missionary power."[3] Ryn actually goes a step further, accusing the proponents of democratism, in effect, of cynically using lofty-sounding rhetoric that merely "puts a nice gloss on the will to power."[4] America's will to empire is "lite" only in the transparency of its euphemistic, self-deceiving camouflage.

The term *democratism* captures nicely that popular form of quasi-religious political neofundamentalism that seems to bridge the rhetorical gulf between Republicans and Democrats in foreign policy and substitutes for policy when nothing else comes to mind. I agree that military solutions must always be a last resort, and I don't think much of that Nietzschean (actually, Schopenhauerian) "will to power" that the Nazis so demonically and, yes, cleverly twisted to suit their psychotic purposes.

But Schopenhauer is one thing, Leo Strauss quite another. Ryn accuses the founding father of the neoconservatives, consistently referred to in the book as "neo-Jacobins," of having not only argued that power is everything but of seeking such power for opportunistic reasons. No better than a lowly Sophist, Strauss is charged with having "taught that the insightful who want influence must often dissimulate and seem to hold beliefs that will advance their fortunes."[5] The good professor would be shocked to hear such words. The erudite author of *Natural Right and History* (first published in 1953), who argued that ideas are best understood in their original context, and who also considered the classics indispensable to a complete education, would shake his head in disbelief. It is now the sad duty of his old friend and collaborator, now the executor of Strauss's estate, Joseph Cropsey, professor emeritus at the University of Chicago, to be dismayed on his behalf.

Ryn doesn't hesitate to name names. Those rapacious vultures, militant democratists and worse, include among their ranks the following: Ronald Reagan's secretary of education, a former assistant secretary of defense, a University of Chicago professor, the editor of the *Weekly Standard*, a senior fellow at the Carnegie Endowment for International Peace, the former editor of *Commentary*, and a *Washington Post* columnist who is also the recipient of a prestigious award from the American Enterprise Institute. None of these people is in any danger of being canonized, but in my various interactions with each one of them, I have detected no imperial ambitions among their more visible foibles.[6]

One may agree with Ryn that America should not be in the empire business, especially not under false pretenses, "democratist" or otherwise. Most conservatives, however, take the diametrically opposite stance. While it is true that there are many who dislike America for its preeminence, so be it. We cannot let that stop us. There is no choice but for us to take the helm; the alternative is nothing short of disaster, if not outright apocalypse. British-born Tony Blankley, who was both a speechwriter and policy adviser to President Ronald Reagan and later press secretary to then–Speaker of the House Newt

Gingrich, now the *Washington Times* editorial page editor, captures the sentiment in the title of his new book: *The West's Last Chance: Will We Win the Clash of Civilizations?* No positive answer to that question is even conceivable, argues Blankley, without America taking seriously its responsibility as the West's unanointed last chance. Europe, itself in denial regarding the clicking time bomb in its midst, is hopelessly ill equipped both materially and spiritually to lead the titanic battle with Islamism that Blankley deems altogether unique, entirely unprecedented in both calamitous potential and ideological complexity.

Writes Blankley, "Today, the challenge of America and the West is to remain alert to the fact that today's Islamist insurgency is something different from anything we have experienced before," and only America is to be trusted to both understand this and carry the ball. He cites Abraham Lincoln's call to reject "the dogmas of the past" as inadequate to "the stormy present," appealing to his deeply divided countrymen to "think anew, and act anew." So Blankley exhorts us to try to think anew "about providing our grandchildren with the America we want them to have."[7] Unless America is able to lead now, its own future and that of the West in general will be history. Image be damned; survival is at stake.

But Blankley should have resisted the seduction of Huntington's catchy phrase. America should never declare war on any "civilization" appropriately so-called. Wars happen when "civilization" in some sense breaks down, if only to save it; in the process, both sides are scarred. Words matter, and *war* is not the most appropriate when the challenge is endless. Neither is "winning" the right idea where terror is at stake—only "losing." If America may be said to be the West's "last" chance, it is also the world's. The West cannot win alone any more that it can survive by ignoring "the rest"; it's too late for that. We are all looking at our collective last chance: "America R Us."

Retired Army intelligence officer Ralph Peters is similarly sanguine about America's critical role in defending the freedom and safety of the world. He shares Blankley's disapproval of Western Europeans' cowardice and is not reluctant to express his contempt. Under the circumstances, Peters believes that no amount of diplomacy, public or otherwise, will make much difference. "Those who think that all we have to do is to frame the argument properly to counter the appeal of terror" are kidding themselves. Whether others like it or not, "we have no choice but to fight for our values in a world where our self-appointed enemies are determined to fight to the death for theirs."[8] Like Blankley, Peters advises against being weighed down by the past and suggests aiming instead at "Expanding America's Global Supremacy," the book's subtitle and the last chapter. "The surest way to expand our global supremacy in the twenty-first century," argues Peters, "is to turn our attention from the lands of yesterday and extend a hand to the struggling lands of tomorrow," for "our security does not lie in preserving a loathsome Eurocentric past, but in building a better future elsewhere." He ends on a quintessentially American note: "We can do it."[9] Never mind winning hearts and minds; as Nike's logo cockily exhorts, "Just Do It."

Peters is a no-nonsense guy who's been in places and seen things the rest of us are probably better off not knowing and not asking about. His contempt for "the European model of diplomacy" is not even thinly disguised: let's face it, says Peters, diplomacy is just plain "dead." As if determined to prove it by example, he continues, "Countless zombies continue to populate embassy receptions or feed from the trough at the United Nations, but as an effective tool to solve the world's most important problems,"[10] forget it. How refreshing to see a spade called a spade, and yet I couldn't help noticing that Peters the intelligence officer was looking to solve the world's problems, which diplomacy, at least the public variety, should not be expected to do in the first place. Public diplomacy has, or should have, a more limited purpose, though no less important. It should present us as we are (or ideally as we would prefer to be seen) rather than letting our enemies do the talking. Of course this also means that we need to understand the nature of our enemy as he is, rather than as we wish he were, or imagine him to be. If a problem is created unnecessarily, it may not need to be "solved"; if a problem is not what we think it is, we are in danger of seeking the wrong solution. But if giving up all diplomacy implies merely doing "what is right" without any concern for explaining our actions in ways that others can understand them, we risk creating animosities where they don't have to be. Peters underestimates that old *esse es percipi* adage, namely, that "is" can only be "what is perceived." Give up the microphone, and—at least on the global stage—you might as well give up the show. And anyway, why should the United States, the nation that invented it, wantonly (or rather, arrogantly) give it up?

Unlike most books containing *empire* in their title, let alone those that enjoy rave accolades in the *New York Review of Books*, Niall Ferguson's *Colossus: The Rise and Fall of the American Empire* is neither predicting nor rooting for such a fall—on the contrary. Recognizing that Americans do not want to rule over an empire, Ferguson plays the role of the ruthless physician who must break the news to his protesting patient. Like it or not, an empire we are, however peculiar. Compassionately, he observes that "it is hard enough to be an empire when you believe you have a mandate from heaven, how much harder it is for the United States, which believes that heaven intended it to free the world, not rule it."[11] Ferguson takes heaven's side but carries the argument to its logical conclusion: rule we must, lest no one rule. Our problem is that we never stared cataclysmic anarchy straight in its Medusa-fiery, petrifying eye. Empire lite is not an option; it has to be the real thing or else.

It's no picnic, admits Ferguson. "Sadly, there are still a few places in the world that must be ruled before they can be freed. Sadly, the act of ruling them will sorely try Americans, who instinctively begrudge such places the blood, treasure, and time that they consume. Yet saddest of all, there seems to be no better alternative for the United States and the world,"[12] which is his book's—and, whether they know it or not, everyone's—bottom line. Interestingly, the reason is not only America's unquestionable military and economic superiority. It is not even just a question of "guts," given that George W. Bush has proven undaunted by charges of unilateralism and has confronted terrorism head on, by military force.

It seems that Ferguson considers America's willingness, even preference, to seem to act[13] more or less alone as additional proof that America is best qualified to stand in front. Having demonstrated that, at least under its current leadership, America has the guts it takes to lead, "it is now about grit, the tenacity to finish what has been started." Which leads Ferguson to his confession: "Unlike most European critics of the United States, then, I believe the world needs an effective liberal empire and that the United States is the best candidate for the job."[14] Job description: world emperor. Application: waived. Image problem: negligible. Competition: none. Status: HIRED. Term of Service: preferably in perpetuity (or, alternately, until a new qualified applicant shows up, which seems highly unlikely).

Clyde Prestowitz, president of the Economic Strategy Institute, Boston University professor Andrew C. Bacevich,[15] and the singularly self-described neoconservative intellectual Irving Kristol[16] have been among the more prominent political observers to identify America as a "reluctant superpower." Former Brookings fellow, director of policy planning at the Department of State, and now Council on Foreign Relations president Richard Haass did so a decade ago in his book *The Reluctant Sheriff*, referring to the Clinton administration.[17] A decade later, in the preface to his book *Opportunity: America's Moment to Alter History's Course*, he admits that he "would not write such a book today," for now "the sheriff could hardly be described as reluctant."[18] Yet it is far from clear whether Haass would also claim that the emboldened sheriff is any more likely now to covet, let alone wear, the imperial mantle. It wouldn't match the jeans.

Despite differences of opinion regarding the origins, degree, nature, and implications of Americans' general preference for denim, and for baseball caps over crowns, as Prestowitz puts it, "If it looks, walks, and quacks like a duck, chances are it's a duck."

Well, maybe we don't quack like it, but we do seem to act like it, for "empires are also measured by their ability to project power, to compel or entice others to do their bidding, to set and enforce rules, and to establish social norms."[19] If that is the case, and Prestowitz insists that it manifestly is, we had better be careful what we do and what we say, even—in fact, especially—to ourselves. In endearingly (if perhaps typically) American fashion, he seems to think that realizing our preeminence will suffice. "[T]he only way for America to be what I think is her ultimate, true self is to know and acknowledge the truth," he writes, adding, "and the truth will make her free and what she ought to be." That truth is "an America that stressed its tolerance rather than its might, its tradition of open inquiry rather than its way of life,"[20] in other words, being the benevolent empire that it thinks it is.

That's all very flattering, and thanks—but no thanks. We should resist the temptation of having America likened to the towering statue of Apollo at Colossus, deemed one of the ancient world's "Seven Wonders" and deliberately designed to elicit awe, fear, and trembling before the supernatural omnipotence of a capricious god. How off-putting an image, and how well does it feed the myth of anti-Americanism? No mere semantic discomfort motivates most Americans' emphatic denial that we are an empire, however "benevolent" in the estimation of our well-meaning though misguided friends. The word is dangerous, because it is quite simply false. Not only do we not talk like a duck, we also don't behave like one. Whether or not our geographic presence is imperial (which it is) hardly contradicts that point. Geography is no longer destiny, as the other of the mammoth nations of the world, Russia and China, know all too well. Those two may deplore the fact, and they obviously harbor hopes of future greatness, which is reason enough for us to shun any such analogy.

Taking on the *E* word is definitely no easy task, for it has acquired a whole new dimension, practically beyond rational discussion. For example, Robert D. Kaplan refers to American imperialism as alternately "implicit," "unconscious," and even "a form of isolationism." While admitting that it was foreign dictators who, in World War II, "forced the U.S. out of its self-imposed isolation in order to meet the security threat posed by Nazism and Japanese militarism,"[21] today the empire is up and running whether it realizes it or not, adding that other empires were equally unself-conscious—at least until they were already in a state of decline. Kaplan cites approvingly Bernard De Voto's observation in his 1952 book *The Course of Empire*: "As both a dream and a fact the American Empire was born before the United States."[22] If so, it might outlive it as well, but don't count on it: "post-Americanism" could be an oxymoron.

Kaplan, like others in the academy and the media, are indeed talking about empire. For even when he concedes that American imperialism may be motivated by a kind of postmodern isolationism, what he means is that "the demand for absolute, undefiled security at home leads one to conquer the world."[23] But to conquer is to control, and that usually means to oppress, to run others' lives. The connotations are ominous, which makes *empire* so dangerous a word. Calling this "a kind of isolationism" is to run roughshod over language and common sense. Surely we can do better.

As far as Ambassador Koshore Mahbubani is concerned, the claim that America is already an empire is nothing short of mystifying. On the contrary, protests Mahbubani, America categorically "refused to join the European impulse to colonize the world."[24] Indeed, the United States could have "easily been seduced by the idea of empire in the Age of Empire. But, fortunately for the world, America was not convinced of the merits of empire. Instead, America, consciously or unconsciously, peeled off the European layers of world history and in so doing opened the door for billions of non-Europeans to enter the modern world."[25]

It turns out that Ambassador Mahbubani is correct: the most recent polling data, as reported by Andrew Kohut and Bruce Stokes, indicate that the American public is emphatically devoid of imperial aspirations. Polls in 1993 and again in 1997 found that only one in eight Americans thought that the United States should be the "single" leader in the world—a sentiment that has not abated. The same goes for most of America's elite; while two out of three opinion leaders believe that the United States should play a strong leadership role, fewer than 10 percent believe it should be the single world leader—a finding, moreover, that has remained consistent for over a decade. Kohut and Stokes conclude decisively that "contrary to widespread misconceptions, Americans' pride in their country is not evangelistic."[26]

Paradoxically, the prevailing sentiment that America is the world's last best hope is shared, albeit somewhat reluctantly, by a few writers who nevertheless classify themselves as "left wing." Notable among them is Paul Berman, a political and cultural critic whose highly readable book, *Terror and Liberalism*, captures a sentiment far more prevalent than is openly acknowledged: "Oh how I wish that the entire world would turn out to be rationally explicable, after all—that a [Noam] Chomsky could nail it down for us, and everything could be shown to be the workings of evil oil companies and their media allies, or some other identifiable pestilence." But no such luck; we may as well face it: "Some aspects of a war against terror and totalitarianism can be fought even by people who cannot abide George W. Bush."[27]

It is too late to be disillusioned, as Henry James had been by the Great World War at the onset of the last century, when the war got worse before it was over, only to get far worse yet. There's nothing left to be disillusioned about anymore. Or is there? In a courageous leap away from existential angst, Berman decides that, after all, "we are the anti-nihilists—we had better be, anyway." In other words, what is our choice but to survive, or not? The enemies of America include both the evil and the naive. The former are beyond reason. With the latter, Berman begs to differ: selfish militarism is not the only alternative. "The anti-nihilist system likewise has two sides." It is possible to opt for war for the right reasons. "In the anti-nihilist system, freedom for others means safety for ourselves. Let us be for the freedom of others." If we don't, nobody else will. The power we should always seek must be that of liberalism. But what does that mean? Paul Berman's answer takes a form of enlightened self-interest. The rub is to define that "freedom."

Americans seem curiously oblivious to the difficulty of translating the concept not only in other languages but in other cultures. In addition to the inscrutability of all translation, an even greater obstacle is the lack of experience. Not only do we have more than one word for it—the Latin-based *liberty* comes in handy when we wish to avoid the ambiguity of the Saxon concept, which affably accommodates both "freedom to" and "freedom from"—we have felt its double-edged effects. We know that one can overestimate its allure and exaggerate its promise, but we have also had occasion to witness its splendor. Fortunate as no other people in never having had to lose it completely, Americans come close to taking it for granted. Maybe that's why we have so much trouble understanding it.

Perhaps if we did, and were able to communicate it, our global image might change. But don't bank on it; we may be rich and powerful, but we are also stupid. After 9/11, writes Berman, world opinion was sympathetic to America's taking on the terrorists, which happened to be "in many people's interest. It was not a matter of us against the universe." But then, "having raised the issue of preemptive wars, Bush also raised the issue of American unilateralism—which was bound to make countries all over the world feel that, on matters of war and peace, they had lost their say."[28] In other words, of all the various public diplomacy tools at his disposal, George Bush chose the least effective. Berman's criticism of Bush goes beyond ideology. "Why did he do that? No reason." Giving the benefit of doubt, he speculates, "Maybe out of inexperience. For lack of time to ponder the alternatives." Speaking of "lite," you got it.[29]

Which brings us to the biggest hurdle the United States faces today as the world evaluates the Iraq war and the larger policy it was meant to exemplify, known as the "Bush Doctrine." If the United States chooses to engage in "preemptive conflict," is this not a form of imperial overreach? How "lite" can an empire claim to be if it wages wars on distant shores with insufficiently solid intelligence to justify it? If the United States ends up having a long-term presence in Iraq as well as Afghanistan, as is increasingly likely, what are the implications for public diplomacy?

Despite the postmilitary debacle in Iraq, some good lessons have emerged, notably the need to be more candid with the American public and the world at large about the difficulties that might be faced down the road in the aftermath of such an enormously risky intervention. Instead of proclaiming it a "slam dunk," had the public (both domestic and global) been told that our intelligence was based on what we considered at the time to be highly reliable information, although any estimate might prove incorrect; had we been up front about what might go wrong, even if we turned out to be infallible; and finally, had we been more willing to admit that we were, in fact, mistaken on many counts, we would have come across as less arrogant and more human.

It is difficult to decide whether the "slam dunk" mentality was a matter of rhetoric, policy, or national chutzpah complemented by incompetence. I put my money on the last and cannot but agree with George Friedman's observation that "there was a strange weakness built into the Bush administration at exactly the place where it was supposed to be the strongest: political management and image making. Bush's political advisors were congenitally incapable of managing public perception of the administration's foreign policies in the United States or in Europe. The administration simply seemed bewildered when it came to articulating what the reality of the U.S. position was."[30] That's the bad news. The worse news is that this congenital incapacity is not only a malady that afflicts Republicans; the disease is national, a nasty form of political smallpox that is not merely disfiguring but potentially lethal.

I leave it to others to assess whether the "thousands" of errors in military tactics—Secretary of State Condoleezza Rice's version of the wilted bouquet to former Secretary of Defense Rumsfeld—could have been avoided. I will not examine debates about possible incompetence at the level of administrative or congressional policy, about flawed counterterrorism tactics, intransigence, and egotism at the Pentagon; obfuscation at the State Department; lack of accountability at the CIA; or greedy contractors. There is plenty of evidence that America reacted against terrorist attacks on its soil with vigor, ready to fight back, determined to send a signal to its enemies that we will not be intimidated and that we are serious about addressing the war on terror. If Saudi Arabia needed proof that its noncooperation on Al-Qaeda was ill advised, so be it. Now if we could only get our message out in a credible fashion. That is the war we seem least equipped to fight; unfortunately, it is also the one that will go far into the foreseeable future.

Most analysts, however, seem more interested in giving us tactical and policy advice than in helping us make our case. Maybe it is just too obvious? Josef Joffe has no problem explaining why the U.S. national interest is consistent with a peaceful world order: "A nation that has always defined its own welfare in terms of the right milieu—a liberal order low on violence—will flourish when the rest of the world flourishes." Considering, moreover, that "the contemporary state system with its two hundred members does not abound with understudies eager to slip into America's starring role,"[31] why worry? But his overconfidence, however comforting at first blush, seems shortsighted. For the world is no Hollywood movie; underdogs who don't even get to audition can blow out the set before the script is even written.

Convinced of America's obviously salutary effect on world stability, and with inevitable grumblings to the contrary notwithstanding, Joffe's final advice is almost perfunctory: "To continue on its path, to endure in the twenty-first century if not beyond, this hegemon must surely soften the hardest edge of its power, all with the world's assent"[32]—a strange ending to a superb book that demonstrates both why the world will continue to withhold that assent and why America's power is the softest in all of history. But yes, of course, softening the hard edge is a good idea; the question is how? When all else fails, as a last resort, as my father always says, try common sense.

We must be strong enough to admit that fighting terrorists and lawless regimes is a mighty tough job. America is no oversized statue but a nation made up of remarkable but obviously fallible human beings. We make mistakes, and we should learn from them. We don't always admit them when they happen, but if we are humble enough to recognize that prejudice is no substitute for knowledge, we will do our homework so that we can keep those mistakes at a minimum. Besides mistakes in strategy, military or otherwise, among the most glaring and least comprehensible blunders of American foreign policy are (1) failures of information dissemination and (2) the inability to appreciate the postwar nation-building challenge. The two are intimately related: they are predicated on intelligent, well-thought-out, global strategic outreach. It's not rocket science. That's why it's so hard.

NOTES

1. Claes G. Ryn, *America the Virtuous: The Crisis of Democracy and the Quest for Empire* (New Brunswick, London: Transaction Publishers, 2003), 17.

2. Ryn, *America the Virtuous*, 39.

3. Ryn, *America the Virtuous*, 179.

4. Ryn, *America the Virtuous*, 41.

5. Ryn, *America the Virtuous*, 113.

6. George Friedman points out that Saudi Arabia has also publicly condemned "neoconservatives," by whom they meant "Jewish policy intellectuals in the administration," but Friedman argues that "the administration was controlled not by the neocons but by people who had a history of close ties with the Saudis," men like Vice President Dick Cheney, Colin Powell, and George W. Bush himself, outraged by intelligence revealing substantial Saudi support to Al-Qaeda. Yet "Saudi intelligence knew the truth of the matter and did nothing." George Friedman, *America's Secret War: Inside the Hidden Worldwide Struggle between America and Its Enemies* (New York: Doubleday, 2004), 240.

7. Tony Blankley, *The West's Last Chance: Will We Win the Clash of Civilizations?* (Washington, DC: Regnery Publishing, 2005), 33.

8. Ralph Peters, *New Glory: Expanding America's Global Supremacy* (New York: Penguin Group, 2005), 283.

9. Peters, *New Glory*, 63.

10. Peters, *New Glory*, 122.

11. Niall Ferguson, *Colossus: The Rise and Fall of the American Empire* (New York: Penguin Books, 2004), xxviiii.

12. Ferguson, *Colossus*, xxviiii.

13. Writes George Friedman, "Two interesting notions took hold that Bush could not shake. The first was the idea of unilateralism—that Bush was acting without international support. The second was the idea that he was rushing into the war. Neither idea could be supported empirically. The United States had substantial international support, although not with two of its traditional allies—France and Germany." *America's Secret War*, 279.

14. Friedman, *America's Secret War*, 301.

15. Andrew J. Bacevich, *American Empire: The Realities and Consequences of U.S. Diplomacy* (Cambridge, MA: Harvard University Press, 2002); and *The New American Militarism: How Americans are Seduced by War* (Oxford: Oxford University Press, 2005).

16. Irving Kristol, *The Emerging American Empire* (Washington, DC: American Enterprise Institute, August 18, 1997).

17. Richard N. Haass, *The Reluctant Sheriff: The United States after the Cold War* (New York: Council on Foreign Relations, 1997). Also "The Squandered Presidency," *Foreign Affairs* 79, no. 3 (May–June, 2000): 136–40.

18. Richard N. Haass, *Opportunity: America's Moment to Alter History's Course* (New York: Public Affairs, 2005), x.

19. Clyde Prestowitz, *Rogue Nation: American Unilateralism and the Failure of Good Intentions* (New York: Basic Books, 2003), 25.

20. Prestowitz, *Rogue Nation*, 284.

21. Robert Kaplan, *Imperial Grunts* (New York: Random House, 2005), 6.

22. Bernard De Voto, *The Course of Empire* (New York: American Heritage, 1980), 228; cited in Kaplan, *Imperial Grunts*.

23. Kaplan, *Imperial Grunts*, 5.

24. Kishore Mahbubani, *Beyond the Age of Innocence: Rebuilding Trust between America and the World* (New York: Public Affairs, 2005), 1.

25. Mahbubani, *Beyond the Age of Innocence*, 9–10.

26. Andrew Kohut and Bruce Stokes, *America against the World: How We Are Different and Why We Are Disliked* (New York: Times Books, 2006), 75.

27. Paul Berman, *Terror and Liberalism* (New York: W. W. Norton, 2003), 208.

28. Berman, *Terror and Liberalism*, 202.

29. Lite or not, America's superpower behavior is, in the view of most observers on the political Left, the main source of its image problems. The diagnosis of Harvard psychiatry professor Robert Jay Lifton is *Superpower Syndrome: America's Apocalyptic Confrontation with the World* (New York: Thunder's Mouth Press, 2003). Like any other mental malady, therefore, it's presumably treatable—but not until the patient recognizes his illness. Clinically speaking, the symptoms are manifestations of an "overarching dynamic" that controls the nation: "The dynamic takes shape around a bizarre American collective mindset that extends our very real military power into a fantasy of cosmic control, a mindset all too readily tempted by an apocalyptic mission" (188). Among the symptoms is "a sense of entitlement concerning the right to identify and destroy all those considered to be terrorists or friends of terrorists." Imagine that.

30. Friedman, *America's Secret War*, 280.

31. Josef Joffe, *Überpower: The Imperial Temptation of America* (New York: W. W. Norton, 2006), 238.

32. Joffe, *Überpower*, 241.

Chapter Five

Watch out for the Entertainment

The world loves a spice of wickedness.

—Henry Wadsworth Longfellow

Ever since the histrionic Senator Joseph McCarthy gave the "Hollywood hates America" movement a bad name in the 1950s,[1] it has been harder to discuss in fashionable circles. But there is certainly more than a grain of truth in it; we do not need to reconstitute the deplorably named congressional committee for "un-American" activities to discover that the electronic media, including both movies and television, generally portray Americans in a negative light. Heavy metal and other high-decibel assaults on the auditory nerves offend the unwary listener not only physically and aesthetically but politically, as they portray and cater to an audience addicted to violence spiced with obscenity. No wonder this audience is easy prey to ideological brainwashing (if that's the right way to describe imprinting nearly pristine neurons).

DON'T LEAVE IT TO HOLLYWOOD

The leading analyst of media violence at the University of Pennsylvania's Annenberg School of Communications, George Gerbner, concluded after thirty years of research that characters on network television, for example, fall victim to acts of violence at least fifty times more frequently than do citizens in the country itself.[2] What emerges is a portrait of America that is not only unflattering but blatantly inaccurate.

There is also concern that portraying violence exacerbates it. In a pioneering study conducted by George Gerbner with Nancy Signorielli in 1987, originally as a project for UNESCO (United Nations Educational, Scientific, and Cultural Organization), in response to over 4,600 requests by media scholars and researchers for information relating to violence and terrorism, the annotated bibliography describes past research and current analysis on a variety of issues related to that specific topic. With most of the research compiled in the United States, the study confirms the suspicion that portraying violence and terrorist actions not only reflects world events but influences them. Since then, many more such studies have been conducted reinforcing these results. Other studies disagree, but the possibility cannot be ruled out.

Not only is violence in the media increasingly pervasive, gory, graphic, and appallingly gratuitous, but it also targets younger and younger audiences. The same is true of sexuality, scatological vulgarity—both visual and verbal—and, more generally, a raw, debasing disrespect for others and oneself, demonstrated at all levels of human interaction. The civilizing ideals of compassion, beauty, honor, fairness, courage, and the rest of what are generally called "virtues" are certainly not gone from screens both large and small, but they tend to attract fewer accolades as a jaded audience seems harder to please.

The moviemakers themselves are at least to some extent responsible for the jading, as prizes tend to go to the more cynical of Hollywood's production. A case in point is the movie *American Beauty*, which virtually swept the Oscars (Best Actor, Best Picture, Best Screenplay) in 2000. The title obviously refers to the name of a flower—used as background for the screen credits and the middle-aged main character's sexual fantasy involving a naked pubescent girl—a rose commonly known as "American Beauty."

Movie critic Michael Medved interprets the title as suggesting "that all is not, well, rosy with the American dream." It should come as no surprise, then, if "viewers in Kenya or Kuala Lumpur"—who would obviously miss the allusion to the flower's name—given the entertainment industry's high praise for the production, "understandably assume that it offers a mordantly accurate assessment of the emptiness and corruption of American society."[3]

Medved points out that America began projecting, particularly in the last four or five decades, "a self-loathing, very violent society, antagonistic within itself," which seems to feed a need felt throughout most of the world "to temper inevitable envy with a sense of their own superiority." In other words, the United States may be rich in material terms, but look at the corrosion of its moral fiber, "the violence, cruelty, injustice, corruption, arrogance and degeneracy so regularly included in depictions of American life."[4] We either pathologically relish doing this to ourselves or, more plausibly, in many cases don't even know it.

If one looks only at profits, we aren't doing badly exporting Hollywood. For one thing, so-called action movies have traveled especially well, since explosions and car crashes need no subtitles. Yet those very action movies are partly to blame for the fact that American travelers are routinely being asked how they "survive" living in such a country. The general assumption is that crime in the United States is skyrocketing, that we live in an embarrassingly permissive society, and that, despite our wealth, we lack finesse.

There is no doubt that the entertainment and news media (the latter increasingly blending into the former with alarming, though predictable, speed) have enormous power for both good and bad. The world learned, for example, that all nineteen conspirators responsible for the 9/11 attacks, during their months and years in the United States, rented action videos, went to peep shows, and were otherwise regular consumers of the most degrading products of the American entertainment industry, presumably to stiffen their hatred. Apparently feeling a degree of remorse in the immediate aftermath of the tragedy, some celebrities agreed to meet with top Pentagon and White House officials, including Karl Rove, to brainstorm in an attempt to mobilize Hollywood creativity to combat terrorism. Director William Friedkin (whose credits include such classics as *The Exorcist*, *The French Connection*, and *Rules of Engagement*) was among those expressing their willingness to enlist full time in so worthy a project.

Both the White House and the Pentagon, however, dropped the ball. Instead, the 2005 winner of the Sundance Festival Prize by Eugene Jarecki called *Why We Fight* — deliberately named after Frank Capra's World War II epic answering the question with patriotic conviction — is one more self-flagellating specimen of homegrown anti-Americanism. In this movie, Jarecki asks why — and claims to "explain how — a nation of, by and for the people has become the savings-and-loan of a system whose survival depends on a state of constant war."[5] In other words, America is now an engine for evil. Our detractors couldn't ask for more. Such sterling negative publicity money can't buy.

And then there is the off-the-screen behavior of our demigods and demigoddesses. But it is one thing for the masses to worship physical beauty, fame, and riches, and quite another to let those attributes go to their heads, as so many of these idols of the theater are wont to do. The constant change of persona involved in the act of acting must generate a need to define some kind of self, and what better way than by championing causes, preferably the kind that get you the most positive publicity? And given the media's predilection for political correctness,[6] that means promoting causes that on occasion play right into the hands of our opponents.

How else to describe the effect of movies such as *Syriana*, one of the honorees of the 2005 Oscars, which portrays the philosophy of a Texas oil man, clearly a Republican, as follows: "Corruption is our protection. . . . Corruption is how we win." His soulless mates at the CIA, meanwhile, are shown blowing up a nice, modernizing paragon of Arab moderation, together with his beautiful family, while wining and dining his corrupt younger brother, a puppet of the oil industry. No one captures the outrage of this kind of message better than the master columnist Charles Krauthammer, who castigates the film industry for having lost whatever moral compass it may have had left by honoring such an execrable production. Krauthammer juxtaposes the star-glittered spectacle of the Oscars with the image of brave young American soldiers who, at that very moment, were "fighting, some perhaps dying, in defense of precisely the kind of tolerant, modernizing Muslim leader that 'Syriana' shows America slaughtering." Continues Krauthammer, "I used to think that Hollywood had achieved its nadir with Oliver Stone's 'JFK,' a film that taught generations of Americans that President John F. Kennedy was assassinated by the CIA and the FBI in collaboration with Lyndon Johnson. But at least it was for domestic consumption, an internal affair of only marginal interest to other countries. 'Syriana,' however, is meant for export, carrying the most vicious and pernicious mendacities about America to a receptive world."[7]

With this kind of help from Hollywood, American public diplomacy becomes an unwitting form of suicide bombing, where the enemy is mainly oneself.

THE HEAVY METAL OFFENSIVE

> There's only two ways to sum up music: either it's good or it's bad.
>
> —Louis Armstrong

America the "hyperpower" is appallingly but unavoidably "Exporting the Wrong Picture"—as it happens, the title of Martha Bayles' perceptive editorial in the *Washington Post*, where she commends Benjamin Franklin's superbly deft ability to wage "a subtle but effective campaign of what we now call public diplomacy, or the use of information and culture to foster goodwill toward the nation"[8] to bolster his congressionally mandated job of traditional balance-of-power diplomacy.

A humanities professor at Boston College and a literary critic, Bayles justly, though slightly condescendingly, deplores Americans' preference for the seemingly more straightforward but far less effective, traditional, realpolitik variety. She juxtaposes the finding by the National Science Board that funding for publicly-funded public diplomacy had been cut by more than 30 percent in 2004 with a report by the Yale Center for the Study of Globalization that between 1986 and 2000, the fees generated by the export of filmed and taped entertainment went from $1.68 billion to $8.85 billion—an increase, to spare us the arithmetic, of a whopping 427 percent.[9] Good news for the bottom line, but very bad news for those of us who worry about the kind of picture the United States so lucratively, yet so embarrassingly, regularly broadcasts.

The Center for the Study of American Culture has been outraged for decades by what it views as a shamelessly anticapitalist ideology implicit in most of what Hollywood-based capitalists crank out to the ticket-buying crowd of unsuspecting, educationally challenged masses, both at home and abroad. Others, notably African American Bill Stephney, cofounder of the rap group Public Enemy, are alarmed by the normalization of crime and prostitution in *gangsta* and *crunk* rap. Professor Bayles, also the author of the popular book *Hole in the Soul: The Loss of Beauty and Meaning in American Popular Music*,[10] laments the best-selling vulgarity.

Next to Bayles' Outlook section editorial is a likeness of Benjamin Franklin's face with an expression that indicates he would have undoubtedly endorsed her lament: "American popular culture is no longer a beacon of freedom to huddled masses in closed societies. Instead, it's a glut on the market and, absent any countervailing cultural diplomacy, our de facto ambassador to the world."[11] Amen, and woe is us. Bring back the fur cap; delete the expletives.

It is much easier said than done, of course. Popular culture is just that: popular. The people who gave the world a revolutionary Bill of Rights need no reminder that government cannot and should not prohibit speech, censor art, or dictate taste. Bayles' metaphorical call to diplomatic arms is not only impractical but misguided. On the one hand, it is hard to disagree with her about conveying something closer to a "full and fair picture of the United States," as the U.S. Information Agency wistfully sought to do in a far simpler, pre-Internet era. On the other hand, Bayles' observation that "to succeed even a little, our new efforts must counter the negative self-portrait we are now exporting" must go far beyond a plea for worry. It is well and good to supplement worries about what popular culture teaches our children with "worry about what it is teaching the world about America." Such advice may satisfy the proverbial Jewish mother, for whom generalized worrying is just her job description; it definitely does not amount to a global communication strategy.

Bayles' prescription is vaguely reminiscent of the joke about the pilot who informs his passengers that he has both good and bad news: "The good news is, we are ahead of schedule. The bad news is, we're lost." When it comes to

communication strategy, absent the proper context, the United States is like
that pilot, whose sense of humor was unfortunately better than his sense of direction. But it is not Professor Bayles' job to outline a public diplomacy strategy for the United States. What she has done, and done brilliantly, is refocus
our attention to the critical significance of culture. It is not merely a matter of
prurience: among the most magnificent treasures of Western Civilization are
the barely clad Venus de Milo and Michelangelo's nude, the incomparable
David. What is more, she reminds us that both culture and morality are inextricably connected to foreign policy and global outreach.

Professor Bayles reminds us that Aristotle, who placed art on an even
higher pedestal than did his teacher Plato, was the founding father of political aesthetics. Aristotle gave art "freedom to make its own rules and even, at
times, mock goodness and sympathize with evil. Yet, ultimately, Aristotle saw
art's relation to good and evil as the same as that of all other human endeav-
ors; he certainly did not give it the exclusive power to redefine, or re-create,
good and evil."[12] Hollywood and the music industry, of course, see no reason
to ask Aristotle's, any more than anyone else's, permission for anything. Professor Bayles is obviously not suggesting censorship, but she is correct that
we need to face the fact that confronting the challenge of modernity takes intelligence, strategic thinking, creativity, and perseverance, not to mention a
liberal education.

NOTES

1. It is worth citing George Friedman, who writes in *America's Secret War: Inside
the Hidden Worldwide Struggle between America and Its Enemies* (New York: Doubleday, 2004), 114–15, 117, "The ultimate legacy of [Senator] Joseph McCarthy is that
he left the United States institutionally and intellectually incapable of coming to grips
with Al-Qaeda on a domestic level without reviving a deep national nightmare. . . .
Joseph McCarthy, J. Edgar Hoover, founder of the FBI, and their allies used the search
for Soviet agents to increase their own political power."

2. See, for example, *Against the Mainstream: The Selected Works of George Gerbner*, in "Media and Culture" (New York: Peter Lang Publishing, 2002).

3. Michael Medved, "Think America: Why the Whole World Hates You?" *National Interest*, Summer 2002.

4. Medved, "Think America."

5. www.sonyclassics.com/whywefight.

6. For examples and analysis of this phenomenon, see Bernard Goldberg, *Bias: A
CBS Insider Exposes how the Media Distort the News* (Washington, DC: Regnery
Publishing, 2002); and *Arrogance: Rescuing America from the Media Elite* (New
York: AOL Time Warner Company, 2003).

7. Charles Krauthammer, "Oscars for Osama," *Washington Post*, March 3, 2006, A17.

8. Martha Bayles, "Exporting the Wrong Picture," *Washington Post—Outlook*, August 28, 2005, B1.

9. As expected, the pattern, unfortunately, is reportedly similar for music, TV, and video games.

10. Martha Bayles, *Hole in the Soul: The Loss of Beauty and Meaning in American Popular Music* (Chicago: University of Chicago Press, 1994).

11. Bayles, "Exporting the Wrong Picture," B2.

12. Bayles, *Hole in the Soul*, 390.

Chapter Six

The Nonstarter Solutions: More Pride and Prejudice

> There are two sorts of pride: one in which we approve ourselves, the other in which we cannot accept ourselves.
>
> —Henri Frederic Amiel

The traditional conservative assessment that anti-Americanism is just a form of un-Americanism risks falling into the trap of self-defeating overcompensation. Self-righteously protesting too much tends to confirm precisely what the rightly outraged Right wishes to refute. Pride in one's country, evidenced by displaying various patriotic paraphernalia, can be endearing—at least within limits, and depending on one's personal taste for kitsch. But pride to the point of railing against all criticism is the quintessential counterproductive form of arrogance, which does this nation no good. To be sure, conservatives react to what they often correctly perceive as ill-informed and malicious attacks that sometimes border on the treasonous. But let us at all costs avoid addressing head-on such criticism as is warranted.

In deliciously Buckleyesque prose, former *National Review* (now known as *NR*) board member Neal B. Freeman reports in a memorable article, "*NR* Goes to War," published in the June 2006 issue of the *American Spectator*, his astonishment at his *NR* colleagues' abdication of independent judgment as they turned support for going to war against Saddam into a litmus test for patriotism. Virtually all, with the notable if unsurprising exception of *NR* founder William F. Buckley, had succumbed to "rational herding, which is the modeling of your beliefs on the beliefs of others whom you presume to be better informed."[1] But the worst had yet to come, as the conservative herd turned against one of its own—in fact, a pillar of the movement, mentor to many conservative journalists, including John Fund, Fred Barnes, and Kate O'Beirne,

Robert Novak—for reportorial skepticism about Iraq. Today, reports Freeman, "on each and every point Novak had been right and his opponents had been wrong. In opinion journalism, you would hope that the quality of opinion would count for something. But in those poisonous days, truth was no defense. 'Unpatriotic.' It was the cruelest cut you could inflict on a conservative of a certain age"[2]—or of any age, for that matter. Un-Americanism and anti-Americanism should never be confused with just plain skepticism regarding specific American policies if we hope to learn from our mistakes. *Unpatriotic* is not synonymous with *dissenter*, let alone *skeptic*.

The same admonition must be addressed to those who do not mind the former epithet—except obviously even more so. Reflecting an undisguised, knee-jerk contempt for the strong pro-American sentiment generally presumed to be the province of the uneducated, political correctness has taken hold of the nation's campuses, which largely explains the scarcity of dissenters who might dare question the "blame-America-first" mentality. "Academic arrogance, thy name is Professor; thy price, tenure," goes the conservative lament, and not without reason. Neo-Marxist nostalgia for a utopian world that might have been, if only the Soviet Union had not derailed the Great Dream, hails from hallowed halls. Professors tend to rail against materialism of the nonrevolutionary kind while yearning for the idealistically dialectical.

Nowhere is this more evident than in the barrage of criticisms against "consumerism" and commercialism, against the profit-mongering members of the military-industrial complex who are allegedly getting fatter while the rest of the world is becoming poorer. But the evidence points to the contrary. So why is it that, instead of applauding the improvements brought by innovations unthinkable without the free market, the elite members of the intelligentsia would sooner condemn than applaud the very system that has eased the plight of those on the lower rung of society? Is it a smug distaste for vulgar consumerism that leads to so distorted and unfair a picture? Is it the pride of learnedness that causes such contempt for uncouth materialism? Doesn't the very notion of "cowboy capitalism,"[3] allegedly America's embarrassing legacy to the world, blatantly reveal the snobbery of its proponents?

But the most common charge of arrogance—or hubris, that excessive pride which has traditionally spelled doom for mankind—leveled against the United States comes from those who accuse it of imperial designs against the rest of the world. Some concede that America is *reluctantly* imperial; or that it doesn't realize how imperial its behavior really is; or that, anyway, we are an empire already, regardless whether we know it or not, simply by being the world's most powerful nation, and we therefore can—and do—behave as we please. It all boils down to ethnocentrism, the American form of pride sometimes branded as "exceptionalism," which blinds us to its insidious quality and angers the rest of the world. We think we know what's best for everyone else, according to the more benevolent of America's critics. We don't give a hoot about what's good for anyone but ourselves, say the more self-righteous among our fellow Americans. Most damning, of course, is the charge that we are agents of evil, Satan's instrument on earth. This latter, courtesy of Al-Qaeda, carries the ominous accusation that America embodies the ultimate form of pride by waging war against God himself.

The irony is that all of these charges presuppose the very possession of one or another variety of hubris. How can anyone presume to know what Americans—or their leaders—"really" intend? When the word *empire* as used in any standard political science textbook manifestly does not apply to America, the self-appointed pundits' departure from accepted taxonomy has the suspect odor of pandering to the Zeitgeist. It is not a question of being on the side of America's enemies. In fact, our well-meaning friends who urge us to accept the lofty role of benevolent Emperor, who adopt a "what the world needs now" approach, do us no favors by implying that we would ever take on such a role, properly so-called. America is not now, has never been, and will never be, an empire. Its brief foray in that direction during the late nineteenth century has taught us a lesson we should not forget. Quite simply, a world empire to end all history can mean either totalitarianism or suicide.

The flip side of snobbery, elitism, and arrogance is prejudice, based not only on ignorance but on refusal to learn, for reasons that run the gamut from an obsession with technocracy, scientism, and specialization to a wide variety of parochialisms including linguistic paucity, cultural poverty, and ideological platitudes. The most common form of parochialism, however, is also the most pernicious: the overwhelming number of our fellow Americans, and even their political representatives, content to allow themselves to be entertained by the pseudoreality dished out by Hollywood, television, fictionalized quasi-fact, and the occasional snippet of information sandwiched among glossy ads in magazines. We live in a virtual bubble, remarkably isolated from the rest of the world. Unconscionably ignorant of history, geography, and great suffering, we have so cushioned ourselves from the world that it is now difficult to reconnect. But America, you have no choice: "You've got mail"—from everywhere. *What does the world want from America?* is the title of one recent anthology sponsored by the Center for Strategic and International Studies, a Washington-based think tank.[4] The book's deceptive brevity belies the substance of the answers. Had it asked "What *doesn't* the world want from America?" the whole book might have fit into one paragraph.

It is by no means a hopeless situation. What I plan to do in the rest of this book is, first, to examine some of the origins of that wonderful pride that gave

us the courage to embark on the most successful political and economic experiment in history, but which can and does turn against us when pursued in
excess. The American spirit of "can do," of meeting challenges with immeasurable optimism, unprecedented ingenuity, and unremitting tenacity,
needs to be tempered with the humility required for learning what it takes to
continue to be successful. It is not the humility of the "blame-America-first"
crowd, some of whose members' obsession with self-flagellation seems to
border on the pathological, for that is really just a feigned, ersatz humility. It
is important to remember that Jane Austen considered nothing quite as deceitful as the mere appearance of humility, which, she thought, far too often
reflects merely a "carelessness of opinion, and sometimes [is nothing less
than] an indirect boast." True humility, by contrast, reflects an appreciation of
human limitations, one's own at least as much as that of others, if not more.

Hardest to defeat is the kind of prejudice that prevents us from understanding what it is that we need to know, and what it takes to learn it. The intelligence community, for example, must resist the temptation of a scientism
that accounts for billions being spent on fancy gadgets such as signals intelligence (sigint) and military hardware, and begin to recognize the overly neglected significance of the human factor, whether in intelligence, institution
building, or public diplomacy. It is less sexy and more difficult to measure,
its impact less visible immediately, but it is far more effective in the long
term. The fact that it is also a great deal less expensive should not detract from
its otherwise incalculable value.

National Review editor Rich Lowry was dead-on right when he dismissed
the retired generals' attacks on former Secretary Rumsfeld as basically irrelevant, urging that "instead of a backward looking debate about the number of
post-invasion troops in Iraq, we should be having a forward-looking one
about how we can attain the requisite cultural understanding for any long-
term effort to transform the Middle East."5 Dubbing it "a muscular multiculturalism," Lowry laments its paucity, starting at the very top. He criticizes
President Bush's "anthropologically simplistic rhetoric" as typical of the cultural myopia that spells disaster. A president who "essentially posits that
everyone around the world is the same" must bear at least some of the blame
for perpetrating such myopia. He plays right into the hands of the militantly
under-informed who would have us all believe that everyone is actually a lot
like us, whether they know it or not, and whether they like it or not.

And so here we are, facing the new world disorder, no longer so "new" ourselves. Beyond pride and prejudice, however, there is hope in sensible realism and sheer—if uncommon—common sense. Far from repudiating the idealism that defines America and its dream, we have to find within ourselves
the wisdom, energy, and constructively critical self-examination required for

its fulfillment. Multiculturalism should be "muscular," yes, and also, simultaneously, empathetic. Fortunately, it often is.

Now if we could only convey this very simple message—for starters, to ourselves.

NOTES

1. Neal B. Freeman, "*NR* Goes to War," *The American Spectator*, June 2006, 30.

2. Freeman, "*NR* Goes to War," 32.

3. See Olaf Gersemann, *Cowboy Capitalism: European Myths, American Reality* (Washington, DC: Cato Institute, 2004) for a comprehensive contrast between fact and fiction by comparing European and American economic performance.

4. Alexander T. J. Lennon, *What Does the World Want from America? International Perspectives on U.S. Foreign Policy—A Washington Quarterly Reader* (Cambridge, MA: MIT Press, 2002).

5. Rich Lowry, "For a muscular multiculturalism," *Jewish World Review*, April 17, 2006, www.JewishWorldReview.com.

Part II

THE LEGACY OF PRIDE

Chapter Seven

History of a Paradox

It's a fine thing to rise above pride, but you must have pride in order to do so.

—Georges Bernanos

With characteristic bluntness and understatement, Benjamin Franklin noted in his self-published runaway best seller, humbly titled *Poor Richard's Almanac*, that "pride is said to be the last vice the good man gets clear of." Pride is rumored to have cost mankind its immortality and the peace of Eden, in exchange for the torments of hell and its counterparts, yet still it lingers in most of us, last to go in the cleansing process, if ever. The tempting garb of pride renders its poison all the more insidious. Who else but Shakespeare could have written, "He that is proud eats up himself. Pride is his own glass, his own trumpet, his own chronicle; and whatever praises itself but in the deed, devours the deed in the praise."[1] The Bard had King Agamemnon speak these words; but while quintessentially Greek, the wisdom is manifestly timeless.

America has had a peculiar love-hate relationship with pride. In his journals, particularly from his early youth, John Adams repeatedly confessed to bouts of "vanity," yet both he and Abigail were nothing if not proud of their American values in contrast to the snobbery of both English and French aristocrats. It was, to be sure, pride in an egalitarian system of government. Lesser souls would cross the line to self-righteousness, an intimate cousin of arrogance itself.

Pity the paucity of related words that this complex sentiment deserves. Lonesome *proud* has long ago lost its archaic sibling, the Latin cognate "*orgulous*" (cf. French "*orgueil*," Italian "*orgoglio*," etc.), which is exclusively pejorative, meaning haughty, arrogant, and such. As it is, *pride* does a lot of heavy lifting, the good and the bad in almost equal measure. The good includes satisfaction with work well done, possessions worth having, healthy self-esteem, and even the best of the lot (as in "the pride of the herd"). Vocabulary shortage is in this instance particularly deplorable, when a term of such importance is laden so heavily with ambiguity. For the most part, as usual, the negative wins.

And so it is that wise men have warned against "pride" as far back as our collective memory is allowed to stretch by written testimony. The ancient Greeks had adapted an ancient Indo-European conception of justice, according to which everyone has a fate (*moiré*) assigned to him, marked by clear boundaries that must not be crossed. Within those boundaries, there is much latitude, and plenty of opportunity to exercise courage, generosity, and dignity. Yet we may be induced by folly (that is Ate, the goddess of mischief) to engage in excess, popularly known as "hubris" (or *hybris*), with regard to our individual *moiré*, by imagining ourselves capable of ignoring and hence defying it.

The subject of tragedies, the fatal flaw of hubris, most dangerous among the royal elite, destroyed its hapless host because presumed parity with the Immortals manifestly constitutes sanctionable, brazen irreverence. Though admittedly fashioned in their image, mortals were explicitly not entitled to emulate divine behavior. True, the Gods were often imperfect, while humans occasionally seemed wiser and more prudent. The Gods tricked and cheated one another; they plotted against and shamelessly deceived each other. Caught in the middle, humans often had to foot the bill.

The deities were hardly superior to mortals in all respects. Indeed, when Eros' indiscriminate arrow caused them to crave undivine lovers, the gods were rendered amorously impotent, their passions tormentingly human. But still the Gods, depending on rank, could expect to indulge their pride, generally with impunity, while their mortal counterparts, no matter how privileged, could expect nothing in the end but eternal suffering. The reasons for divine retribution (Nemesis) may not have been immediately obvious to mankind (humankind, if you must) in all cases, yet mythical examples were deftly described by crafty poets to make the point without elaborate explanations. The Gods were, after all, Gods.

As Hesiod, Homer, and their fellow bards described it, Mount Olympus could be a rowdy place, its inhabitants mercurial, lusty, and ferocious when snubbed. Bad enough it was to be snubbed by a fellow divinity, but should the culprit be a mere mortal who even inadvertently, let alone deliberately, would dare counter the will of an Olympian, the sinner's merciless sentence might reach no end. Even a superhuman creature like Tantalus, son of Zeus and the nymph Pluto, would be tortured in the shadowy afterlife of the underworld in perpetuity, by way of punishment for his transgressions.

Tradition has it that his guilt consisted of one or more of at least four instances of insubordination: whether divulging some secrets entrusted to him by Zeus; or daring to steal the Gods' food, ambrosia and nectar (which accounted for their immortality and was strictly forbidden to nondeities); or other similar demonstrations of deadly insolence, he would be condemned to eternal thirst and hunger. The foolish delinquent was to face eternal temptation in the form of food and drink always just barely out of his reach. Thus cruelly tantalized, his only contribution to civilization would amount to nothing beyond an entry in the etymological history of that sorry verb.

The inhabitants of ancient Greece were well aware that all who presumed to defy the Gods in general and the Fates (Moirae) in particular would meet their comeuppance at the heavy hand of Vengeance (the goddess Poena). And why indeed would anyone in his right mind dare disobey any of the mighty immortals, even when encouraged by some in opposition to other, often mightier, gods? For heaven, too, had its hierarchies. The Trojan Paris, for example, who had been persuaded by Aphrodite to defy and defile the law of hospitality (*xenia*) most dear to Zeus by stealing and then marrying the wife of his Greek host Menelaus, would end up being punished, together with his entire nation. The brutal butchering and fall of his beloved Troy would become the subject of Homer's monumental *Iliad*, written around the eighth century B.C.

Roughly around 700 B.C., Hesiod too described in the *Theodicy* a view of life centered on the idea that man's inescapable lot was assigned to him directly by Zeus. Man has to resist temptation by the spirits of insubordination and pride, in strict obedience to both Aidos and Nemesis, the goddesses of shame and retribution, respectively. A century or two later, Aeschylus' tragedy *The Persians* illustrated the perils of hubris as exemplified by foolish King Xerxes, whose presumptuous attempt to do the humanly impossible—turning sea into land by building a bridge of ships across the Hellespont—insured his eventual absolute defeat. In this case, offending Athena, the peerless goddess of justice and virgin daughter of Zeus, born from his own cranium, carried the ultimate penalty.

The Greek respect for the quixotic whims of the Gods was typical of ancient man. The awe felt by our prescientific ancestors before the unknown, unknowable, and unpredictable forces of the universe reflected an understandably terrifying impotence. Primitive man could ill afford to enrage the powers that be: taunting them would be not merely risky to the foolish iconoclast himself, but it could—and usually would—endanger an entire family, a whole city, or even all mankind. Unwarranted pride, the dreaded hubris, could spell calamity or worse. Humility was not simply virtuous; it was prudent.

Wrathful as the Greek Gods may have been, however, they couldn't hold a candle to Jehovah, the Maker of the universe depicted in the Torah, Whom man was forbidden to call by name. Jehovah, the sole Author and Keeper of the universe, is merciful but prone to extraordinary anger. The very first act of human hubris doomed us all, when His prize creatures, though fashioned in His image, rejected His admonition by tasting the fruit that He had explicitly and unequivocally forbidden them to touch. Endowed with free will, man—encouraged by woman, herself tempted by Satan reified as articulate reptile—proceeded to misuse it by implicitly placing his own judgment against (which is to say, above) that of the Almighty.

The devil-serpent had explained to his newfound human friends the reason for God's warning against eating the magic fruit. The point was not so much that the couple would die but rather that God knew "that as soon as you eat of it your eyes will be opened and you will be like divine beings who know good and bad" (Genesis 3:5). The serpent had shrewdly left out a small detail: once the humans' eyes were "opened," they would not actually *be* but would merely *believe themselves to be* "like divine beings," a subtle but crucial epistemological distinction predictably lost on the beguiled innocents. And so it was: his eyes opened, presumptuous man proceeded to judge the work of the Lord. Assuming himself armed with divine knowledge, he covered his nakedness, "ashamed."

"Ashamed" of what? metaphorically thundered Jehovah. What could possibly be shameful—and thus implicitly imperfect, bad, and flawed—about His creation? How dare Adam think himself godlike by passing judgment on God's workmanship? Indeed, reasoned his Maker, if Adam fancies himself capable of judging good and bad, he might go as far as to judge himself worthy of eating from another tree, the ultimate Tree of Life, which confers immortality. The Hebrews knew, as did the ancient Greeks, that man would never be allowed this privilege.

Anger and thunder aside, Jehovah's reported decision was fair and justified, the argument proceeding something like this: if man feels that he can tell the difference between good and bad actions, presuming to either disregard or overrule divine advice, well then so be it; let him fend for himself. And given man's chutzpah, daring to override God's prohibition against tasting but one of countless fruits in Eden's lush garden, hardly to assuage the pangs of hunger, why should God trust that man would ever listen to His advice again? Only centuries later, according to biblical chronology, did Jehovah finally relent and, recognizing man's desperate need for mentoring and direction, chose the loyal and pious, if highly reluctant, Moses to receive His commandments and help guide the lost, confused, and suffering people of Israel.

The Old Testament contains other admonitions against pride besides the Torah, or the first five books of Moses. A later section known as "Kethuvim" ("The Writings") states, "Pride goes before ruin, / Arrogance before failure" (Proverbs 16:18). The same sentiment is echoed shortly thereafter: "Before ruin a man's heart is proud; / Humility goes before honor." (Proverbs 18:12). How very closely this resembles the wise remark from Publilius Syrus' *Moral Sayings*, written around the first century B.C.: "There is but a step between a proud man's glory and his disgrace." In short, beware of chutzpah.

The one Jew who took this warning to heart most profoundly, Jesus of Nazareth, proclaimed the virtue of poverty and meekness, the imperative of compassion, promising salvation to those who find holiness in humility and repentance, and repudiate all sin. Pride was thereafter declared absolutely anathema to Christianity as the first and foremost of the seven deadly sins. Some went so far as to consider it virtually synonymous with sin. Thus Jeremy Taylor, writing in 1647, emphatically endorsed "Epiphanius [who] makes pride to be the *onely* [*sic*; emphasis added] cause of heresies." Or, expressed somewhat differently, "Pride and Prejudice cause them all, the one criminally, the other innocently."[2]

To be sure, Jesus was not crucified for preaching humility. Rather, he paid with his mortal life for engaging in what the Roman judges considered to be the highest form of insubordination: declaring that he was the Messiah, son of God, the Lord incarnate. His executors accused Jesus of no ordinary haughtiness or arrogance (as in the French "*orgeuil*") but of hubris, which implies presumption, irreverence, and impiety. Both Socrates and the Christian champion of humility and piety would be executed for the very sin they denounced. To the authorities, insubordination and a threat to the status quo spelled treachery, pure and simple. But in reality, the executioners were inadvertently engaging in the very sin they presumed to condemn, for it is precisely the glorification of man-created order that constitutes the presumption of quasi-divine knowledge. Ironically, both Socrates and Jesus were condemned to death for having the temerity to expose the hubris of their prosecutors.

Both Socrates and Jesus preached self-examination and deference to the genuine Truth, of which man can only hope to gain an occasional glimpse. Such intellectual humility is deeply offensive to the ignorant proud and may well be mistaken for cowardliness or its very opposite, excessive pride. Yet it constitutes by far the wisest course and, in a deeper sense, requires the greatest courage. It is no coincidence that both Socrates and Jesus died as a result of their faith in the higher cause whose humble servants they saw themselves to be, and which both identified with Truth. It is in this spirit that Americans have tended to trust their own judgment and their conscience—prepared, as were the two great icons of freedom and virtue, for any consequences, however dire.

It is a hard legacy, much harder than it may appear to the unaided eye. The great historian Richard Hofstadter discussed the ensuing American dilemma in his classic work *The American Political Tradition and the Men Who Made It*. Humility and Christian virtue, writes Hofstadter, were difficult to reconcile and adapt in the New World for the simple reason that "the demands of Christianity and the success myth are incompatible. The competitive society out of which the success myth and the self-made man have grown may accept the Christian virtues in principle but can hardly observe them in practice. The motivating force in the mythology of success is ambition, which is closely akin to the cardinal Christian sin of pride."[3]

Hofstadter's insights were meant to elucidate the enigma of the gaunt president who first opened the American promise to men of every color; but in the chapter entitled "Abraham Lincoln and the Self-Made Myth," he explores the dilemma at the very core of our culture: "In a world that works through ambition and self-help, while inculcating an ethic that looks upon their results with disdain, how can an earnest man, a public figure living in a time of crisis, gratify his aspirations and yet remain morally whole?"[4] Given the profoundly religious and intensely private character of our Civil War president, whose public persona was simultaneously a solace and a burden, his natural sensitivity exacerbated by personal loss and ensuing depression, "the stage [wa]s set for high tragedy."[5] Lesser mortals, too, seduced by the deceptively heroic self-sufficiency of the self-made myth, at times fell victim to what turned out to be merely a kind of self-imposed exile. Miraculously, however, a special alchemy produced within the crucible of this New World a creature who somehow managed to transcend the contradiction.

NOTES

1. William Shakespeare, *Troilus and Cressida*, 2.3.155–59.

2. Jeremy Taylor, *A Discourse of the Liberty of Prophesying* (London: Printed for R. Royston, 1646), xii, 185.

3. Richard Hofstadter, *The American Political Tradition and the Men Who Made It* (New York: Vintage Books, 1974), 121.

4. Hofstadter, *The American Political Tradition*.

5. Hofstadter, *The American Political Tradition*.

Chapter Eight

Self-Exiled to Self-Sufficiency

He that is proud eats up himself.

—William Shakespeare, *Troilus and Cressida*

Not long after their eviction from Eden for insubordination, one of the biblical first family's sons killed the other, from envy and spite. So did Cain become the proverbial ancestor of all who slay from a purely evil motive, proud and unprovoked. One interpretation of the reason that God spared his life is that Cain had no concept of death.[1] But murder was added to the first family's— and hence mankind's—list of inheritable burdens.

Cain would go on to marry and beget children, who in turn begat children of their own—a chain that, symbolically, according to some, includes those responsible for the carnage that defines human history. The presumed descent from Cain is no less powerful for being metaphorical; the biblical story captures the idea that God had intended humans to live in harmony, free of envy and revenge. This sacred truth is central not only to the Abrahamic triadic tradition of Judaism, Christianity, and Islam, but also to virtually all other religions. Always a misnomer, so-called fundamentalism—putatively legitimized by anachronistic textual deconstruction—invariably sugarcoats hatred and intolerance, both offsprings of pride.

As recorded in the Torah, God is outraged by the moral obtuseness betrayed by the murderer's arrogantly rhetorical question: "Am I my brother's keeper?" How, God wonders, could Cain fail to realize that indeed he is just that? Like every other human being, Cain is categorically not allowed to be his innocent brother's executioner. Thus does God thunder against Cain: "You shall be more cursed than the ground, which opened its mouth to receive your brother's blood from your hand" (Genesis 4:11). Yet, for centuries to come, notwithstanding God's furious admonition against fratricide, countless more brothers, sons of brothers, and the sons of their sons' sons would slaughter each other throughout the world, across every continent, including the most sophisticated capitals of "highly" civilized Europe.

The bloody, sinful legacy of the Old World was only one reason why some of the first pilgrims decided to risk crossing the treacherous Atlantic on precarious ships, but it was certainly among the more important. The aptly named Puritans thought themselves "purer" than other men (which earned them both the respect and contempt of lesser mortals). It would be a mistake, however, to dismiss them as but another self-styled "chosen" people, afflicted with garden-variety ethnocentrism. While Stanford philosopher Richard Rorty's undisguised contempt for them as "self-flagellating sickos" is unjustly offensive, the Puritans undoubtedly regarded their uniqueness as a hard challenge rather than a coveted prize. Historian Andrew Delbanco, who hails from Harvard, captured (in language rather more in keeping with the decorum of that institution) this peculiar self-conception in his 1989 work, *The Puritan Ordeal*: "The myth of America, if it persists at all, has always rested on a precarious foundation. It is precisely its fragility, not its audacity—the perpetual worry of its believers, not their arrogance—that has made it something different (dare we say, something better?) than just another version of nationalist pomp."[2]

What made America truly exceptional is the power of that myth. In the same vein, historian Perry Miller explains that, even more than other Christians, "the Puritans were gifted—or cursed—with an overwhelming realization of an inexorable power at work not only in nature but in themselves, which they called God"[3] and which gave them an aura of otherworldliness. They were bold and unforgiving, not only with others but above all with themselves. They expected a great deal of man, who is supposed to "live in the world, but not of it." Their vision may be captured simply as an attempt to make the world a better, more holy place. Simple, yes, but there was no uniform idea, then or now, of how the world could be made better, any more than how a person can live "in" the world without losing his self. It was nevertheless the first version of the "dream" that brought so many others to these shores. It demands of the dreamer that he trust himself to be able to turn it into reality.

If the phrase itself, "the American Dream," is of recent coinage, the denotation is not, for it defines the very idea of "America," its founding premise. Historian Jim Cullen reiterates its connection to the concept of freedom, all of whose applications "rest on a sense of *agency*, the idea that individuals have control over the course of their lives."[4] And, paraphrasing Henry David Thoreau, "the Dream assumes that one *can* advance confidently in the direction of one's dreams to live out an imagined life."[5] It is impossible to understand America without a thorough appreciation of this idea, the paradoxes at its core, and the contradictions that it came to embrace.

The most striking of these paradoxes was the predestinarian or determinist legacy of Calvinism, referring to the belief that individual fate was sealed from birth, which also implied that salvation or damnation had already been decided. The "catch" was that no one could know whether it was one or the other. Evidently, it was far preferable, far more comforting, to behave assuming the best rather than the worst. In practice, therefore, Puritans behaved *as if* they were headed for salvation, while rationally accepting the possibility that fate had sealed that door for any one of them in particular. Another way of expressing this strange reality is to say that they imagined themselves saved, and hence they behaved that way and thus transformed a "dream" into "reality." The result is, on one level, perfectly simple, though on another level it is extraordinarily complex. In brief, on the assumption of predestination, the American Dream turned into its exact opposite: the belief in personal agency, the conviction that imagination can become reality. He who accepts the fact that his life has already been directed by God and acts in accordance with an optimistic assumption that God's goodness and mercy will prevail may be more likely to trust his dream.

But the original logic took an unexpected—though perhaps predictable—conceptual and emotional trajectory. Writes Cullen, "One of the greatest ironies—perhaps *the* greatest—of the American Dream is that its foundations were laid by people who specifically rejected a belief that they did have control over their destinies." The dream was then passed on to "successors who later declared independence to get that chance, to heirs who elaborated a gospel of self-help [eventually] promising they could shape their fates without effort, and ends with people who long to achieve dreams without having to make any effort at all."[6] However oversimplified, this analysis captures with remarkable acumen the challenge of contemporary America, the dilemma facing the dreamers of today. If we consider ourselves "chosen" as were the Puritans before us, is it enough for us to wait for God's will to be done on earth as it is in heaven merely because we happen to be Americans? Or will the current version of the passionately disciplined early Americans' determinist dream, absent their stoic humility, lead America to a rude awakening?

The first logical step in the effort to play out each individual's God-ordained destiny is to make sure that no one, no other human being, interferes with the divine plan. It follows that independence and self-determination must be gained and then preserved. Once in charge of his own fate, however, man has to work at fulfilling his God-given destiny by obeying the laws of

God. By the eighteenth century, those laws were presumed to be discernible through reason—the faculty reenshrined by the Scientific Revolution, formerly worshiped as the goddess of Athens. Countering it were the traditional nefarious passions, weaknesses, and vices. Reason and discipline made a fine couple; the American Dream was the offspring they deserved.

Independence did not imply monadic individualism, let alone a quasi-psychotic solipsism—the idea that the world is our idea, that we alone exist. The Puritans conceived of themselves as a community first, a "people" with a common God, by no means a collection of "atomized" individuals. They would unquestioningly accept Aristotle's belief that man is by nature a "social"—certainly a "paired" or "coupled"—animal, and whoever thinks otherwise must be either a god or a beast. Perhaps it was precisely because the Puritans believed salvation to be the fate of each solitary soul that community was even more important. Being alone in the world is easier when we are alone together.

Governor John Winthrop of the Massachusetts Bay Colony was the first to express this sentiment in 1630 in a sermon, published after his death, by appealing to an enlightened sense of self-interest that embraced the community: "No man is made more honorable than another or more wealthy, etc., out of any particular and singular respect to himself, but for the glory of his creator and the common good of the creature, man. . . . [Therefore] we must delight in each other, make others' condition our own . . . having before our eyes . . . our community as members of the same body."[7]

There would always be comfort in community and fellow feeling. Eventually, however, the New World would breed a radically new kind of self-sufficiency, both material and spiritual, tending more toward the solitary individual. Along with the newfound independence that shunned all shackles, including the closest ties that bind without coercion, there developed a spirit of the righteous lone ranger who had boldly abandoned the Old World with its intrigues and false idols. The dream of the new American was to be free; he believed he had what it took to find his own path to peace and salvation. Almost imperceptibly, the new American slipped into his own peculiar form of solipsism: "The world may be shaped by my will; my world is my idea reflected by my will; the world can be different if I will it so." This was no German-style, romantic idealism, but a new form of realism based on a newfound faith in the power of agency. If this seems close to blasphemy, well yes, it could be read that way.

But outright blasphemy it definitely was not, at least not quite, and certainly not at first. Eloquently captured by the philosopher-poet Ralph Waldo Emerson in his celebrated essay "Self-Reliance," published in 1840, the American Dream of making it on one's own was more saintly than arrogant;

this world should offer a preview of the ultimate, heavenly serenity. And that can only be attained through inner strength: "Nothing can bring you peace but yourself." The reason is clear: "Self-existence is the attribute of the Supreme Cause, and it constitutes the measure of good by the degree in which it enters into all lowers forms. . . . Nature suffers nothing to remain in her kingdoms which cannot help itself." More specifically, "the vital resources of every animal and vegetable are demonstrations of the self-sufficing and therefore self-relying soul."[8]

This is not an expression of simplistic "atomistic" individualism but in many ways its very opposite. Rather than alone, we are all "one," not only before God but before one another. "All men have my blood and I all men's."[9] Emerson's humanism, better known as "transcendentalism," implied that not only Christ but everyone lives through all of us; it is the blood of God we all share; it flows through us, within us. Wild idea, this American-style pantheism, and widely it resonated. "In yourself is the law of nature," declared the orator; "in yourself slumbers the whole of Reason; it is for you to know all; it is for you to dare all."[10]

So spoke Emerson in 1837, standing before a mesmerized audience consisting of Phi Beta Kappa Society students attending Harvard University. Oliver Wendell Holmes later dubbed "The American Scholar," as Emerson's eloquent address came to be known, "our intellectual Declaration of Independence." There were reasons aplenty for according it such a revolutionary status: in this address, Emerson proclaimed not only the preeminence of a unique form of universal individualism, but also the necessary superiority of American over European education. "We have listened too long to the courtly muses of Europe. The spirit of the American freeman is already suspected to be timid, imitative, tame."[11] Heaven keep us from such a charge. We will be bold: "We will walk on our own feet; we will work with our own hands; we will speak our own minds" and build an unprecedented society. And so "a new nation of men will for the first time exist, because each believes himself inspired by the Divine Soul which also inspires all men." Could a message offer loftier inspiration—and project more self-confidence?

But to his surprise, Emerson would soon find an even bolder kindred soul. In 1855, a man of sensuous, raw rebellious temperament would publish an extraordinary book of verse echoing the pagan version of Emerson's humanist pantheism. The man was Walt Whitman, and the book was *Leaves of Grass*. The irreverent virility, revolutionary style, and brazenly unrepentant power of this stunning work, printed by its author, could not fail to mesmerize Emerson, at least initially. In large measure, it was Emerson's immediate, unqualified endorsement that facilitated Whitman's entrance on the American literary stage. Eventually, America would recognize in the ruggedly handsome "carpenter" poet its own true voice: the roar of a raw new breed of man, set on settling a brand-new continent and ready to remake, rename, and revel in himself.

In his monumental epic "Song of Myself," Whitman rephrased Emersonian theocentric universalism in more explicitly egocentric, material terms: "I celebrate myself, / And what I assume you shall assume, / For every atom belonging to me as good belongs to you."[12] The semireligious overtones of shared "blood" are by no means discarded, but they are subtly transformed, as Whitman invokes atoms—indeed, atoms of energy: "Urge and urge and urge / Always the procreant urge of the world." He means by "energy" exactly what it implies: creation, life, and light where there had been night. "Out of the dimness opposite equals advance, always substance and increase." And in the 1892 edition, he is emboldened to add, too, "always sex"—that is, the alchemy of human creation. So does the ghost of Parmenides from pre-Socratic times return, invoking "the many-in-the-one": "Always a knit of identity, always distinction, always a breed of life."[13]

This expansive humanist universality implies, too, that America itself is a microcosm of all the world, now a microcosm for all of history, present and future. Thus Whitman: "There was never any more inception than there is now, / Nor any more youth or age than there is now, / And will never be any more perfection than there is now, / Nor any more heaven or hell than there is now."[14] There is no need to look beyond oneself to know the world, to feel it, to sing it. More dramatically still, he proclaims, "The past and present wilt—I have fill'd them, emptied them, and proceed to fill my next fold of the future."[15] Aware of the paradox, he hastens to embrace it, with light defiance: "Do I contradict myself? / Very well then . . . I contradict myself; / I am large. . . . I contain multitudes."

Whitman's raw, earthy sexuality embraced all: hermaphroditic and cosmic; life and death; all of time, in its infinity; yin and yang; and energy itself—containing the positive and the negative, not to cancel one another but to give birth to the orgasmic splendor of Creation. I am that I am; I am, and therefore I feel; I feel the world, and therefore the world is infinite! So goes Whitman's quasi-biblical cry—well-nigh blasphemous were it not his peculiar, idiosyncratic tribute to God's magnificence and workmanship. More particularly, it was his tribute to America. In his preface to the 1855 edition of *Leaves of Grass* (omitted from subsequent editions perhaps because of its embarrassing gushiness), Whitman writes, "The United States themselves are essentially the greatest poem. . . . Here at last is something in the doings of man that corresponds with the broadcast doings of the day and night."[16] America is "not merely a nation but a teeming nation of nations," its "genius" found not among its elite but "always most in the common people," whose accolades

Whitman sings, deserving "the President's taking off his hat to them not they to him," in brief, "unrhymed poetry" all. Heretofore, "the largeness of nature or the nation were monstrous without a corresponding largeness and generosity of the spirit of the citizen"[17]—at long last achieved in America.

The odd clumsiness of his prose is more than compensated by Whitman's groundbreaking, exquisite poetry, testimony to his genuine, boundless love for his country and what it represents. He spoke for millions who would have scratched their heads at his metaphors, and he spoke from their hearts. Concluding his preface, he passes judgment on himself and his nation, simultaneously: "The proof of a poet is that his country absorbs him as affectionately as he has absorbed it."[18] Absorbed by Whitman, America became his idol, to whom he dedicated his talent and his passion. Whitman the individual symbolized America the supreme, where the individual reigned above no one but himself, and so did Whitman sing his song: to himself. Whitman glorified and worshiped his universal nation with all the ardor worthy of that self-worship sometimes known as freedom. But Whitman's deity was nothing other than mankind in its highest expression, its timeless beauty.

Both Whitman and Emerson assumed that every man reflects all mankind: the universal not only mirrors the particular as an instantiation of a Platonic idea, but in a much more literal, existential sense *is* that idea. Not only is America everywhere, but anywhere: all is each, and each is all. Or, as modern-day positivists might put it, the logic of the universal quantifier is non-exclusive, captured by either expression, meaning both. Each of us instantiates the predicate of "Being" regardless of location, each a prototype of the divine, whether in Manhattan, Calcutta, or Mecca.

The curious practical, not to say mundane, corollary of this concept is a decided antipathy to travel. Why bother roaming aimlessly in strange, faraway lands? Writes Emerson, "Traveling is a fool's paradise. . . . The rage of traveling is a symptom of a deeper unsoundness affecting the whole intellectual action." Why copy foreign ideas? "Beauty, convenience, grandeur of thought and quaint expression are as near to us as to any, and if the American artist will study . . . the wants of the people, the habit and form of the government, he will create a house in which all these will find themselves fitted"[19]—so why travel? In brief, "the soul is no traveler; the wise man stays at home" and minds his own business.

Emerson was not merely advising the cultivation of inward-looking wisdom. In fact, he was reflecting what had become a unique conception of freedom that traced its roots to the man whose words expressed it most famously: Thomas Jefferson. For even as he proclaimed the universality of man's rights, he was also conscious of the corrosive influence of ill-conceived ideas. What Americans had been able to carefully nourish was a classical conception of virtuous freedom that cherished independence in a manner that men of other nations could not fathom. Long before immigration was to be curtailed for much more base reasons, Jefferson had feared the deleterious effect on the brave New World of those who might "bring with them the principles of the [monarchical] governments they leave, imbibed in early youth," and would "infuse into [America] their spirit of subjection and 'licentiousness.'"[20]

America was to incubate the man who both wanted and could be free, whose natural thirst for self-realization had not been extinguished by the sclerotic ideas and feudal arrangements of old Europe. Being free implies more than a celebration of the human potential—which it surely is, above all else. It is also a solemn responsibility, simultaneously to oneself, the nation, the world, and ultimately to God Himself, whose instrument every man is, whether he knows it or not. But if he does not, the risk is not merely loneliness; it is self-destruction.

No one demonstrates this better than Gatsby—mockingly described as "Great"—the doomed protagonist of F. Scott Fitzgerald's masterpiece. I wholeheartedly agree with Azar Nafisi: *The Great Gatsby* is "in many ways the quintessential American novel,"[21] and not only because Gatsby is the prototypical Great American Dreamer—which he is—but because he demonstrates what can happen when the dreamer seeks to translate his dream into reality. Some dreams are best left untouched by the blinding light of day. Past dreams that come true invariably betray the preconceived silhouette of their promise. Nafisi urges learning "from the lonely, isolated Gatsby, who also tried to retrieve his past and give flesh and blood to a fancy, a dream that was never meant to be more than a dream,"[22] which cost him his life. Once the dream is no longer a life-giving source of inspiration, having become a pathological obsession defying reality and common sense, its author is already doomed, his soul cremated by the flames of its own delusions.

NOTES

1. Rabbi Joseph Telushkin, *Jewish Literacy: The Most Important Things to Know about the Jewish Religion, Its People, and Its History* (New York: William Morrow Company, 1991), 28.

2. Andrew Delbanco, *The Puritan Ordeal* (Cambridge, MA: Harvard University Press, 1989), cited in Jim Cullen's *The American Dream: A Short History of an Idea That Shaped a Nation* (Oxford: Oxford University Press, 2003), 13.

3. Perry Miller, *The New England Mind* (1939–1952), cited in Andrew Delbanco, *The Real American Dream: A Meditation on Hope* (Cambridge, MA: Harvard University Press, 1999), 41.

4. Cullen, *The American Dream*, 10.

5. Cullen, *The American Dream*.

6. Cullen, *The American Dream* (text in brackets added).

7. John Winthrop, "A Model of Christian Charity," in *The Puritans in America: A Narrative Anthology*, ed. Alan Heimert and Andrew Delbanco (Cambridge, MA: Harvard University Press, 1985).

8. Ralph Waldo Emerson, "Self-Reliance," in *Selections from Ralph Waldo Emerson*, ed. Stephen E. Whicher (Boston: Houghton Mifflin, Riverside Editions, 1957), 159.

9. Emerson, "Self-Reliance," 159.

10. Ralph Waldo Emerson, "The American Scholar," in *Annals of America*, vol. 6, *1833–1840, The Challenge of a Continent* (Chicago: Encyclopaedia Britannica, 1968), 378.

11. Emerson, "The American Scholar," 6:378.

12. Walt Whitman, *Whitman's "Song of Myself"—Origin, Growth, Meaning*, ed. James E. Miller Jr. (New York: Dodd, Mead & Co., 1964), 2. The later version, published in 1892, adds "and sing myself" after "I celebrate myself" in the first line.

13. Whitman, *Whitman's "Song of Myself,"* 5.

14. Whitman, *Whitman's "Song of Myself,"* 5.

15. Whitman, *Whitman's "Song of Myself,"* 94–95.

16. Walt Whitman, *Leaves of Grass* (Oxford: Oxford University Press, 1998), 439.

17. Whitman, *Leaves of Grass*.

18. Whitman, *Leaves of Grass*, 462.

19. Emerson, "Self-Reliance," 164.

20. Thomas Jefferson, "Notes on the State of Virginia," in *The Portable Jefferson*, ed. Merrill Peterson. ed. (New York: Viking Press, 1975), 125.

21. Azar Nafisi, *Reading Lolita in Tehran* (New York: Random House, 2003), 109.

22. Nafisi, *Reading Lolita in Tehran*, 114.

Chapter Nine

Exceptionalist Nationalism

> The patriots are those who love America enough to wish to see her as a model to mankind.

> —Adlai E. Stevenson

It took a while for the settlers of the new continent to acquire a national identity. They thought of themselves as Virginians, New Yorkers, Pennsylvanians, or Vermonters; at a broader level, they were British subjects or colonists. "American" nationality as such emerged mainly as a result of political necessity. It was unrealistic to expect the separate colonies to be capable of maintaining any kind of "sovereignty" when faced with the great powers of Europe who would defend their people, feudal estates, and protectionist policies without batting an eyelash against encroachments by brazen upstarts, no matter how articulate. To fight effectively for their principles and hard-earned profits, Americans quickly understood that they needed to mobilize and pool their assets; fighting one another at home would have spelled disaster. At least their fight had to be contained within a broader political unit. And so were born "the United States of America." Although it would take more than a century for the name to start being used as a singular noun, a people was emerging, hopeful.

Inherently drawn to the ideology of capitalism as articulated by Adam Smith in his seminal tome, *The Wealth of Nations*, published in the same year—*anno mirabilis*—as Jefferson's Declaration of Independence, most Americans put their trust in the Invisible Hand whose mysterious wisdom they believed would bring prosperity to all mankind, and in particular to their own newly settled lands. George Washington captured that natural national faith in his first inaugural address, delivered on April 30, 1789: "No people can be bound to acknowledge and adore the Invisible Hand which conducts the affairs of men more than those of the United States. . . . [May] the pre-eminence of free government be exemplified by all the attributes which can win the affections of its citizens and command the respect of the world [since] there is no truth more thoroughly established than that there exists in the economy and course of nature an indissoluble union between virtue and happiness."[1]

It seemed self-evident to the impatiently self-assured Americans that free markets guaranteed not only prosperity and happiness but also world peace and liberty, the ideal society where men could pursue their individual interests for the common good. The evils of mercantilism were obvious; if only governments would start pursuing the public interest and set aside the petty rivalries of the decadent European courts, all those costly wars and unnecessary bloodshed would come to an end.[2] This, at least, was the ideal; reality should at least try to come close.

But why couldn't other nations realize the plainly visible benefits of letting the Invisible Hand play Its cards? And why didn't they also recognize the universal advantages of trading with America? John Adams was especially upset by the slowness of the European courts to establish commercial relations with the United States. He was convinced that it was the system of free exchange of goods between nations that constituted America's most critical, certainly most profitable, message to the world.[3]

So too did most of his colleagues, notably the ever-frugal epicurean Benjamin Franklin and his friend Silas Deane: "Tyranny is so generally established in the rest of the world, that the prospect of an asylum in America for those who love liberty, gives general joy, and our cause is esteemed the cause of all mankind. . . . We are fighting for the dignity and happiness of human nature. Glorious is it for the Americans to be called by Providence to this post of honor." The messianic passion of the newly "chosen people" for liberty, joy, and dignity was inseparable from their devotion to free trade. America's abundance of raw materials along with the colonists' industrious energy should easily explain the almost self-righteous aggressiveness and quasi-religious zeal of its new citizens, eager to buy and sell far and wide.

Even long before Adam Smith, almost a century earlier, John Locke had easily succeeded, with his impeccable logic, in convincing educated Americans that life, liberty, and property constituted an indissoluble trinity that he identified by one word: *estate*. Locke had declared the right to equal freedom to be God given, unquestionable, and prior to the establishment of worldly civil society both temporally and theoretically.[4] Not in his wildest dreams could Locke have imagined that his ingenious thought experiment, the theoretical construct he called "the state of nature," would become reified so soon, on a new continent almost as pristine as his ingenious premises.

John Locke's American disciples followed in his footsteps. Thomas Jefferson did not substitute "the pursuit of happiness" for "property" in Locke's tripartite notion of "estate" to modify the idea but to underscore, and even explicate, the synonymy. Property, after all, is what makes possible the pursuit of whatever we each call "happiness." Patently necessary as life and liberty undoubtedly are to that pursuit, they are hardly sufficient. Once the conditions for its realization were philosophically justified and the territory settled, the American Dream was ready to be dreamt. All it needed was to carve out a political homeland.

The colonists were convinced, in their hearts, that Providence had ordained them to found an ideal polity in accordance with the principles of reason. Men like Benjamin Franklin, John Adams, and Thomas Jefferson fervently, and not a little immodestly, believed they were on a sacred mission on behalf of all humanity, even if humanity in general happened not to know that. But in order to implement the divine experiment, reason had to be set free to test the validity of specific political policies by establishing an institutional governing structure based on the consent of the governed, not on tyrannical rule by corrupt princes.

That structure was to take root on the continent that Christopher Columbus fatefully, if accidentally, stumbled upon on his roundabout way to India. The moment was ripe, and the feisty European settlers, who had left behind their ancestral heritage and most of their worldly goods, were prepared—and, in any event, were required—to give it their all. The lofty purpose of the New World was captured best by pamphleteer Thomas Paine's runaway best-seller *Common Sense*, in which he predicted that America would become nothing short of "an asylum for mankind." Beyond becoming an unprecedented near-utopian political and economic entity, the United States was assumed to be meant to be, not only by its inhabitants but also by many of its friends, the anointed herald of a new world.

Among the newborn nation's most ardent admirers was the English parliamentarian Thomas Pownall, a former governor of Massachusetts, whose opinion carried considerable weight as he spoke from intimate acquaintance with America. In a tract published anonymously in July 1780 entitled "A Memorial Most Humbly Addressed to the Sovereign of Europe on the Present State of Affairs, between the Old and New World," Pownall observed that "the acquirement of information in things and business," which circumstances forced Americans to seek and develop, "thus sharpened and thus exercised, [causes] a turn of inquiry and investigation which forms a *character peculiar to these people* [italics in original], which is not to be met with, nor ever did exist in any other to the same degree, unless in some of the ancient republics."[5] Speaking not only for himself, but for everyone else who has known Americans "and has viewed them in this light will consider them as animated in this New World . . . with the spirit of a new philosophy," comparing them to "eaglets" who "commence the first efforts of their pinions from a towering advantage."[6]

Most importantly, their advantage comes from the boldness of experiment in commerce and all areas of economic activity, due in large measure to the absence of any "laws that frame conditions on which a man is to become entitled to exercise this or that trade, . . . the manner in which, and the prices at which, he is to work"; in brief, "there are none of those oppressing, obstructing, dead-doing laws here," which guarantees that manufacture "will take its shoot and will grow and increase with astonishing exuberance."[7]

America's economic success was seen as only one aspect of its special spirit. Pownall compared America to "the infant Hercules," young and strong. Indeed, "its strength will grow with its years, and it will establish its constitution, and perfect adultness in growth of state." The young country proved him right in less time than even her sanguine admirer might have anticipated. By the end of the next century, the grown-up Hercules that was America stretched from one end of the continent to the other, convinced that if it flexed its muscles, the world would shudder with admiration, in awe of the omniscient hand's eminently visible might.

Naturally, most if not all national dreams consist of a fair amount of embellishment, and America is no exception. But the famous "city on a hill" metaphor is generally misunderstood to reflect the American version of run-of-the-mill ethnocentrism. The record indicates, however, that John Winthrop was not exactly starry-eyed. He knew the price of conspicuously located real estate. Ostentatiously shining, and propped up on a hill to boot, the city would inevitably lose its anonymity. Winthrop warns the proud inhabitants that now "the eyes of all people are upon us, so that if we shall deal falsely with our God in this work we have undertaken," they (or, rather, we) will all be in pretty deep trouble. "We shall open the mouths of enemies to speak evil of the ways of God . . . we shall shame the faces of many of God's worthy servants, and cause their prayers to be turned into curses upon us till we be consumed out of the good land whither we are agoing." The sentiment was echoed by Reverend Peter Bulkeley, a minister at Concord, Massachusetts, who declared that the people of New England should "in a special manner labor to shine forth in holiness above other people . . . [for] we are as a city set upon a hill," and shame will befall us if we "walk contrary to our covenant."[8]

How better to express the burden of the "chosen," the paradox of awe inseparable from fear and humility? If America intends to stay on top of the hill, shining away, the upkeep will require constant polish and eternal vigilance. But have we perhaps taken on too heavy a burden? Is Beacon of Hope to All the World not too grand a self-appointed task, a mission impossible for anyone other than God Himself? Have we been overselling ourselves, even (perhaps especially) to ourselves? Are we the great white whale itself, the mighty mammal of the earthly ocean, whom misguided Ahabs mistake for an evil shark bent on swallowing its lesser creatures on the food chain? Herman Melville captured our remarkably lofty self-image with legendary clarity:

> We Americans are the peculiar, chosen people—the Israel of our time; we bear the ark of the Liberties of the world. Seventy years ago, we escaped from thrall, and besides our first birth-right—embracing one continent of the earth—God has given to us, for a future inheritance, the broad domains of the political pagans, that shall yet come and lie down under the shade of our ark, without bloody hands being lifted. God has predestinated, mankind expects, great things from our race; and great things we feel in our souls. . . . And let us always remember that without ourselves, almost for the first time in the history of the earth, national selfishness is unbounded philanthropy; for we can not do a good to America but we give alms to the world.[9]

The idea of American exceptionalism was keenly understood by many an outside observer, notably Edmund Burke, known best as the merciless critic of another, far more murderous revolution, across the English Channel, which he found revoltingly detestable. Contemptuous of idle utopia, Burke realized that Americans were a very special breed, no mere transplanted Englishmen but the idiosyncratic architects of a remarkably efficient, self-regulating, and altogether novel society. In an impassioned speech on March 22, 1775, he urged his colleagues in the House of Commons to let these fiercely independent, industrious, and able men across the ocean continue to govern themselves without dictates from a distance.

Burke saw the colonists' independence, built steadfast on Protestant religion, as "the most adverse to all implicit submission of mind and opinion"[10]—a spirit that elevates freedom to "a kind of rank and privilege." Yet, ever the realist, Burke hastens to dispel the impression that he means "to commend the superior morality of this sentiment, which has at least as much pride as virtue in it,"[11] but merely to assess the "fierce" nature of the colonists' "spirit of liberty," which Parliament would seek in vain to squelch.

With similar compassion, the Frenchman Michel-Guillaume-Jean (known in America as J. Hector St. John) de Crevecoeur, eventually opting for American citizenship himself, answered the question "What is an American?" by noting the paucity of "words of dignity and names of honor"[12] to address the "upper" classes—indicative of an individualism more famously observed and praised by another Frenchman. More than anyone else, however, it was Charles-Henri Clerel (better known as Alexis) de Tocqueville who, after visiting the colonies for the first time in 1831–1832 with his friend Gustave de

Beaumont, gave the world a remarkably accurate and sympathetic picture of American exceptionalism, its participatory civil society, and widespread self-government, in what became the wildly popular *Democracy in America.*

An intrinsic component of that exceptionalism was the moral conviction that America is somehow God's chosen bride, better than all other societies, and the only one worth bothering about. Sometimes the accolades would highlight America's fertility, as did Captain John Smith in 1616, who was awed by the variety of flora and fauna. Reverend James Smith, writing in 1797, was wildly impressed by "the finest beef and mutton," to say nothing of the hogs which "fatten in the woods in a most surprising manner . . . [while] the rivers produce an infinite number of fish."[13] America has often been commended as an example to the rest of the world for its natural prosperity enhanced by the energy of unregulated commerce, its enviable GDP, the lightning-like speed of its Internet connections, the sprawl of its exurbs, and the happiness of its seemingly endless pursuits.

But right there alongside the economist's hard milk-and-honey data is invoked the nation's vaunted moral uniqueness, a spirituality that if not acquired is at the very least aspired to and is historically unprecedented in both scope and sincerity. Hence American idealism can become so excessive as to turn against itself. Thus Seymour Martin Lipset argues that American values are complex to the point of paradox. "The American Creed," writes Lipset, "is something of a double-edged sword: it fosters a high sense of personal responsibility, independent initiative, and voluntarism as it also encourages self-serving behavior, atomism, and a disregard for communal good."[14] Citing both patriotism and opposition to war, both greed and philanthropy, he nevertheless concludes on a positive note, observing that most Americans view their country as rewarding personal integrity and hard work. A survey conducted by the Hudson Institute, for example, found that despite serious concerns on a wide range of issues, three-quarters of the population agree that, "as Americans, we can always find a way to solve our problems and get what we want."[15]

To this day, American nationalism carries messianic overtones that are sometimes mistaken for imperialism, whether conscious or not. Robert D. Kaplan, for example, observes that the Army Special Forces sergeants he met on his world tour of America's alleged empire "saw themselves as American nationalists, even if the role they performed was imperial."[16] This is no mere semantic disagreement. The United States cannot be understood in terms that apply to any other nation. Yes, we are patriotic and nationalistic, but no, we are not imperial. Our nationalism is exceptionalist in exceptional ways. Melville had it right: we see ourselves as the "peculiar" chosen people. That peculiarity is not inscrutable; it deserves not to be mislabeled.

NOTES

1. *Annals of America*, vol. III, *1784–1796, Organizing the New Nation* (Chicago: Encyclopaedia Britannica, 1968), 344–45.

2. Paul Varg, "The Economic and Ideological Framework," in *Foreign Policies of the Founding Fathers* (Baltimore, MD: Penguin Books, 1963), 1–10.

3. Varg, "The Economic and Ideological Framework," 3.

4. John Locke, "Of Property," in *The Second Treatise on Government*, edited by C. B. Macpherson (Indianapolis, IN: Hackett Publishing Company, 1980), 18–30.

5. *Annals of America*, vol. II, *1755–1783: Resistance and Revolution* (Chicago: Encyclopaedia Britannica, 1968), 553.

6. *Annals of America*, II:553.

7. *Annals of America*, II:553.

8. *Annals of America*, II:537.

9. Herman Melville, *White Jacket: Or, the World in a Man-of-War*, chap. 36. www.gutenberg.org/dirs/1/0/10712/10712.txt.

10. Edmund Burke, "Speech on Conciliation with the Colonies," in *The Portable Edmund Burke*, ed. Isaac Kramnick (New York: Penguin Books, 1999), 262.

11. Burke, "Speech on Conciliation," 263.

12. J. Hector St. John Crevecoeur, *Letters from an American Farmer* (New York: Dolphin Books, 1963), 46–47. He first published his *Letters* in 1782, later supplemented by newly found letters in France in 1925.

13. *Annals of America* II:540.

14. Seymour Martin Lipset, *American Exceptionalism: A Double-Edged Sword* (New York: W. W. Norton, 1986), 268.

15. Lipset, *American Exceptionalism*, 287.

16. Robert D. Kaplan, *Imperial Grunts* (New York: Random House, 2005), 14.

Chapter Ten

Too Proud to Play Hardball at the UN

The fewer the voices on the side of truth, the more distinct and strong must be your own.

— William Ellery Channing the Elder

John Quincy Adams, in his Independence Day Address of 1821, wrote that "America, in the assembly of nations, since her admission among them, has invariably, though often fruitlessly, held forth to them the hand of honest friendship, of equal freedom, of general reciprocity." He was talking about an informal "assembly," but he could as well have referred to the more formal organizations that have since proliferated. America, Adams went on, "has uniformly spoken among them, though often to heedless and often disdainful ears, the language of equal liberty, equal justice, and equal rights"—more or less to no avail. That was 1821; in the ensuing century, Americans became increasingly tired of speaking "fruitlessly," and instead of learning how to talk more effectively, they proceeded to turn within.

When Woodrow Wilson first proposed establishing the League of Nations, the U.S. Senate flatly rejected it. The former professor was so set on putting into practice the theories he had embraced so ardently, with the intense pride of Platonic certitude, that he neglected to do the prerequisite politicking, assuming that any politicking would have worked to persuade his decidedly more grounded colleagues, especially the traditionally more empirically minded Republicans whom Wilson didn't much care to consult.

From its abortive inception, the League of Nations certainly had all the markings of Immanuel Kant's quasi-utopian community of virtuous nations. Outlined in his seminal, celebrated, if misleadingly titled essay "Perpetual Peace," published in 1795, such a community was a metaphysical ideal that we must all seek, not necessarily a reality attainable on earth. "When we consider the perverseness of human nature which is nakedly revealed in the uncontrolled relations between nations," wrote Kant, "we may well be astonished that the word 'law' has not yet been banished from war politics as pedantic."[1] It is the concept of ideal law that Kant meant to elucidate by envisaging a possible state of "perpetual peace," not its actual implementation. It may have been Kant's turgid prose that seems to have prevented Wilson from noticing the wise philosopher's admonition to the effect that such a community, while not a logical impossibility, was highly improbable.[2] And even a monkish academic could have predicted that Wilson's lack of political savvy in his dealings with Senate members of the opposing party would guarantee that his starry-eyed plan would lead nowhere.

It would be another quarter of a century before a league of sorts would come together. Winston Churchill's idea was rather closer to Immanuel Kant's vision of like-minded nations genuinely "united" in the pursuit of peace predicated on democratic freedom. Franklin Delano Roosevelt's conception was grander but no less idealistic. Joseph Stalin's agenda was another story altogether, but the wartime alliance and perhaps a heavy dose of wishful thinking obscured that fact. In the end, a global organization did emerge from the smoke-filled chambers where the Founding Fathers, some much older than others, nursed their brandies and vodkas. The result was more or less crammed down the collective throats of the world noncommunity—a motley crew of more-or-less ravaged regimes, most considerably farther from rather than closer to the Kantian ideal.

There were those who from the outset considered the United Nations a mistake or worse, having to look no farther than its name to be convinced that it had been conceived with deliberate deception or, at the very least, self-deception—perhaps a more defensible but in fact more dangerous affliction. When idealism slid into blatant hypocrisy is hard to say, since the two are too often intertwined anyhow. So goes the scathing indictment by a recent American inmate of the asylum on Turtle Bay known as the UN Secretariat: "There was thus no avenue of escape from incompetence at the United Nations. Incompetence was expected. Nobody with a serious plan for reform could get anywhere because the system was deliberately maintained in a dysfunctional state by the big powers."[3] It would eventually be the turn of some small powers to do the same.

The author of these unminced remarks is Pedro A. Sanjuan, first appointed in 1983 by then-vice president George H. W. Bush to join the ranks of the international civil service—which turned out to be anything but civil. The title of his book barely contains his revulsion not only at the shenanigans that go on under our very eyes but, far more, at the inexplicable indifference of its host, the superpower that bankrolls it all. *The UN Gang: A Memoir of Incompetence, Corruption, Espionage, Anti-Semitism, and Islamic Extremism at the UN Secretariat* is a funny book. But it is also a sad and frightening indictment of its wealthy and powerful host, who is either too stupid or too arrogant to realize that the joke is on him, and it's getting to be increasingly less funny.

Sanjuan's testimony is the latest in a long string of credible, well-documented accounts of espionage, subversion, and corruption taking place right under own noses. Daniel Patrick Moynihan, America's candid, flamboyant ambassador appointed by Jimmy Carter in the late 1970s, captured his experiences in a well-written memoir that sent shivers up many an idealistic spine. The colorful Moynihan was followed by another Democrat of a decidedly antitotalitarian bent, the brilliant, and no less eloquent and undaunted, Georgetown professor Jeanne Kirkpatrick.[4] In 1981, the Heritage Foundation launched an ambitious United Nations Assessment Project whose reports would land on the desks of every congressman and senator, and of top policy makers in the administration, think tanks, academia, and the press, with dizzying speed and astonishing regularity, documenting the vicious anti-Americanism, anti-Semitism, and general political decadence of an organization that many preferred to dismiss as merely useless.[5]

At the time that I started the United Nations Assessment Project, I recall how little investigative work had been done to uncover what was really going on inside that peculiar building. Most Americans had no clue. It is true, New Yorkers knew about the thousands of dollars in unpaid traffic tickets by ambassadors who pleaded diplomatic immunity. College or even high school students who participated in "Model United Nations projects" engaged in a fantasy facsimile with little relationship to the corrupt real thing. The United Nations Association was so open in its pro-UN bias that I had to look elsewhere for hard facts. I found them initially in three places. First, there was the African American specialist at the Library of Congress, a paragon of professionalism, fairness, and cordiality, whose genuine love for the United Nations never interfered with her objectivity. Next were the Americans working at the UN, inside the secretariat, notably Pedro Sanjuan, who was always glad to have someone with whom to share his frustration and outrage. The Americans inside the U.S. Mission could always be counted upon to help at any time of day or night. They told it like it was, and not just to me but to the whole world. The late ambassador Charles Lichenstein, subsequently for many years my colleague at the Heritage Foundation, will go down in history for calmly but firmly telling the UN that, if it doesn't like it in New York, we will gladly wave it good-bye. Meanwhile, the current president of the National Endowment for Democracy, Carl Gershmann, was confounding the Third

Committee, tasked to address human rights. Both—and indeed the rest of the mission—stood as a valiant boulder in the path of the rhetorical avalanche coming from the malodorous political culture of the UN.

Rather more unexpected was the third source of my information, and certainly the most significant, for it included a wide variety of UN diplomats themselves, sometimes from European nations whose home governments—to the chagrin of their New York–based representatives—would opt to keep a low profile and abstain rather than boldly reject preposterous resolutions. Surprisingly, some represented small nations, principally African ones, such as the Ivory Coast, Sierra Leone, and Ghana, who were almost routinely instructed to vote for every resolution directed against the United States, practically on automatic pilot. The diplomats spoke mostly off the record, relieved to be able to reveal their frustration with the United States for its seemingly condescending indifference to the United Nations and its members, and for its failure to realize that it was being dealt significant, albeit rhetorical, blows.

Anger would have been preferable to contemptuous neglect. There was strong, widespread consternation at the way American ambassadors had consistently failed to call other governments to task, whether through bilateral discussions or any other means, for their anti-American harangues inside the halls of the General Assembly and for hostile votes on behalf of one-sided, vicious resolutions. They told me about Soviet tactics behind the scenes, pressuring weaker countries to vote, and even introduce resolutions, on their behalf. Meanwhile, America watched with a seeming noblesse oblige haughtiness that resembled the benevolent tolerance of a parent toward a naughty child. It was in fact not only offensive but shortsighted and self-defeating.

It was this political culture that Ambassador Jeanne Kirkpatrick and her team tried to change in the 1980s. She used to love telling the story of an incident that took place when she first arrived at the United Nations, which I heard repeated on many occasions by members of her staff. It happened that, once again, a whole herd of putatively nonaligned nations voted on the opposite side from the United States on one of the many outrageous resolutions on which the United States found itself in the usual minuscule minority. Ambassador Kirkpatrick did something absolutely unprecedented: she contacted their respective representatives and asked why they voted the way they did. It so happened that many if not most of these governments were recipients of some form of American largesse, so the response came quickly, echoing the same theme, expressing surprise, even astonishment, at the fact that anyone in the U.S. government cared! Why didn't we tell them that these votes mattered? Ambassador Kirkpatrick made it quite clear that to her, at least, they did.

But it was too little too late. The U.S. Mission to the UN in the 1980s may have gathered a pretty formidable team, led by a remarkable orator, but it wasn't enough. Congress didn't start to care until the 1980s, when the Kirkpatrick team and the Heritage Foundation's exposure of voting patterns resulted in a legislative requirement to take UN voting behavior into consideration as a factor in determining who gets foreign assistance and how much. Since the U.S. contribution to the UN, which at 25 percent already amounted to a larger chunk of the budget than any other country by far, came in hard, convertible currency (meanwhile, the Soviet Bloc's was in nonconvertible "silly money"), this meant that insult had been self-inflicted in addition to the increasingly routine injury. The United States was bankrolling the daily spectacle of flagellation, apparently having convinced itself that it all comes with the territory, in a somewhat perverse version of *richesse oblige*.

The diplomatic beating to which the United States ritualistically exposes itself is only the more obvious, more tangible expression of a far greater danger represented by this Trojan piece of enormously profitable real estate in the heart of Manhattan, which happens to lie entirely outside the jurisdiction of the U.S. government. During the Cold War years, the crimes being committed on this extra-American territory were mainly espionage, especially conducted by the Soviet Bloc intelligence services, particularly the KGB, and drug trafficking on a massive scale. The Palestinian Liberation Organization's (PLO's) "observer" mission to the UN (giving it a status on a par with the Vatican) was certainly a security concern, as were the activities of Muslim extremists inside the secretariat.

Not many Americans realize that inside the UN Secretariat building, the headquarters donated to the world by an American businessman, on American soil that we have voluntarily exempted from our own laws and prohibited the FBI from entering, UN staffers reacted to the 9/11 massacre with open satisfaction, declaring that at last America was getting what it deserved.[6] Indeed, this was not Ramallah but New York City; nor was it an isolated incident in an organization dominated by blatant anti-Semitism. What is especially galling is that Islamist extremists connected with the UN are able to use the headquarters with impunity and even diplomatic immunity.

When it comes to America's dismal image in the United Nations, there is plenty of blame to go around. It is true that the so-called nonaligned governments allowed themselves to fall under the influence of the Soviet Union, which had deftly succeeded in co-opting the vast majority of their votes to support their routine anti-Western and progressively more blatantly anti-American resolutions in the General Assembly (or the GA, for short). But the USSR had been running virtually unopposed. The United States was obviously correct in its assessment that the posturing taking place in the halls of that "debating society"—as the UN was known to it its more jaded, if utterly naive, friends—had little to do with debate. The political culture that had slowly and deliberately emerged over the course of about two decades was becoming a potent instrument in the war of words, not always distinguishable from the war of ideas. Whether it cared or not, and it certainly didn't care enough to prevent what soon became an irreversible reality, the United States was losing the war inside the UN. The GA's perennial resolutions reflected with chilling accuracy the inanities spewed by the lackeys of tyrants, parading as representatives of their "peoples."[7]

While it is also true that UN resolutions "passed" by the GA fail to translate in the way of action, since only the Security Council is empowered to engage in peacekeeping operations, it is tempting to dismiss them as mere verbiage. In his new book on the United Nations, Joshua Muravchik, American Enterprise Institute senior fellow and Institute of World Politics professor, may seem somewhat lenient with the Third World members of the Non-Aligned Movement (NAM). Established in 1961 by a quartet of staunchly socialist heads of state, NAM was quickly and cleverly co-opted by the Soviet Union. Muravchik allows that its anti-Western, and specifically anti-American, rage has "at least a patina of logic."[8] And so it does, certainly by the twisted rules of the time-tested brand of demagogy that passes for public diplomacy at Turtle Bay. Muravchik is right not to put the bulk of the blame on the Third World. More culpable by far is the United States, which early on had decided to treat the whole circus as a kind of Turkish bath where hot air circulated mainly to soothe tired political muscles. Even a decade after the end of the Cold War, the anti-U.S. sentiment at the United Nations persisted, with no discernible price to pay. A study by the Heritage Foundation released on June 12, 1998,[9] examining voting records in the UN found that three quarters (74 percent) of all the states that received U.S. assistance were still voting on the opposite side of the United States.

The current U.S. permanent representative to the UN, John Bolton, describes the American response to the pro-Soviet, anti-Western turn of the organization with somewhat greater sympathy, noting that "within just a few years after its founding, the UN was so obviously ineffective that the United States, and those in the world who shared our values, turned to more realistic approaches to protecting our basic national interests."[10] Realistic they may have been, but also shortsighted. Once again, America in its self-righteous pride decided not to stoop to oratorical devices. Whatever "realism" we thought we were pursuing, it wasn't pragmatism. We abdicated, having decided that we would sit on the bench and let the others play.

The result was a perverse game in which we agreed to subject ourselves to scathing accusations that we knew to be preposterous, watching as the nation whose birth was the work of the United Nations itself, the only ally who consistently voted alongside the United States, Israel, was being castigated as the most vile and dangerous menace to civilization since Nazi Germany. When Yasser Arafat, ostentatiously sporting a holster when addressing the international body in 1974, championed the "armed struggle" of his people—which meant killing Israeli civilians—he was hailed with a standing ovation. The United States, as usual, did essentially nothing.

The mountains of paper spewed out by the presses of the UN, while obviously unknown in the United States, proved useful to the enterprising Russian government whose skill in public diplomacy was as well honed as ours was nonexistent. Among Pedro Sanjuan's many revelations, during his ten-year stint at the UN, one came on a trip to the Soviet Union where he happened to watch a popular TV news program *Vremya* (Time) featuring a UN news segment on a daily basis. It helped that he spoke Russian; he thus learned, for example, that "Soviet food and medicine and other forms of humanitarian aid is going to Africa with strong UN support, while America is providing weapons to the entire strife-ridden African continent to promote reactionary regimes and apartheid."[11] Never mind that the opposite was true.

The United States had never protested, because "the U.S. State Department apparently saw no particular harm in it. The U.S. has an embassy in Moscow equipped with numerous television sets."[12] Indeed, one may argue that Soviet citizens were used to propaganda, and anyway, American protests would be entirely useless in Moscow. The problem is that the same propaganda was being beamed elsewhere, as pivotal Soviet officials were being posted to most, and certainly in the most pivotal, of the UN Information Centers (UNICs) throughout the world.

This included especially "the most amazing condemnation of U.S. policy," with emphasis on the wrongness of U.S. support for Israel and on the correctness of the PLO version on the situation in the Middle East. It was being beamed throughout the world and disseminated by all the UNICs, including the Washington bureau. Israel[13]—and the United States—were being routinely accused of racism and genocide. Nor is the Third World alone; our presumed Western allies use the UN to score points in public diplomacy. In 2001, for example, the European Union (in all probability at France's instigation) colluded with Cuba and China in the Economic and Social Council to ensure that the United States would lose its seat on the Commission on Human Rights. Libya—and of course Cuba and China—could sit on the commission, but not the United States.[14] Again, it would be funny if it were not so preposterous.

It serves us right, implies Sanjuan, for we willingly, inexplicably, dropped the ball. Just to clarify, we had put the ball in the UN's court ourselves; many of its features that later proved to give us the most trouble turned out to have been our own initiatives. The Economic and Social Council, for example, had been based on the idea that economic problems need to be addressed first if peace is to be assured. Was it really too difficult to predict that such a forum would eventually be hijacked by demagogues on the payroll of shrewd kleptocracies that unflinchingly would utter the baldest lies? Also, the headquarters itself became a nest of spies,[15] drug dealers, and Islamic militants, smack in the middle of the largest metropolitan center of the country. The price of undue pride can be, and usually is, mighty high.

As Ambassador John Bolton points out, the decision made during the years of the Carter administration, and later the Clinton administration (he could also have added that of George Bush *le pere*), to treat the UN General Assembly as "just a way for the Third World 'to let off a little steam'"[16] was hardly the right approach. In fact, it was merely a different kind of pride—the condescending variety—arguably even more infuriating behind its disingenuous veneer. The realization that the UN really could be used to advance U.S. interests—at the very least, that it could seriously hamper our ability to straighten out falsehood from fact—came far too late, if it came at all. Bolton is now trying to do what he can, but it is long after the UN's fall—in fact, its second fall, judging by the title of Bolton's 1997 essay about "The Creation, Fall, Rise, and Fall of the United Nations."

It certainly does not help that even inside the State Department there is disagreement about what the United States is trying to do at the United Nations. For example, in early April 2006, the Bush administration decided not to seek a seat on the Human Rights Commission, to protest the UN's refusal to reform itself by admitting only members with acceptable human rights records, which would imply excluding dictatorships. Ambassador John Bolton cast the U.S. vote against seeking a seat on the commission, where it had previously lost to the likes of Cuba and Libya. But the public message got badly scrambled. *Washington Post* columnist Robert Novak notes that the State Department's explanation, "given in un-attributed statements to reporters, made it appear that course was taken because the U.S. candidate for the council might lose. 'It's a question more of tactics than principle,' a senior U.S. official was quoted as saying in a Reuters dispatch. The same official then went on to say 'we'll probably run for a seat later on,'" leading Novak to wonder just "who really runs the State Department."[17] A far more important question is why anyone in the U.S. foreign affairs establishment would want to sabotage such a message being sent to one of the world's most important public diplomacy forums. No wonder we keep losing this game, when so many of us don't want to play ball in the first place.

What is worse is that some may even think, on the contrary, that *that* is playing ball. America is so powerful that it doesn't have to stoop to the under-the-belt tactics of its dictatorial fellow governments. Why, so the reasoning goes, take them to task for making of mockery of human rights? The problem is that this kind of condescension, which may seem benevolent and peace loving at first blush, is in fact disrespectful—indeed it should be seen as offensive—and many see it just that way. For it is not only the United States that loses when we play the game disregarding the real rules; it is the people of the world whose rights the UN's hypocritical members blatantly disregard while we look the other way.

NOTES

1. Immanuel Kant, *Perpetual Peace*, ed. Lewis White Beck, Library of Liberal Arts (Indianapolis: Bobbs-Merrill Company, 1957), 17.

2. A brief, excellent discussion of Kant is to be found in W. B. Gallie's *Philosophers of Peace and War: Kant, Clausewitz, Marx, Engels and Tolstoy* (Cambridge: Cambridge University Press, 1978).

3. Pedro A. Sanjuan, *The UN Gang: A Memoir of Incompetence, Corruption, Espionage, Anti-Semitism, and Islamic Extremism at the UN Secretariat* (New York: Doubleday, 2005), 2.

4. Kirkpatrick was in many ways the female equivalent of King Arthur, her knights including luminaries such as the late Charles Lichenstein, a distinguished senior fellow at the Heritage Foundation; Carl Gershmann, the long-time president of the National Endowment for Democracy (NED); political scientist Mark Plattner, who heads up NED's International Forum for Democratic Studies and coedits the *Journal of Democracy* along with Larry Diamond of the Hoover Institution; Kenneth L. Adelmann, later head of ACDA; and Allan Gerson, expert in international law and terrorism.

5. These reports are now available in the archives of the Heritage Foundation on its website, www.heritagefoundation.org.

6. Sanjuan, *The UN Gang*, 174.

7. Among the first exposés of the General Assembly's rhetorical excesses and the overwhelmingly anti-American voting pattern of UN members was my own study, "Through the Looking Glass: The Political Culture of the U.N.," Heritage Foundation Backgrounder, August 27, 1982.

8. Joshua Muravchik, *The Future of the United Nations: Understanding the Past to Chart a Way Forward* (Washington, DC: AEI Press, 2005), 83.

9. Bryan T. Johnson, "U.S. Foreign Aid and United Nations Voting Records," Backgrounder 1186, June 12, 1998.

10. John Bolton, chapter 3 in *Delusions of Grandeur: The United Nations and Global Intervention*, ed. Ted Gale Carpenter (Washington, DC: Cato Institute, 1997), 46.

11. Sanjuan, *The UN Gang*, 112.

12. Sanjuan, *The UN Gang*, 112.

13. See the author's "The United Nations' Campaign against Israel," Heritage Foundation Backgrounder, June 16, 1983.

14. Muravchik, *The Future of the United Nations*, 86.

15. The UN Secretariat, together with the Soviet missions to the UN, constituted the largest continent of spies in the United States. See the author's "Moscow's U.N. Outpost," Heritage Foundation Backgrounder, November 22, 1983, Executive Memorandum 54: "It's Time to Curb U.N. Based Spies," June 7, 1984, as well as "The Many Ways the U.N. Serves the USSR," May 3, 1984. A very important firsthand account is Arkady Shevchenko's memoir as the highest-ranking Soviet employee in the UN Secretariat who defected to the United States.

16. Bolton, *Delusions of Grandeur*, 46.

17. Robert D. Novak, "Behind the U.N. Council Boycott," *Washington Post*, April 10, 2006, A17.

Chapter Eleven

Strategic Public Diplomacy: For Dummies?

The American people never carry an umbrella. They prepare to walk in eternal sunshine.

—Alfred E. Smith

George Washington University professor Jarol B. Manheim, who coined the concept of "strategic public diplomacy" fifteen years ago, recently wrote a book tantalizingly entitled *Strategic Public Diplomacy and American Foreign Policy: The Evolution of Influence*. The title's systematic ambiguity seems deliberate, leading some to expect a study of American strategic public diplomacy. Not so. However important, such a book, as Professor Manheim politely intimates, cannot be written; "the inquiries [he has] made over the years, with professionals at the United States Information Agency and at other points in the federal establishment where one might expect such activities to center as well as with outside observers, have led [him] to the preliminary conclusion that, when it comes to strategic public diplomacy, the United States gives far less than it gets."[1] That is diplomatic talk for "*oy vey, gevalt*,"[2] or, let's not talk about it.

Manheim hastens to add that he certainly doesn't mean to imply that, just because it's short on strategy, the United States does not engage in *any* public diplomacy. On the contrary, "it is quite active in this area." Which only makes his next comment more devastating: "The argument applies only to the sophistication of those efforts that are implemented."[3] In other words, no offense to his many friends who engage in them, the United States government doesn't know squat about how to communicate effectively on a global scale. It is not clear whether the reason is because the United States is too sure of its premier status and considers strategic public diplomacy beneath it—or, as

Manheim says more diplomatically, "it feels less dependent on the largesse of its partners in the international system and is therefore less inclined to attempt this form of political management across national borders[—]or perhaps because it has not learned to appreciate the power of strategic communication as much as some others have, [but] the United States does not appear to engage in these activities either regularly or systematically."[4] Translation: Whatever we think we are doing in "public diplomacy," either it's not terribly strategic, or insofar as it is, it isn't worth much.

This is all the more frustrating when one considers that for nearly half a century it has become increasingly clear that "a government, to survive, must supplement formal government-to-government relations with an approach to the people."[5] John Lee said so clearly in the preface to *The Diplomatic Persuaders*, published in 1968, in the midst of the decolonization of the African continent. "To meet this challenge governments around the world have turned to a totally new concept of international diplomacy." Briefly, and dramatically, he concludes, "This is the age of public diplomacy." And since international opinion wields such incredible power, there is simply no choice but to inform the people of other nations, "allies and enemies alike," lest we find ourselves "inarticulate in the face of world opinion."[6] Maybe even worse— we let falsehoods and prejudices triumph, unaddressed.

Subsequently, Congress got into the act as well by holding hearings a decade later in 1977, and then again, before another mere decade went by, in 1987. The conclusion was that public diplomacy activities could productively be expanded and improved. But it was a 1979 report by the U.S. General Accountability Office (GAO) that summarized the public diplomacy activities of seven countries—France, Great Britain, Japan, West Germany, China, and the USSR, along with the United States—assessing their implications for U.S. foreign policy. The GAO report echoed Lee's finding, a decade earlier, that public diplomacy had become a very important instrument of foreign policy in all of these countries, but that the U.S. effort was the smallest. It therefore recommended a number of improvements.

Manheim mentions these recommendations with barely veiled, certainly understated, disapproval, for not only did they display the "bean counter" mentality typical of congressional reports, but they were also grounded in the belief that "relatively straightforward" efforts to disseminate information are altogether sufficient. This somewhat simplistic point of view is perhaps unsurprising in a government context. But Manheim also (however indirectly) blames those scholars who focused primarily on issues relating to the management, general content, and direction of a public diplomacy whose integration with foreign policy interests and initiatives rendered information dissemination secondary at best.[7]

Hoping to influence the American media, public, and elite opinion, foreign nations engage in outright "political campaigns" designed to obtain military, economic, or at least diplomatic and even psychological support from the U.S. government; "framing" or shaping public impressions through carefully selected words or images; and staging "megaevents" assured of reaching worldwide audiences for national foreign policy objectives, to mention but a few such techniques. It comes as no great surprise that strategic public diplomacy that benefits foreign interests—whether states or foreign-owned corporations—involves the use of sophisticated techniques developed mainly in the United States. Both the social and political technology of strategic public diplomacy is made in the USA; "indeed," claims Manheim, "it is one of our most successful exports on the world market."[8] It is therefore especially unfortunate that we not only make little use of it ourselves but that we fail to protect ourselves adequately when others use it to manipulate us or others against us. Is it perhaps because we think ourselves immune to manipulation? It's not out of the question. Such is the price of overconfidence, of which we have too much in stock.

Most countries have traditionally made extensive use of bureaus designed specifically to influence decision makers inside and outside targeted foreign governments. In addition, particularly after the introduction of rapid and effective technological advances in media, their scope was broadened to include public diplomacy. Thus, other countries appreciated from the outset the importance of radio, and most took direct control of the structure and content of radio broadcasting as it expanded throughout the 1920s. The United States was the exception.[9] This is not necessarily to imply that the United States should have followed suit, but it does underscore America's failure to appreciate radio's potential given its enormous reach. While other governments saw the power of broadcasting to affect public opinion not only at home but abroad, the radio market in the United States was almost exclusively domestic. Commercial broadcasters, after all, had no reason to reach beyond the national audience, to people who couldn't buy what their advertisers had to sell.

In fact, one of the earliest advocates of using radio for political ends was the first dictator of the Soviet Union, V. I. Lenin, at first for domestic purposes, followed within a short time by foreign-language broadcasts reaching neighboring countries and eventually the entire globe. Next in line was Nazi Germany, which installed shortwave transmitters capable of reaching even into Asia and the Western Hemisphere. The British and French governments, meanwhile, were targeting primarily their colonies in Africa and Asia. The United States was the last to use international broadcasting in its foreign outreach. When, in 1939, the Federal Communications Commission sought to limit foreign transmissions by U.S. broadcasters to programs that "reflect the culture of this country and which will promote international goodwill, understanding, and cooperation," it had to back down in response to fierce opposition by CBS, NBC, and the American Civil Liberties Union [ACLU] on First Amendment grounds.[10] At the time of Pearl Harbor, the United States had fewer than a dozen shortwave transmitters capable of overseas broadcasting.

It was Edward R. Murrow, head of the U.S. Information Agency during the Kennedy administration, who realized the significance of strategic information outreach. Murrow realized that younger people had been a primary target for Soviet propaganda for decades. For several decades, the USSR had been conducting all-expenses-paid "World Youth Festivals" where future Communist leaders were being groomed. So Murrow turned his attention to university student leaders. "Youth officers" assigned to various USIA posts usually spoke the local languages and established good rapport with the young people there.

But it was also possible to reach foreign audiences right here at home, within the borders of the United States, a fact that seems to have pretty much escaped us for most of our history. Foreign correspondents stationed in the United States had been virtually ignored by the White House, the State Department, and other agencies. While other countries paid a great deal of attention to members of the press, especially from large news organizations, it was not until the 1960s that Foreign Press Centers were opened first in New York and later in Washington.

The same has been true of overseas educational and cultural programs. The United States, again, was the last of the major powers to officially promote its cultural wares abroad.[11] The French subsidized the immodestly named *mission civilisatrice*; the Germans peddled their forthrightly dubbed *Kulturpolitik*; the Soviet Union engaged in heavy-handed but certainly not unsuccessful propaganda; and even the more subdued Brits created a special organization in 1934, the British Council, devoted to the management of an extensive program of academic and artistic exchanges. It was not until 1947 that the United States started the Fulbright scholarship program, funded by the sale of surplus war equipment abroad. Finally, in 1948, with the passage of the Smith-Mundt Act, cultural exchanges rose to the rank of diplomatic tools in the United States, a role long recognized by other nations.[12]

"Strategic," however, is a word that tends to raise blood pressures, or at the very least eyebrows, among the tenderhearted in this country, particularly outside military circles, and most certainly the media. So, for example, when the *Washington Post* got wind of a couple of slides from a briefing prepared for General George Casey, the top U.S. commander in Iraq, describing a strategic communication strategy regarding the late Abu Musab Zarqawi, the journalistic eyeballs popped. The *Post* was unable to estimate the precise cost of this ominously orchestrated "Zarqawi campaign, which began two years ago and is believed to be ongoing,"[13] so hang on to your hats, folks. The *Post* did learn that "U.S. propaganda efforts in Iraq in 2004 cost $24 million, but that included extensive building of offices and residences for troops involved, as well as radio broadcasts and distribution of thousands of leaflets with Zarqawi's face on them," according to "the officer speaking on background," since the Pentagon is mandated by law to make sure that no "propaganda" reaches Americans.

The fact that Zarqawi was among the most vicious terrorists on earth did not stop the *Post* from using the word *propaganda*; after all, it has such a catchy sinister ring to it, only further exacerbated by *strategic*, which adds that irksome quasi-military touch. General Casey's slides, moreover, referred to "*aggressive* Strategic Communications" designed to "*eliminate* popular support" for the terrorists and "*deny* ability of insurgency to 'take root' among the people" (italics added). All of which are very nasty words, definitely not suited for sensitive domestic ears—not, at least, according to the *Washington Post*.

Conceding that the military's "propaganda program largely has been aimed at Iraqis," the *Post* should have known better. They call it "bleed-over," and it sure is hard to avoid. What with satellite television, e-mail, and the Internet, what's to be done? There isn't even any need to be coyly off the record here. Army Colonel James A. Treadwell states the obvious: "There's always going to be a certain amount of bleed-over with the global information environment." Draw your own conclusions: whether you like it or not, you too are a target of American "propaganda." The fact that none of the information, which the Pentagon considered important enough for the Iraqi people to know, turned out to be false was no consolation. For one thing, it does not deter journalists, who dutifully guard their version of the objectivity of your news, from insinuating otherwise. Some of you might feel at least some relief that "the people of al-Anbar—Fallujah and Ramadi, specifically—have decided to turn against terrorists and foreign fighters," according to Major General Rick Lynch, indicating that the Pentagon's operation may have delivered at least some bang for your buck. But don't let that lower your guard.

Sarcasm aside, how can genuinely *strategic* communication be conducted in such an atmosphere? The situation has been summed up with remarkable—and chilling—accuracy in the Report of the Defense Science Board Task Force on Strategic Communication of September 2004:

Strategic communication is a vital component of U.S. national security. It is in crisis, and it must be transformed with a strength of purpose that matches our commitment to diplomacy, defense, intelligence, law enforcement, and homeland security. Presidential leadership and the bipartisan political will of Congress are essential. Collaboration between government and the private sector on an unprecedented scale is imperative. To succeed, we must understand the United States is engaged in a generational and global struggle about ideas, not a war between the West and Islam. It is more than a war against the tactic of terrorism. We must think in terms of global networks, both government and non-government.[14]

The report concludes that we need, above all, "in-depth knowledge of other cultures and factors that motivate human behavior." Mazel tov.[15] (Or, as my father would say, "And how much did they get paid to come up with that?") That is the good news: we have been told what's wrong. Now for the bad news: when asked what is being done about it, one of the contributors to the report stated succinctly, "Zilch." Since he is still on the payroll of the Pentagon, this is off the record. But he need not worry; the silence of nonaction is deafening enough.

NOTES

1. Jarol B. Manheim, *Strategic Public Diplomacy and American Foreign Policy: The Evolution of Influence* (New York: Oxford University Press, 1994), 11.

2. Jewish Proverb: "Man comes into the world with an *Oy!*—and leaves with a *gevalt!*" Leo Rosten, *The Joys of Yiddish* (New York: Pocket Books, 1970), 134.

3. Manheim, *Strategic Public Diplomacy*, 11.

4. Manheim, *Strategic Public Diplomacy*, 11.

5. John Lee, *The Diplomatic Persuaders: New Role of the Mass Media in International Relations* (New York: John Wiley & Sons, 1968), ix–x.

6. Lee, *The Diplomatic Persuaders*, ix–x.

7. Among these scholars were Fitzhugh Green, *American Propaganda Abroad: From Benjamin Franklin to Ronald Reagan* (New York: Hippocrene Books, 1988); Gifford Malone, *Political Advocacy and Cultural Communication: Organizing the Nation's Public Diplomacy* (Lanham, MD: University Press of America, 1988); Anthony Smith, *The Geopolitics of Information: How Western Culture Dominates the World* (New York: Oxford University Press, 1980); and Hans N. Tuch, *Communicating with the World: Public Diplomacy Overseas* (New York: St. Martin's Press, 1990).

8. Manheim, *Strategic Public Diplomacy*, 13.

9. Wilson P. Dizard Jr., *Inventing Public Diplomacy: The Story of the U.S. Information Agency* (Boulder, CO: Lynne Rienner Publishers, 2004), 23.

10. Dizard, *Inventing Public Diplomacy*, 24.

11. Dizard, *Inventing Public Diplomacy*, 147.

12. For a superb history, see Richard T. Arndt, *The First Resort of Kings: American Cultural Diplomacy in the Twentieth Century* (Dulles, Virginia: Potomac Books, 2005).

13. Thomas E. Ricks, "Military Plays up Role of Zarqawi: Jordanian Painted as Foreign Threat to Iraq's Stability," *Washington Post*, April 10, 2006, A1 and A14.

14. "Report of the Defense Science Board Task Force on Strategic Communication," Office of the Under Secretary of Defense for Acquisition, Technology, and Logistics, Washington, DC, 20301, September 2004, 2. See also chap. 2, "The New Strategic Environment," 33–47.

15. A writer bragged to another whom he knew to be more than a little jealous of him, "You have no idea how popular my writing has become. Why, since I last saw you, my readers have doubled." "Well, *mazel tov!*" came the answer. "I didn't know you got married." See Leo Rosten, *The Joys of Yiddish* (New York: Pocket Books, 1970), 227–29.

Chapter Twelve

The Price of Pride

There is but a step between a proud man's glory and his disgrace.

—Publilius (aka Publis) Syrus

Like Elizabeth, whose hostility to Darcy was almost instantly kindled by his outrageous good looks and palpable self-assurance, the world is ready to believe the worst of us. Hence, how convenient that our clumsiness sometimes enhances the plausibility of that presumption, which is then further reinforced by those in our midst who masochistically give them additional ammunition. Many will start believing the message, so widely prevalent even in the Western media, that the rich care nothing for the poor in America; that we would pollute to our heart's content were it not for the Lord's angels cleverly disguised as environmentalists; that we would—indeed, already do!—rule the entire globe from Sixteen Hundred Pennsylvania Avenue (or Wall Street, for is that not the same thing, *mon cher*?); that American biased support for the Israelis indicates our view of them as "heroic cowboys" fighting against Palestinian "savages";[1] and so forth; the list goes on. Meanwhile, Americans—not unlike Darcy—sulk in disbelief, oscillating from feeling alternately mystified, penitent, and clueless.

The world, of course, is no Elizabeth. The clever young woman had cared nothing for a rich suitor; as self-sufficient as Jane herself, she enjoyed chuckling at the spectacle of others' innocent and not-so-innocent follies, lightheartedly and slightly detached. There is nothing "detached" or lighthearted about a great many of our fellow earthlings; a grab-as-you-can mentality reigns supreme, whether what is grabbed is money, fame, sex, or the blood of the infidel and his children. And yet we wish to woo what there is out there on the planet that is full of wonder and majesty, innocence and beauty, history and suffering.

It is not simply that we want to be safe and to "win hearts and minds" so as to avoid future terrorist acts against our countrymen, especially on our own soil. This is not just a form of isolationism, whether simplistic or enlightened. Nor is it the contrary, that we want to conquer the world as smoothly as we can. The interdependence of the United States must be understood far more deeply, in a profoundly human dimension. America may be the promise and the strength, but, like the mythical two halves of the severed hermaphrodite seeking their original Siamese unity, which embodied Love in Plato's immortal *Symposium*, America needs "the other" to become fulfilled. We are human beings, hence condemned to solitude. Our only escape is one another. Existentialist guru Jean Paul Sartre had it only half right when he said, in the play *No Exit*, that "hell is other people." Hell—admittedly of a different sort—is also their absence.

Of all the riches coveted by man, recognition and affection seem to rank highest. Why would we Americans wish to take advantage of others, or even think meanly of them? If we were to do so, as Mr. Darcy was "almost" taught to do by his unsuspecting, well-meaning parents, it would gain us, beyond an ephemeral sense of superiority, little but the direst solitude, distrust, and hostility. Self-righteousness eventually tends to be undermined by a gnawing suspicion that one may be wrong. In the end, one is left unsatisfied, curmudgeonly, holding a grudge against the world as one feels misunderstood.

Like Mr. Darcy, we may not be selfish in principle, but insofar as we are perceived to be selfish in practice, the difference hardly matters. And so we Americans vacillate from one extreme to another, from abject repentance to haughty, neojingoistic resentment, protesting that we mean well and always have. Not quite certain of our sins, Americans are certainly willing to be humble, or at the very least to be seen as such. The more common folk are not content to emulate the haughtier, somewhat less ingenuous elite who populate academia as well as the media, and who engage in ostentatious self-flagellation. There is a sincere desire in this motley nation to accept others at their true worth. The trouble is that we had thought we were already doing that. So, what is to be done?

Remember that the Darcy/Elizabeth composite is akin to a playing card, as Professor Mark Schorer had astutely revealed. Flip it, and you will see the characters precisely reversed through the mirrors of their intra-twinned souls, divided against themselves. Like Elizabeth, America originally stood "below," proudly penniless. We were all poor once, for whatever status we may have previously enjoyed had been abandoned. Once landed here, we all had to pull ourselves up by our respective bootstraps.

And those boots, in a way, still fit. Whoever doesn't like us because we lack "refinement," well, who do those highfalutin think they are? Self-tutored and self-reliant, we can see through affectation and the pretension of rank. Yet flip that card and see the prejudice take top billing—a proud variety, at that. "Our country, love it or leave it," is slightly more than an idle threat. The sentiment it describes is meant to stop the questioning, the introspection, and the doubt. Patriotism can far too easily slide down the proverbial slippery slope to jingoism, especially among those who can't spell *jingoism* without looking it up.

We must, and do, take comfort from the fact that Jane Austen's story ended on a happy note. Mr. Darcy's prejudice against "the meaner" of his fellow humans was easily overcome when experience showed him otherwise. This was especially true with regard to Elizabeth, whose worth shined in her comely eyes as it did in her kindly actions and well-turned phrases. That Elizabeth's prejudice against Mr. Darcy took considerably longer to evaporate than his against her should not surprise: her stakes were arguably higher. For, however temporarily tempted, she loved no other man, and her meager worldly possessions promised little by way of choice among suitors likely to attain her sterling standards. Her negative presumptions against Mr. Darcy also persisted in no small measure due to the ineptitude with which he presented his own case. But in the end, having not only the means but also the will and the ability to demonstrate beyond doubt his unimpeachable character and crystal-pure motives, a satisfying denouement was all but certain.

In vain would we Americans consider ourselves as lucky as Jane Austen's winsome characters. We are nowhere near as limitless in resources as to satisfy the various and, as it happens, contradictory, global expectations proclaimed by self-appointed spokesmen of sundry peoples, nations, or "imagined communities." (This is Benjamin Anderson's apt term for the elite-driven mythologies usually designed to legitimize boundaries created by politicians oblivious, if not outright hostile, to matters of ethnicity and culture). We occasionally mumble, even grunting a bit, that the billions we have already expended on humanitarian foreign aid should have resulted in a greater bang—if not an explosion to awaken Jupiter's more sluggish satellites, at least a thunderous applause or two.

We must convince the world that our intentions are ultimately good. While Ambassador Kishore Mahbubani believes that the "inherent American desire to liberate rather than to subjugate the world" has already gained us much goodwill, we're beginning to slip. How can we persuade others when our own pundits in academia and the media tell us otherwise? To be sure, our vaunted liberating instinct does not exempt us from failing to deliver. The proverbial road leads to hell with no less certainty if its bricks are built with nothing but the best of intentions. Accordingly, if subjugation should happen to be the unintended consequence of our actions, we must face the consequences and own up to them, correcting if at all possible not only the results but their inadvertence. That is true pride, informed by the ability to recognize mistakes.

By contrast, those who would have us fall on our knees beating our breasts, to beg forgiveness for our presumed imperial behavior, often favor relinquishing sovereignty. But entrusting the euphemistically dubbed "international community" to decide what is in the global public good, subsuming America's national interest to an amorphous "global interest"—defined by whom? international bureaucrats?—is exactly the wrong answer. Such self-flagellation is not only potentially suicidal; there is simply no evidence that could possibly support it. When, in all of human history, did this "international community" ever save humanity from anything? Such elitist anti-Americanism is common to those who think themselves superior intellectually as well as morally to the ignorant, flag-waving patriots who define "Red America."

But homegrown Western-variety anti-Americanism is no less dangerous for being insidious, articulate, and oblivious to the harm that it causes to the very civilization that protects it. Similarly, transnational civil society organizations can undermine the very institutions that nurture them. We must find a way to learn our lessons constructively, being able to maintain our rightful confidence in the democratic process and at the same time uphold the principle of national sovereignty. In the apt words of Hudson Institute senior fellow John Fonte,

> The United States should be prepared to champion not simply generalized notions of building democratic institutions and promoting "human rights" and "democratic values" that are susceptible to post-democratic manipulation, but the principle of democratic sovereignty within the institution of the liberal democratic nation-state.[2]

There is no doubt that it can be done, but it will not be easy. America has been too complacently proud, imagining itself more self-sufficient than it may be. Its enemies are lurking where it—and indeed even they—least expect it. The first step is to recognize the nature of our own goals. If we want to "sell" America, are we looking for buyers or soul mates? For universal prosperity and freedom, or for the dream of its possibility? If what we want is not for America to rule the world but for the world to rule itself by humane, classical liberal standards, how can we convincingly explain the difference? How can we persuade those who merely want the world to leave us alone that we no longer have that option? Finally, what price are we willing to pay for our inability or unwillingness to address these questions honestly and effectively?

America is both a country and a dream, an ideal and a political reality; it reaches across a vast, rich, if sometimes ravaged territory, yet it also transcends this territory both literally and figuratively. American products and its ideas are certainly "for sale," but its future lies in recognizing that its greatest asset not only must not but indeed cannot be sold. From this paradox we should emerge more humble in our pride and wiser from acquiescing in the time-old prejudice that we cannot be wrong as long as we accept at least some element of fate in our manifest, human destiny. The wisdom of the Greeks—and all religions in some fashion—that warns humanity to temper its predilection for self-deification is well worth recalling, relearning, and taking to heart.

Unless, of course, the end comes first—a cataclysmic possibility whose high probability we must admit on pain of self-delusion. The resemblance between the current war of the worlds and former squabbles among kingdoms and empires, while not entirely coincidental, is negligible. This is not merely the United States versus Al-Qaeda, America or perhaps the Judeo-Christian world against Islamist extremism, or the West clashing with "the rest"[3]—alias superego-tyrannized "civilization" in turn tyrannizing the "discontents." It is not just modernity contra traditionalism, or profane versus sacred. It is not a simple dialectic of the world defined by globalization, individualism, a vision of progress, and an American-led pursuit of consumerism, on the one hand, facing a loosely defined collection of the militantly unassimilated on the other. We may well wish that it were so clear-cut, but it isn't. We must continue to be proud enough to recognize America's uniqueness but not so proud as to declare it either divine or diabolic. Moreover, our war is with ourselves no less than with our sworn external enemies.

The novelty of the current state of affairs does not imply that history has nothing to teach us—far from it. Without learning all that can be learned from past encounters among cultures, ethnicities, and nations, we are bound to commit unnecessary mistakes, some of which have been made before and needn't be repeated. The floundering that inevitably accompanies rough new roads on the journey of history is enough without added potholes for which the map has already been drawn. Fighting the real enemies should more than suffice; we should avoid boxing with chimeras.

This elementary truth appeared in the most ancient treatise on strategy entitled *The Art of War*, presumed to have been written over two thousand years ago by Chinese warrior Sun Tzu. His wisdom is aptly illustrated by this aphorism: "Know the enemy and know yourself; in a hundred battles you will never be in peril."[4] The corollary, that "if ignorant both of your enemy and of yourself, you are certain in every battle to be in peril," comes painfully close to describing the nature of our predicament in the current war with terror. Not that "the enemy" is not also ignorant, at times perhaps willfully so, underestimating our sincerity while simultaneously assuming our near invincibility. To our dismay, time and again we find him attributing to us rapacious imperial motives and malevolent intentions when we least expect it, when we had thought that everyone knew what we were about. But the consequences of such misinterpretations and misinformation are no less fatal for being at times inadvertent. By failing to imagine that we would be grossly misunderstood, we are, to use the quaintly simple, blunt words of Sun Tzu, "in peril."

Surely the most glaring recent example of the dangers lurking in America's highly vaunted self-confidence, its cocky pride in its military prowess, has been evidenced in the ongoing war in Iraq. To some extent, that self-confidence was justified: the military victory over Saddam was rapid and elegant. That we miscalculated the postinvasion atmosphere is now well known; wars are always difficult, and the Iraq war is certainly more complicated than most. But to have been so utterly unprepared for handling the probability of something going wrong is inexcusable. Even a modicum of modesty might have made the United States look just a little less foolish before the world. When we are too proud to admit that our forecast was wrong and led to unanticipated results, others may be justified in assuming that we are as infallible as we think ourselves to be and that we had in fact anticipated those very results but pretend otherwise. Either way, we lose.

The most exasperating lesson is that overconfidence can blind us to what is staring us in the face. In many cases, even after the fact, deeply entrenched modes of thinking will prevent our grasping the obvious. For example, *National Review* editor Richard Lowry, in his astute review of three recent books on the Iraq war—to wit, *New Yorker* contributor George Packer's *The Assassins' Gate: America in Iraq*; *Cobra II* by *New York Times* reporter Michael R. Gordon and retired marine lieutenant general Bernard Trainor; and *No True Glory*, by marine veteran and author Bing West—points out how foolish we still are when we quarrel about the numbers of troops we should have sent into Iraq, when the problem was much simpler: how could we imagine that military prowess would allow us to dispense with old-fashioned knowledge of the world around us? What America could have used is not simply more boots on the ground but "a delicate cultural touch, of the sort it is difficult to have without spending time on the ground," without which, more troops "could be counterproductive."[5]

It goes without saying, although Lowry is to be commended for saying it, that, in the United States, time, and the requisite intellectual patience, happen to be in legendary short supply. The price of our pride in being able to deliver quick results by sheer strength is not only that we look foolish when it turns out otherwise, but that the impression is justified. It follows that one of America's main challenges, self-confident in its motives, is to present itself more accurately without at the same time feeling obliged to demonstrate either infallibility or moral impeccability. Arguably, this is the most important first step. But the task is not easy, nor will it yield immediate results. Madison Avenue surely doesn't have the answer, for the simple reason that it is addressing the wrong question. Knowing that fact—knowing how, when, and of whom to ask what—was Socrates' rightful claim to wisdom. Before one can learn, however, it is also absolutely necessary to rid oneself of prejudice, which is far more dangerous even than ignorance. We turn to that next.

NOTES

1. For this and other accusations, see, by senior associate at the Carnegie Endowment for International Peace Anatol Lieven, *America Right or Wrong: An Anatomy of American Nationalism* (Oxford: Oxford University Press, 2004).

2. John Fonte, "Democracy's Trojan Horse," *The National Interest*, Summer 2004, 125.

3. Samuel Huntington, "The West and the Rest: Intercivilizational Issues," in *The Clash of Civilizations and the Remaking of World Order* (New York: Simon & Schuster, 1997), 183.

4. Sun Tzu, *The Art of War*, translated and with an introduction by Samuel B. Griffith (Oxford: Oxford University Press, 1971), 84 (III–31).

5. Rich Lowry, "Writing the War," *National Review*, April 24, 2006, 52.

Part III

THE LEGACY OF PREJUDICE

Chapter Thirteen

Why Learn about Others?

If a nation expects to be ignorant and free, it expects what never was and never will be.

—Thomas Jefferson

The incumbent first lady of public diplomacy, Karen Hughes, during her first international fact-finding mission through the Middle East in the fall of 2005, told reporters that she had not realized how people overseas can get so riled by American television programs or newspaper columns that have nothing to do with the administration.[1] By her own account, international affairs are not exactly her expertise: Hughes is a former television journalist with extensive public relations and campaign experience. But she speaks for millions of Americans who are astonished to find themselves misunderstood throughout the world. They expect foreign publics to differentiate among different segments of American society, and they expect global audiences to know us, even to know us well.

But then again we generally don't bother to know very much about them ourselves. "Hughes Misreports Iraqi History," announces another *Washington Post* headline.[2] Leave it to our own media to pounce on the gaffes of our leaders, especially if it involves a member of a Republican administration. Limited knowledge of world history and geography is in fact an equal-opportunity disability that afflicts Americans across the ideological spectrum—hardly a reason for celebration.

On closer examination, our failure to communicate with other cultures is intimately connected to the shortsighted pride in our visibility, power, and presumably manifest benevolence. The same pride blinds us to the importance of fostering a better understanding of America—so as to avoid misjudgments of

141

what we do and what we say—while guaranteeing that we are not only ignorant about our audience but come across as arrogantly uninterested. In brief, the
flip side of assuming that others know us is that we in turn don't know them.[3]
It is hard not to infer that we believe ourselves to be alone important. Impressions aside, we are bound to operate with presumptions that often turn out to be
just plain wrong. To judge prior to knowledge is not only rude; it is highly unwise. When we act without serious forethought, we witlessly engage in run-of-
the-mill prejudice.

Whether English, Greek, Latin, or Sumerian, obviously the more widespread the use of any language, the easier it is for people who speak that language to communicate, a fact recognized by the Abrahamic tradition. According to the Old Testament, everyone had originally spoken the same
tongue.[4] It was not long before these lucky monoglot humans built themselves a mighty city complete with "a tower with its top in the sky," an ominous expression of arrogance, predating the skyscraper by several millennia,
ostentatiously intended by their architects to "make a name for
[them]selves."[5] God responded as usual when confronted with overt displays
of hubris, by punishing the shameless upstarts, first by confounding their
speech and creating many languages, and then, for good measure, scattering
the race over the face of the entire planet. The infamous tower would hence-
forth be called "Babel," from the Hebrew word *balal*, meaning "to con-
found."

Once spawned and spread, the languages never unscrambled; occasional
extinction aside, they were doomed to stay. While often borrowing from one
another in reaction to political and cultural evolution, conquest, scientific
progress, and miscegenation, complete linguistic convergence seems as elusive now as on the day Babel caught God's attention and kindled His formidable ire. The course of linguistic entropy by now seems irreversibly set,
notwithstanding the ever-growing proliferation of Anglo-American as it rides
high upon the global tentacles of outsourcing and the relative resilience of the
ubiquitous dollar.

Most of us prefer oneness, inexorably (if subconsciously at best) indebted
to the Ionian philosopher Xenophanes of Colophon (alive around the sixth
century B.C.). If Aristotle is to be believed, Xenophanes' claim to fame rests
on being "the first to postulate a unity . . . [and] with his eye on the whole
heaven [declaring] that the One is god,"[6] although the credit for this idea
sometimes goes to his slightly better known student Parmenides, who recon-
ciled the opposites of light and darkness into one transcendent synthesis.
Classicists aside, most survivors of the 1960s are familiar with Eastern versions—whether Buddhism, Taoism, or other variations on the archetypal
theme—which state simply that harmony, peace, and oneness are inexorably

interconnected. This timeless truth was rediscovered and refashioned by Emerson and Whitman in new words, new metaphors, fit for a brave and great New World. It seems particularly appropriate in the age of globalization, when standardization is no longer an option but a rude, irreversible reality.

The eloquent *Autobiography* of that most reluctant of world travelers, John Adams, whose competing desires—to serve his country, and to be with Abigail—would torment him for nearly a lifetime, is sometimes cited to illustrate America's early propensity to isolationism. Referring to the debates of the congressional forerunner of Senate and House foreign relations committees, established in June 1776 for the purpose of establishing economic treaties, Adams advised to "avoid all Alliance, which might embarrass Us in after times and involve Us in future European wars."[7]

But Adams was by no means alone in expressing a general antipathy to joining forces with other nations unless absolutely necessary, let alone presuming to change their systems of government. So too did Washington, despite the fact that America's independence could never have been won without military as well as financial support from abroad. That detail aside, both Adams and Washington hoped to secure the defense and welfare of their new country with the least possible assistance from others.

Adams' reasoning is plainly revealed in a letter to his friend John Jay on May 8, 1785: "It behooves the United States to knit themselves together in the bands of affection and mutual confidence, search their own resources to the bottom, form their foreign commerce into a system, and encourage their own navigation and seamen, and to these ends their carrying trade," which should make them one strong "United States of America, destined beyond a doubt to be the greatest power on earth, and that within the life of man."[8] While not entirely foolhardy, Adams' patriotism tested the bounds of realism. He trusted the power of peaceful, and specifically commercial, bonds far beyond those of a military and coercive nature.

But he was no utopian. His education had been solid, instilling few illusions about human nature. Adams anticipated that even as America reached unprecedented success, "we shall be more an object of jealousy than any other upon earth. All the powers know that it is impossible for any, the proudest of them, to conquer us; and, therefore, if we should be attacked by any one, the others will not be fond of undertaking our defense."[9] Yet conquest was the farthest thing from his mind. It is with reluctance that he concedes the need to centralize power so that all the states may be required to act in harmony, for the common good: "I am much afraid," confessed Adams to his friend Jay, "we shall never be able to do this unless Congress are vested with full power" to enter into commercial treaties—hardly the mindset of a Caesar.

The largely defensive stance of American foreign policy was evident even in what looks otherwise to all the world like protoimperialism, namely in the Spanish-American war, the assumption that the United States was entitled to most if not all of the northern continent. Partial to an expansive reading of that doctrine, Theodore Roosevelt would launch the twentieth century with a grand vision of America dominating over the entire Western Hemisphere. For that propensity, Boston University professor David Fromkin appropriately branded the charismatic, if somewhat egomaniacal president "an instinctive internationalist."[10]

It was his Democratic successor, however, an otherwise "instinctive isolationist" college professor, who not only led the United States into World War I in 1917 but set the tone of the nation's foreign policy for the century that followed. Wilson's rationale, insofar as it has any coherence,[11] may be summarized as proclaiming that if America is required, against its will, to become militarily involved outside the Western Hemisphere, the intervention may only be justified if it changes the world for the better. Lofty as this end may have sounded to many—though by no means all—who heard it at the time, what later came to be known as the "Wilson Doctrine" lacked one critical component: its namesake, who was soon to suffer a debilitating stroke, had not managed to think out the means. He would prove not to have been the only president to exhibit such deficiency. As for the caveat that America would wage war only when "forced," critics of internationalism and militarism, both then and later, would find little comfort in what seemed to them, and (so they thought, with some justification) to all the world, as either self-delusional or disingenuous.

It fell upon another Roosevelt to involve America in the second great war of the century, and to his hapless vice president who was left to sweep up after him. Having constitutionally inherited the office for which he felt grossly underqualified, Harry Truman rose to the occasion with his own form of internationalism, which sought to reconcile power politics with America's democratic mission.[12]

Half a century later, President George W. Bush would define America's mission as the deliberate, quasi-messianic spread of democracy throughout the world. We seem to have come full circle from the Founders' antipathy to proselytizing by force, their widespread expectation that the American example would take root on its own through the inexorable laws of the free market and that a democratic (that is, republican) world order was just around the corner. And yet the common thread is clear: the monist vision, the ONE eye at the top of the pyramid of history gazing upon us all. *Ex pluribus, unum*: from polypolis to monocracy, one system of government *über alles*. Call it "freedom," or "democracy," or "civilization," or "modernity," the new regime should guarantee all God's children the unhampered pursuit of happiness, no matter how they pronounce or define or spell it.

The United States, in other words, would make it possible for others to seek the American Dream, even if they were not American nationals. How could we convey the idea that America was not simply a country but an idea? Would anyone believe us when we protested that we want others to be "just like us" in the sense of becoming believers? And would that be possible without occasional military intervention? Or is it rather a more modest proposition that motivates American foreign policy—namely, that we wish to be left to our own visions, we insist on being left to pursue our American Dreams without anyone denying us that right, and this is impossible without striking against the enemies of our national vision. The long visa application lists of people asking permission to join us in partaking of that vision provide proof enough that large numbers wish they might be allowed to come along.

There is, of course, one problem that accelerated throughout the twentieth century. Early on, immigration defined us, and for much of our history we welcomed it, presupposed it, and even glorified it. The Statue of Liberty ostensibly proclaimed it to all who would care to read the message engraved on its proud torch. But Americans have often proved less open armed, with ensuing quotas and a variety of other restrictions on immigration for reasons based on ideology, national security, morality, economics, or just plain bigotry. Before long, Americans found that they had to limit access to their nation, still mighty vast, but whose frontier no longer seemed indefinitely extendable.

As the ongoing debates on immigration legislation plainly demonstrate, we are ambivalent. On the one hand, we recommend the American Dream to all, but on the other hand, we expect most of the world, with occasional exceptions made for those whose skills we can use, to pursue that dream in the comfort of their native abodes. Nor is there anything legally or even morally wrong with such a stance: a nation-state has the right to confine its citizens territorially, no matter how economically and culturally shortsighted such a policy may be (which more often than it is politically correct to admit, it is not). Still more to the point, America the nation is by no means identical with America the dream, not even to its own people.

But even if we inhabited paradise on earth—which we decidedly do not—we should not avoid the tree of knowledge as if we had been commanded to do so. Knowledge of others is not only prudent—although it certainly is that—but interesting, life enhancing, wonderful. Not to appreciate that fact is a kind of premature death, not only for the individual but for the community he represents. Prejudice is doubly lethal: to both its victim and its perpetrator. It betrays a certain lassitude and decadence best captured by F. Scott Fitzgerald in his seminal novel *The Great Gatsby* by the idea of "carelessness":

> They were careless people, Tom and Daisy—they smashed up things and crea-
> tures and then retreated back into their money or their vast carelessness, or what-
> ever it was that kept them together, and let other people clean up the mess they
> had made.[13]

In this context, the true antonym of *carelessness* is not *careful* but *caring*. *Caring*, in turn, has an emotional dimension—captured by the term *empathy*—and an intellectual, or cognitive aspect, which requires gathering the relevant information to understand someone else. People who care do not make a mess; they don't smash things up; they take *care* of them. They don't neglect their responsibility to look before they act.

We are prejudiced against those we do not know and do not care to know. Nafisi explains that "carelessness [or] lack of empathy appears in Jane Austen's negative characters," and certainly in Fitzgerald's: "Empathy lies at the heart of Gatsby; like so many other great novels—the biggest sin is to be blind to others' problems and pains. Not seeing them means denying their ex- istence."[14]

In social terms, prejudice prevents us from seeing a human being in his or her full complexity. Prejudice blinds, both literally and figuratively. In the end, failing to learn from others means failing to know even oneself. Singu- lar, solipsistic self-knowledge in the absence of other-directed knowledge is as impossible as is the concept of a private language. It is the sound of one hand clapping. The joke, in this case, is on us.

NOTES

1. "Campaign Methods Put to Test in Tour to Boost U.S. Image," *Washington Post*, September 30, 2005.

2. *Washington Post*, October 22, 2005.

3. In her recent book, *Friendly Fire: Losing Friends and Making Enemies in the Anti-American Century*, Julia Sweig coins the term "green zone" mentality to refer to a self-inflicted isolation from the world's masses, a lack of "access to or human in- telligence about the 80 percent of the country's population," which is usually poor and—except for Anglophone countries—does not speak English (New York: Public Affairs, 2006), 37. She laments the fact that even State Department officials usually prefer staying within their compounds rather than reach out to the local population, which leads to ignorance and prejudice.

4. Genesis 1:1.

5. Genesis 1:4.

6. G. S. Kirk and J. E. Raven, *The Presocratic Philosophers: A Critical History with a Selection of Texts* (London: Cambridge University Press, 1969), 171.

7. For this and other contemporaneous policies see Paul Varg, *Foreign Policies of the Founding Fathers* (Baltimore, MD: Penguin Books, 1963), esp. 20.

8. *Annals of America*, vol. III, *1784–1796, Organizing the New Nation* (Encyclopaedia Britannica, 1968), 23.

9. *Annals of America*, 3:23.

10. David Fromkin, *Kosovo Crossing: American Ideals Meet Reality on the Balkan Battlefields* (New York: The Free Press, 1999), 56.

11. For an excellent analysis of the contradictions and confusions contained in Wilson's Fourteen Points, see Fromkin, *Kosovo Crossing*, 118–19, as well as the useful—if a bit overly demonizing—critique of Wilson by Jim Powell, *Wilson's War: How Woodrow Wilson's Great Blunder Led to Hitler, Lenin, Stalin & World War II* (New York: Crown Forum, 2005).

12. See the excellent, well-documented study by Anne Pierce, *Woodrow Wilson and Harry Truman: Mission and Power in American Foreign Policy* (Westport, CT: Praeger Publishers, 2003), 2:7.

13. F. Scott Fitzgerald, *The Great Gatsby* (New York: Charles Scribner's Sons, 1925), 180–81.

14. Azar Nafisi, *Reading Lolita in Tehran* (New York: Random House, 2003), 132.

Chapter Fourteen

No Place Like Home

The less America looks abroad, the grander its promise.

—Ralph Waldo Emerson

If little Dorothy had to learn the hard way that even Oz isn't all that it's cracked up to be, so did the considerably less sheltered Thomas Jefferson. The most learned author of the Declaration, who felt as comfortable in Paris as in Monticello, wrote to his friend John Banister that Americans had no reason to wander the world in search of education, with the possible exception of acquiring foreign languages. Notwithstanding the vaunted salubrious effect of travel, Jefferson warned even against that dubious excuse for meandering beyond one's borders, noting that homegrown schooling—particularly at the College of William and Mary—was perfectly well suited for that sort of training.

He grudgingly admitted of one area where Europe still had the edge on America, namely medicine. But that is where he drew the line, concluding most emphatically that enumerating all the disadvantages of sending a youth to Europe "would require a volume"[1]—manifestly a wasted effort when a cutting verdict will do. Not one to mince words, Jefferson concludes that "an American coming to Europe for education *loses* [emphasis mine] in his knowledge, in his morals, in his health, in his habits, and in his happiness."[2] By contrast, the best men in America—the most learned, beloved, trusted, and eloquent—are those "whose manners, morals, and habits are perfectly homogeneous with those of the country." Admitting to excessive zeal on the subject, Jefferson coyly expresses hope that Banister is still "sufficiently American"[3] to forgive him.

The well-nigh jingoist prejudices exhibited by the patrician polyglot from Virginia were not demonstrations of blind xenophobia but constituted the expression of a new educational philosophy, much touted throughout the Enlightenment, which emphasized the critical significance of experience rather than tradition in shaping ideas and attitudes. The passionate antipathy against the imagined advantages of European breeding also serves as a powerful reminder of the pride felt by our ancestors in their unprecedented experiment, coupled with a desire to keep the country strong and see it flourish in future times, possibly (many thought, even probably) throughout the world.

Indeed, Jefferson was by no means alone in his concern to strengthen native education by having American teachers nurture the minds of American youth. Following Jefferson's letter to Banister by less than a year, Dr. Benjamin Rush would send his own missive to the well-known British moral philosopher Richard Price, advancing his own plan for "general education," which he firmly believed "alone will render the American Revolution a blessing to mankind." He called upon Price to urge American leaders, perhaps by means of a small pamphlet, to establish compulsory public schooling designed to teach "the law of nature and nations, the common law of our country, the different systems of government, history and everything else connected with the advancement of republican knowledge and principles."[4] Like Jefferson, John Adams and Benjamin Franklin also founded colleges in their home states; education was clearly held in the highest esteem by the men and also women who were instrumental in creating the American nation. They knew it would provide the key to self-reliance, national security, and true greatness.

The Founders were admittedly not unanimous in opposing study abroad with the ferocity displayed by Jefferson. But they basically agreed on the paramount significance of encouraging homegrown education to nurture the virtues required to sustain a democratic form of government. Besides a strong practical component, including science and technology, they thought the ideal curriculum should not neglect the liberal arts, since the American citizen, empowered by a brand-new Constitution, had to be duly prepared for the serious task of deciding not only his own but also his many fellow countrymen's political life.

Never before in the history of the world had so far-reaching a democracy, involving so many issues open to public scrutiny, spread across so large a territory. The Roman Empire, notwithstanding its liberal citizenship laws, was not an appropriate precedent, both too diffuse and chaotic to emulate. Yet the constant reminder of its disastrous fall was never far from the minds of America's Founders, all of whom understood only too well the critical importance of a well-educated public to maintain the health of the body politic, no matter how masterfully crafted its legal framework and its institutions—economic, political, and social.

In broad outline, this had been the lesson of America: out of the cacophony of the Old World, with its tribal hatreds and history of intolerance, decadence, and oppression, the colonies had evolved into a centralized federation, one nation emerging surprisingly strong and confident, heralding a new age. But the unity was surely fragile and needed building by a new breed of men and women nourished on its virtually virgin soil, who believed in the American Dream and helped to realize it for themselves, for their families, and, in the process, for (presumably most of) their countrymen. But if their dreams were American, why not their education?

The fact that America thought of itself even at the outset as different from, and even in many ways superior to, all other nations did not necessarily imply that all education had to be exclusively homegrown, yet the idea that travel abroad was not only dispensable but possibly even harmful would become entrenched within the American psyche, if only subliminally. Among the first to use this uniquely American form of iconoclasm was this nation's celebrated ambassador, the craftiest, most versatile American genius, Benjamin Franklin. Having perfected his bespectacled bonhomie and ostentatious simplicity to a virtual art form, he seduced his Parisian admirers young and old. Simultaneously, he implicitly taught his countrymen not to be intimidated by the arrogant display of sophistication so typical of the Old World, and especially its often sclerotic aristocracy.

It wasn't hard to do, for Americans were already skeptical enough. Abigail Adams, upon meeting King George and his queen with their powdered entourage, found them all basically boring. To an American, a member of the European elite was like the Wizard of Oz, whose pomposity did not escape the skeptical, if not outright scornful, republican eye. Like Dorothy, who wanted nothing so much as to get back to Kansas, Abigail and John Adams longed for their farm in Massachusetts while being wined and dined at a fancy royal palace.

Speaking for Dorothy and her relatives one century after Jefferson had so thoroughly refuted the proposition that Americans must be educated in Europe, Samuel Clemens would convey that message even better in his celebrated best seller *The Innocents Abroad*, published in 1869, with the humor that proposition deserved. Here is how he describes the hapless Bostonians whom he hardly considers improved as a result of their experiences in what they called "Yurrup":

> They never talk to you, of course, being strangers, but they talk to each other and at you till you are pretty nearly distracted with their clatter; till you are sick

of their ocean experiences; their mispronounced foreign names; their dukes and
emperors; their trivial adventures; their pointless reminiscences; till you are sick
of their imbecile faces and their relentless clack, and wish it had pleased Providence to leave the clapper out of their empty skulls.[5]

Mark Twain's contemporary, Ralph Waldo Emerson, wholeheartedly, and
no less bluntly, concurred. In his essay "Self-Reliance," Emerson writes, "It
is for want of self-culture that the superstition of Traveling, whose idols are
Italy, England, and Egypt, retains its fascination for all educated Americans."[6]
Mark Twain's holier-than-thou disdain for hypocrisy, especially when based
on the pretense of "culture," was hard to distinguish from run-of-the mill ignorance; the "superstition of Travel," he declared, is the soul's way of running
away from its own emptiness. Emerson warns against the man who "travels
away from himself, and grows old even in youth among old things. In Thebes,
in Palmyra, his will and mind have become old and dilapidated as they."[7]

The aura of history and tradition loses much of its luster, charm, and power
when described as "old and dilapidated." The New World was seen as vigorous, virile, and virtuous—or at the very least, young. Moreover, like Peter
Pan, it refused to grow old—not only in order to postpone, if not outright
obliterate, senescence, but to repudiate it. Correlative to American youth worship is antiageism. That is to say, we are urged to refrain from calling someone "old" not only in deference to political correctness but to echo our society's conscious opposition to the idea. America is beautiful, and it is young;
long live.

Closely related to our narcissistic domesticity, however, is a relative indifference to the opinion that others have of us. Two and a quarter centuries ago,
on June 25, 1787, a South Carolinian member of the Federal Constitutional
Convention in Philadelphia, Charles Pinckney, stated, "We mistake the object
of our government, if we hope or wish that it is to make us respectable
abroad." The object should be not even "superiority among other powers," let
alone—heaven forbid—conquest; rather, if our representatives "are sufficiently active and energetic to rescue us from contempt and preserve our domestic happiness and security, it is all we can expect from them," and all we
should expect.

That was then, however, and this is now. At the end of the eighteenth century, it was entirely legitimate and indeed critical for Americans to worry
mainly about strengthening a government that was barely being created. But
it is equally critical, at the outset of the twenty-first century, not to rest content merely with being "rescued from contempt." We should expect more;
notably, we Americans should seek not to be misunderstood, to be appreciated for who we are. That means that we should be eager to travel, and learn
to appreciate how others live, and also how they perceive us. That so many

of our congressional representatives and other government officials do not even own a passport is worrisome. But even more is the fact that some brag about it.

In some respects, we are among the most globally connected people in the world. Gross numbers aside, only the British equal us in the percentage of its population—about a quarter—who own computers, and in the percentage of them who go online—90 percent.[8] That's the good news. Now for the bad news: while both Americans and Europeans believe that traveling is good for their country and for their families, Americans don't do much of it, and not only because we are geographically isolated. Kohut and Stokes report that only one in five Americans traveled outside the United States between 1997 and 2002, and only one in four phoned, visited, or corresponded with people in another land. The effect is predictable: "Such isolation produces an inward-looking perspective, such as a distinct indifference to learning a foreign language, that has undeniable, real-world implications for the United States and for Americans as they attempt to understand and deal with other peoples."[9]

The real-world implications are twofold: first, Americans are far less likely to be able to understand other cultures, and second, people from foreign countries not only—and justifiably—get the impression that we are not interested in them, but they in turn are deprived of firsthand knowledge of Americans. Everyone ends up making judgments on the basis of impressions gathered from highly flawed sources such as media, hearsay, and politicians. The point is not to start a PR popularity campaign to "win" hearts, minds, or anything else. The point is to make sure that the world knows who we are. But for that, we will have to make a greater effort, in turn, to know them. Otherwise, by the time we find out that we are addressing them at the wrong address in the wrong language, it's too late to say sorry.

NOTES

1. "Thomas Jefferson: An American Education for American Youth," October 15, 1785, in *Annals of America*, vol. III, *1784–1796, Organizing the New Nation* (Chicago: Encyclopaedia Britannica, 1968), 41.

2. "Thomas Jefferson," 42.

3. "Thomas Jefferson," 42.

4. "Benjamin Rush: On the Need for General Education," in *Annals of America*, vol. 3, *1784–1796, Organizing the New Nation* (Chicago: Encyclopaedia Britannica, 1968), 55.

5. Mark Twain, *The Complete Humorous Sketches and Tales of Mark Twain*, ed. Charles Neider (New York: Doubleday, 1961), 103.

6. Ralph Waldo Emerson, "Self-Reliance," in *Selections from Ralph Waldo Emerson*, ed. Stephen E. Whicher (Boston: Houghton Mifflin, Riverside Editions, 1957), 163.

7. Emerson, "Self-Reliance," 164.

8. Andrew Kohut and Bruce Stokes, *America against the World: How We Are Different and Why We Are Disliked* (New York: Times Books, 2006), 161–62.

9. Kohut and Stokes, *America against the World*, 162–63.

Chapter Fifteen

Biased against Intelligence

He who is not sage and wise, humane and just, cannot use secret agents.
And he who is not delicate and subtle cannot get the truth out of them.

—Sun Tzu

Malcolm Gladwell's best-selling *Blink: The Power of Thinking without Thinking*, offers fascinating case studies that demonstrate how, in many situations, not only do we "know" before we know that we know, but we categorically must do so in order to save our lives. For purposes of survival, man is no less fortunate than his fellow animals, being providentially "programmed" to react more rapidly than his conscious brain would allow him to do. Experience and knowledge can help him react correctly, and sometimes too much conscious thinking can literally get in the way. Gladwell compiles evidence that illustrates how complex the thinking process really is: our instinctive reactions often have to compete not only with conscious "reason" but also with other interests, emotions, and sentiments. But "when our powers of rapid cognition go awry," we can find out why.[1] In other words, prejudices are not always wrong; but when they are, we can correct them, at least in principle.

In time, the word *prejudice* itself, if clearly not the practice, shed most of its positive connotations, keeping only the pejorative. (Gladwell's book offers plenty of such examples, as do Richard Heuer[2] and John Hughes-Wilson[3]). Its best-known synonym, *bias* (as it happens, also of Latin origin—the French "*biais*" meaning slope, or slant), shares the implication that a prejudgment is in certain respects slanted, predisposed toward one rather than another interpretation of the facts, and hence possibly, if not probably, wrong. John Bright typifies the most common meaning, both then and now; as he wrote in the

Times of July 18, 1861, "Ignorance is the mother of prejudice, whether among nations or individuals." Putting a still finer point on it, acting on presumed rather than actual knowledge is that nefarious form of "pride" called hubris, the infamous tragic flaw, the ultimate mortal sin.

An objection may be adduced that *hubris* refers primarily to presumption of knowledge regarding values, the nature of good and bad, rather than empirical or descriptive knowledge (known to philosophers as the "is/ought distinction"). The objection is fair enough, but acting is an implicitly normative event. We do something because we believe it to lead to good results, or at least results that we consider to be good. To be sure, actions may well lead to felicitous consequences in the absence of "true" or complete knowledge, and even in the absence of knowledge altogether, as in the case of soldiers following orders given by their generals, who implement decisions made by their commander in chief. The commander himself consults with his top advisors, who in turn have the requisite facts. At some point, all of these people must act on the basis of incomplete information. Yet at each juncture, data has to be evaluated with wisdom, caution, and background knowledge. A critical element in that evaluation is sifting through information to separate "legitimate" facts from outright disinformation. Obviously, the same process takes place on the enemy side. Hence, at its most sophisticated, this information game is called "counterintelligence."

"Counterintelligence" is defined to include both "passive (personnel and property security activities) and active (counter subversion of counterespionage) defense efforts against foreign intelligence services."[4] Lest the reader do a double take and see double as the double negatives pile up, this is merely spook talk for fighting military deception. If even the "active" elements seem defensive, this is because we have traditionally been very uncomfortable with "subversion" of any kind. It goes against our up-front, "what-you-see-is-what-you-get" nature. Not that Americans have been above deception; the War of Independence could never have been won without some measure of it. But, again, we try to avoid it when we can.

Sun Tzu's homespun insight to the effect that intelligence revealing your enemy's motivations and plans is indispensable is so deceptively simple that it becomes too easy to dismiss with a "well, duh." For some reason, however, we have found it much harder to take to heart its corollary, namely that one should definitely not feel squeamish about using every possible means to preempt war, including, specifically, deception of an enemy prepared for murder. Sun Tzu never wastes words: "All warfare is based on deception."[5] Meaning what, you say? "Therefore," Sun Tzu anticipates, "when capable, feign incapacity; when active, inactivity." And, of course, "pretend inferiority and encourage his arrogance."[6]

Whoever said that common sense was common? Sun Tzu's quintessentially Eastern perspective has remained counterintuitive for Western societies throughout much of recorded history, but especially for Americans. The brilliant student of politics and culture, the late Adda B. Bozeman, has made this point in many of her writings. So, despite the fact that knowing "the other" is the primary intelligence requirement—and has been so for millennia—we have dropped the ball for a variety of complex reasons, none of which amounts to justification. "In our zeal to relegate conflict to a marginal detour in an otherwise peaceful march of history," writes Bozeman, "we have engaged in political warfare sporadically and clumsily, mainly because 'peace' and 'war' are conceived as opposites in the West, and in law as well as in religion—quite in counterpoint to non-Western mind-sets in which these concepts interpenetrate."[7] In international relations, alas, counterpoint makes for cacophony.

The concept of "counterintelligence" itself seems etymologically biased against preemption: we somehow cannot bring ourselves to do it until it's done unto us. The United States, in this regard, is even more reluctant than most of its Western colleagues.[8] As the seasoned student (and practitioner) of intelligence analysis Cynthia Grabo writes in the long-overdue unclassified version of an older handbook *Anticipating Surprise: Analysis for Strategic Warning*, "There can be no question that, at least until quite recently, deception has been one of the least understood, least researched and least studied aspects of both history and intelligence."[9] (For one thing, as Bozeman explained and Grabo confirms, deception tends to be forgotten and neglected between wars.)

In the age of cyberspace "chatter" and increasingly surreal high-tech sigint (spook acronym for "signals intelligence"), the intelligence problem has acquired a whole new dimension. At the same time, the cast of usual suspects, nation-states such as Iran and North Korea, have been joined, even if not outright supplanted, by terrorist organizations, with Al-Qaeda topping the sinister list. The barrage of jumbled "factoids"—a mixture of half-truths, inaccuracies, outright bald-faced lies, plausible-sounding rumors, imagined facts, and wishful thinking parading as data—has been exacerbated by the otherwise felicitous explosion of information through the Internet and other modes of communication, ranging from rapid to instantaneous.

The mass of material leads to what Grabo calls "analyst fatigue" and the need for technological sophistication in sifting through the pile, with the result that "the analytical system can literally be overwhelmed to a degree that some important and valid facts become lost in the mill, and others are not accorded their proper weight."[10] This fact has been demonstrated all too keenly by the 9/11 fiasco. Classified prejudice is the worst kind; it manages to hide behind the lofty curtain of "national security." The result is not only that America's image is tarnished, but its—and the world's—real security is greatly, perhaps lethally, jeopardized. The stakes could not possibly be higher.

The National Intelligence Strategy (NIS) released to the public by the office of John Negroponte in October 2005 promises a few changes.[11] Mission objective (MO) number 4 recognizes the need for "improving human intelligence," and MO number 5 authoritatively pronounces that the intelligence community (IC) not only should but will "promote deeper cultural understanding, better language proficiency, and scientific and technological knowledge among personnel at all levels." Sure to enrage the professional spooks, enterprise objective number 2 is to "strengthen analytic expertise, methods, and practices; tap expertise wherever it resides; and explore analytic views," spelling out the need to "utilize expertise from outside the Intelligence Community to inform judgments and to bolster areas where knowledge is lacking in the Community." All right, so it doesn't say that the community *will* do that, only that it *must*. A cynical friend of mine with a mere half century of experience inside the community doesn't put much stake in the strategy; he says that nobody in the IC will read anything that isn't stamped at least "Top Secret." Let's be grateful, though, even if it's all just rhetoric for public consumption; the public should be encouraged to consume all the sensible food for thought it can get. At some point, it may trickle up to the experts.

Quite aside from the intelligence failures prior to 9/11, compounded by the not-exactly-slam-dunk assessments that led to the war in Iraq, failures of analysis regarding other strategic environments are innumerable.[12] In many, though admittedly not most, cases, they are not unavoidable. A recent report published in *Studies in Intelligence* that deals with U.S. intelligence collection strategies concludes as follows: "Looking for information on a particular subject with a preconception of what is needed is almost certain to result in data that reinforces existing assumptions."[13]

In the same vein as the NIS, the report concludes that "the acquisition of 'softer' intelligence on societal issues, personalities," and so forth, though it "may be equally, if not more, important," has been systematically and deliberately neglected. Yet some of this information can be found in databases, as well as in "the minds of groups of people who are accessible but not easily approachable and who do not fall into the category of controlled agents."[14] By way of remedy, the authors of the report concur with the NIS: emerge from old habits; shake off your old prejudices; talk to others outside the IC; think out of the box. Does it seem too much to ask?

Stopping all or even most surveillance of U.S. citizens, whether "authorized by Congress" or not, is certainly not the answer.[15] As Alexis de Tocqueville observed almost two centuries ago, democracy abhors secrecy, which is but one of the system's handicaps. The astute Frenchman noted that "foreign politics demand scarcely any of those qualities which are peculiar to a democracy; they require, on the contrary, the perfect use of almost all those in which it is deficient."[16] Not only is it reluctant to embark on offensive actions, "it cannot combine its measures with secrecy or await their consequences with patience." America's early presidents, George Washington and Thomas Jefferson, whom Tocqueville cites at length, articulated plain principles "to be easily understood by the people," which have admittedly "greatly simplified the foreign policy of the United States." The result, however, is that "the foreign policy of the United States" appeared to Tocqueville to be "eminently expectant; it consists more in abstaining than in acting."[17]

This is clearly not the ideal scenario for conducting robust counterintelligence. Former CIA expert Frederick L. Wettering's assessment of the situation today is not encouraging; he finds it alive, but deeply ailing. Among the reasons are American cultural traits, or "mores," which have assumed the importance of fixed and binding customs, notably "the sad truth that Americans do not like or respect secrets."[18] Yet some secrecy is required for protecting national security. It certainly does not help when classification turns out to have been used as a tool for masking politicization and bureaucratic incompetence.

In fact, bureaucracies can be more than incompetent; they can sabotage the very security of the United States. In brief, observes Wettering, "basic bureaucratic behavior consistently precludes developing an efficient counterintelligence system." The example he uses dates from the Reagan era, when, during a period of seven years, the Intelligence Senior Director on the National Security Council staff, Ken DeGraffenried, tried to improve U.S. counterintelligence. He failed: "Even with his incredible talent, and despite his best efforts and the authority of his office, [DeGraffenreid] was able to achieve only minor, piecemeal reforms."[19] Wettering had no way to know that DeGraffenreid would live to try again, during the administration of George W. Bush, this time also joined by the eminently capable Michele Van Cleave, but with no greater success.

George Friedman is convinced that a principal reason for "the failure to anticipate first-order events [which] is hardwired into the U.S. intelligence system . . . is the obsession with the collection of information rather than with its analysis," the latter being considerably more complex. The system "has a great deal of difficulty not only building the big picture but filling in the blanks through logic, inference, and intuition"[20]—in other words, the quintessentially human component that no superfancy equipment can ever supplant. This is not to say that humans do not make huge mistakes of logic, inference, and intuition, further exacerbated by a penchant for overconfidence in their own infallibility. But the human component cannot be ruled out; analysis is indispensable.

So, the bad news is that the United States has had trouble with the "big picture." But the worse news is that it has also failed on the ground, as the "small" picture, or "actionable intelligence," is eluding us as well. Richard Shultz, director of international security studies at Tufts University, and Georgetown University professor Roy Godson have just completed an extensive, eighteen-month on-the-ground "tutorial" with senior intelligence and security officers from several countries, to whom they first explained the enduring organizational culture that prevails in the U.S. intelligence community, which is still focused on threats posed by states, and still overreliant on technology rather than case officers who do local intelligence work. One of the tutorial experts reacted bluntly: "Academic nonsense! The United States needs to get serious with what you call 'intelligence dominance' in Iraq, or suffer the strategic consequences."[21]

The main lesson learned by Shultz and Godson was that "it was necessary to create an architecture of security . . . [which] would involve establishing physical control of territory and introducing intelligence operatives into areas within this territory who knew the language and culture and who were ready to stay on the ground for a prolonged period of time." These findings were presented to senior officials in the Defense Department, the Joint Chiefs of Staff, the National Security Council, Senate staff, and the intelligence community. The consensus, at least for now, is that it can't be done. One particularly striking objection was that "Americans look different from our enemy, don't live next door, and don't know the language or culture."[22]

NOTES

1. Malcolm Gladwell, *Blink: The Power of Thinking without Thinking* (New York: Little, Brown & Co., 2005), 15.

2. Richard Heuer, *Psychology of Intelligence Analysis* (Washington, DC: CIA, Center for the Study of Intelligence, 1999).

3. Colonel John Hughes-Wilson, *Military Intelligence Blunders* (London: Robinson Publishing, 1999).

4. *Intelligence Warning Terminology* (Washington, DC: Joint Military Intelligence College, 2001), 11.

5. Sun Tzu, *The Art of War* (London: Oxford University Press, 1982), 1:17.

6. Sun Tzu, *The Art of War*, 1:23.

7. Adda B. Bozeman, *Strategic Intelligence and Statecraft* (Washington, DC: Brassey's [US] Inc., 1992), 12.

8. "When viewed in historical perspective, the approach of the United States government to covert foreign policy activities is relatively unusual. Most states regard the overt and covert influencing of politics abroad as part of the normal functioning of the entire foreign policy bureaucracy." Richard H. Schultz and Ray Godsun, *Dezinformatsia: Active Measures in Soviet Strategy* (McLean, VA: Pergamon-Brassey's International Defense Publishers, 1984), 14.

9. Cynthia M. Grabo, *Anticipating Surprise: Analysis for Strategic Warning*, ed. Jan Goldman (Washington, DC: Joint Military Intelligence College, 2002), 119.

10. Grabo, *Anticipating Surprise*, 128.

11. http://www.dni.gov/publications/NISOctober2005.pdf.

12. George Friedman lists a few: "Since World War II, the U.S. intelligence community has failed to predict the North Korean invasion of the South, the Chinese intervention in Korea, Khrushchev's plan to place missiles in Cuba, the fact that U.S. strategy in Vietnam would fail, the fall of the Shah of Iran, the collapse of Communism, or the breakup of the Soviet Union. . . . U.S. intelligence has never been very good at forecasting the big things," in *America's Secret War: Inside the Hidden Worldwide Struggle between America and Its Enemies* (New York: Doubleday, 2004), 61.

13. Richard Kerr, Thomas Wolfe, Rebecca Donegan, and Aris Pappas, "Issues for the US Intelligence Community," *Studies in Intelligence* 49, no. 3 (2005): 50.

14. Kerr et al., "Issues for the US Intelligence Community," 51.

15. For a lucid defense of the constitutionality of the Bush administration wiretaps, see Roger Pilon, "The War Powers in Brief: On the Irreducible Politics of the Matter," 2 *Cardozo Public Law, Policy & Ethics Journal* 49 (2003).

16. Alexis de Tocqueville, *Democracy in America* (New York: Vintage Books, 1945), 1:243.

17. Tocqueville, *Democracy in America*, 1:243.

18. Frederick L. Wettering, "The Broken Triad," in *Strategic Intelligence: Windows into a Secret World; an Anthology*, ed. Loch K. Johnson and James J. Wirtz (Los Angeles, CA: Roxbury Publishing Company, 2004), 339.

19. Wettering, "The Broken Triad," 241. He also cites Kenneth DeGraffenried's "Building for a New Counterintelligence Capability: Recruitment and Training," in *Intelligence Requirements for the 1980s: Counterintelligence*, ed. Roy Godson (Washington, DC: National Strategy Information Center, 1980), 161–272; and Mark Riebling, *Wedge: The Secret War between the FBI and the CIA* (New York: Alfred A. Knopf, 1994), 349, 364, 393, 395, 399, 455–56, 450.

20. Friedman, *America's Secret War*, 62.

21. Richard H. Shultz Jr. and Roy Godson, "Intelligence Dominance: A Better Way forward in Iraq," *Weekly Standard* 11, no. 43 (July 31, 2006).

22. Shultz and Godson, "Intelligence Dominance."

Part IV

PUBLIC DIPLOMACY
THE HARD WAY

Chapter Sixteen

Soft Power for Softies?

American diplomacy is easy on the brain but hell on the feet.

—Charles G. Dawes

The man who coined the term "soft power" in 1990, then dean of Harvard University's Kennedy School of Government and former Chairman of the National Intelligence Council, Joseph S. Nye Jr., blames our leaders, or at least "some of them," for failing to "understand the crucial importance of soft power in our reordered post-September 11 world."[1] High on his list of culprits is former Defense Secretary Donald Rumsfeld, who seemed to mistake "soft" for "weak," and opposed it on the grounds that "weakness is provocative."[2] Nye denies that wishing to persuade through attraction rather than coercion is a weakness. Isn't seduction more effective than force?

Without doubt, we cannot afford to dispense with a more sophisticated approach to the dangers of the post–Cold War era. Nye is right that hard power is not only insufficient but often the wrong approach altogether. He argues that the changing context of power in international politics is the main reason why soft power is not less but indeed "becoming more important than in the past."[3] Winning the war on terror depends on winning hearts and minds; it takes friends, argues Nye. After all, the United States cannot possibly hunt down every suspected Al-Qaeda leader hiding in caves or wherever; nor can it "launch a war whenever it wishes without alienating other countries and losing the cooperation it needs for winning the peace."[4] Nye agrees wholeheartedly with the *Financial Times* editorial claim that "to win the peace, therefore, the US will have to show as much skill in exercising soft power as it has in using hard power to win the war."[5]

Table 16.1. Comparison of Resources for Public Diplomacy and Defense

Country	Public Diplomacy	Defense	Year
United States	$ 1.12 B	$347.9 B	2002
France	$ 1.05 B	$ 33.6 B	2001
Great Britain	$ 1.00 B	$ 38.4 B	2002
Germany	$218 M	$ 27.5 B	2001
Japan	$210 M	$ 40.3 B	2001

But soft power continues to be a low priority for this administration, writes Nye, citing "the paucity of resources" devoted to producing it, particularly when compared with other countries. He uses Table 16.1 to illustrate his point.[6]

While he commends a few good initiatives, such as "an Office of Global Communications . . . created in the White House," he argues that "much more is needed," in the area of exchanges and generally a two-way communication with the rest of the world. He warmly endorses the recommendations of the Council on Foreign Relations' Public Diplomacy Task Force report, released in July 2003,[7] which urged that public diplomacy be coordinated from the White House or else through the creation of a Corporation for Public Diplomacy modeled on the Corporation for Public Broadcasting.

The CFR report is only one of a plethora offering suggestions on how to improve U.S. public diplomacy. Another was produced in September 2004, after the so-called Task Force on Managed Information Dissemination was charged with determining the feasibility of a coordinated U.S. information dissemination capability. The task force had been tasked to examine the strategic information activities of the departments of Defense and State. Sponsored jointly by the Office of the Assistant Secretary of Defense for Special Operations and Low Intensity Conflict (OASD/SO/LIC) and the Office of the Under Secretary of State for Public Diplomacy and Public Affairs (DOS/R), the lengthy final report was endorsed by the Defense Science Board Task Force on Strategic Communication.

In a useful appendix, the report lists several major studies by both government and independent organizations on the topic of strategic communication and public diplomacy following 9/11.[8] Additional reports continued to be released after September 2004.[9]

It would be impossible to offer a complete overview of all these reports, but what must be noted is a general consensus that "we cannot succeed if we tinker at the margins."[10] Included among the latest putatively posttinkering ideas are the following:

- Creating a Center for Strategic Communication (CSC) modeled on federally funded research and development centers, such as the RAND Corporation and the National Endowment for Democracy.[11] The task force specifically recommends that the national security advisor's current deputy for strategic communications should be an ex officio member of the CSC's board, which in turn should appoint the center's director.
- Developing a strategy by the secretary of state to guide department efforts to engage the private sector in pursuit of common public diplomacy objectives.[12]
- Establishing an agency within the Department of State and the National Security Council process, to be known as the U.S. Agency for Public Diplomacy (USAPD), to manage the U.S. government's civilian information and exchange functions and to coordinate all U.S. government public diplomacy efforts.[13]

The recommendations of the latest report on public diplomacy—specifically focusing on the Middle East—released by the General Accountability Office in May 2006, are not substantially different from its predecessors, but they do highlight the urgent need for "lessons learned." Above all, the report castigates the State Department for the fact that "State currently lacks a systematic mechanism for sharing best practices," demanding that it consult with the White House, affected government agencies, and outside experts to come up with "written guidance detailing how the department intends to implement its public diplomacy goals,"[14] particularly for Muslim audiences.

Apparently reluctant to take on the challenge of thinking out of the box, most reports recommend mainly more money for the tried-and-true methods that seemed to work for many decades when USIA was still around. These include cultural exchanges and "American Centers" to provide videos, printed and recorded books, and, more recently, Internet outlets to the information hungry in foreign countries. The common general assumption behind all of these recommendations is that by knowing us, the world is bound to feel better about who we are and what we mean to them. The consensus seems to be that winning hearts and minds is mainly a matter of organizing the dissemination of information. In many ways, this assumption is pretty safe; cultural exchanges are always welcome, as is "information," admittedly a word whose connotations vary wildly, depending on the beholder. But much more far-reaching changes are required if the United States is to relate effectively with the rest of the world.

For starters, "soft power" is a misnomer. There is nothing harder than genuine, human communication—softies need not apply. Commending "soft" over "hard" power—that is, military and other types of coercion—seems to imply not only that love is better than hatred, peace better than war (neither proposition particularly controversial), but that war should be avoided at all costs. Often, the proponents of soft power oppose hard power altogether: "winning hearts and minds" is always the tactic of choice; winning battles, never.

On second thought, is "winning" the right word? Not according to Colonel Ralph O. Baker, division chief for the Middle East of the Strategic Plans and Policy Directorate, who reports that "duty in Iraq has a way of debunking myths and countering ivory tower theories with hard facts on the ground."[15] Those hard facts made him rethink the way we describe our soft power strategy. His detailed comments are worth citing in full:

> We have all heard about "winning hearts and minds." I do not like this phrase, and I liked it less and less as experience taught me its impracticality. The reality is that it will be a long, long time before we can truly win the hearts and minds of Arabs in the Middle East. Most of the people have been taught from birth to distrust and hate us. Consequently, I did not like my Soldiers [*sic*] using the phrase because it gave them the idea that to be successful they had to win the Iraqis' hearts and minds, which translated into attempts at developing legitimate friendships with the Iraqis. However, in my view, even with considerable effort it is possible to cultivate friendships with only a small segment of the Iraqis with whom we have frequent contact.
>
> Unfortunately, befriending a small portion of the population will not help us convince the remaining Iraqi citizens to begin tolerating or working with us. For us, given the amount of time we had to influence our target population, the more effective plan was to prioritize our efforts toward earning the grudging respect of our target population with the 12 months we would occupy our AO [area of operation]. This was a more realistic goal. If we could demonstrate to our population that we were truthful and that we followed through on everything we said we would, then we could earn the respect of a population and culture that was predisposed to distrust us.
>
> Conversely, I felt that it would take considerable effort and time (resources we did not have) to develop legitimate friendships—assuming friendships were possible on a broad scale. So, by replacing "winning the hearts and minds of the Iraqis" with "earning the trust and confidence of the Iraqis," I attempted to provide a mental construct to guide our Soldiers and leaders in all aspects of the IO [information operations] campaign.[16]

There is more wisdom in this excerpt than in thousands of footnoted pages produced by many a comfortably perched inhabitant of the Ivory Tower and in ghost-written precleared speeches by senior members of the government, let alone in densely written reports recommending the creation of new slots for information gurus skilled in dense wordsmithing. Colonel Baker is suggesting that trust is a critical aspect of defeating cunning adversaries whose nontraditional strategies must be addressed on all levels, "hard" and "soft." But trust can only be won by delivering, by keeping promises and telling the truth. The fact that we must and will defend ourselves against attackers, that we will pursue Al-Qaeda and other enemies with vigor, is a given, and there is nothing "soft" about that. Of course there will be times when, during the course of military action, disinformation proves useful. But tactical lies should be used with very great care, and only as a measure of last resort. When the goal is winning trust, self-contradiction and inaccurate information guarantee failure. It is what Colonel Baker and his colleagues call "IO fratricide."[17] The texture of trust is neither soft nor hard; we got our metaphors mixed up.

Disagreements among proponents of "hard" as opposed to "soft" power boil down to a matter of tactics: the latter believe that we can attain our objectives better with carrots than with sticks, while the former disagree. Neither camp rejects the idea of "winning." Neither rejects the model of power outright. And therein lies the rub, for the concept of power is intrinsically intransitive: if A exercises power over B, at least at that point and in that relationship, B is passive. Power defines the agent-subject relationship. Whether soft or hard is not the issue; it's the whole picture that's wrong. This is by no means to deny the importance of power, of winning, of strength, and of preeminence. But it is to remind ourselves that outreach is an altogether different kettle of fish than warfare. Until that is appreciated, public diplomacy will continue to be the hardest kind of business—the kind that files for bankruptcy.

NOTES

1. Joseph S. Nye Jr., *Soft Power: The Means to Success in World Politics* (New York: Public Affairs, 2004), ix.

2. John Barry and Evan Thomas, "Dissent in the Bunker," *Newsweek*, December 15, 2003, 36.

3. Nye, *Soft Power*, xii.

4. Nye, *Soft Power*, xi.

5. "A Famous Victory and a Tough Sequel," *Financial Times*, April 10, 2003, 12.

6. Nye, *Soft Power*, 124. Unfortunately, it is not clear what is supposed to be included in the "public diplomacy" column, nor how the information was obtained.

7. Council on Foreign Relations, *Finding America's Voice: A Strategy for Reinvigorating U.S. Public Diplomacy*, report of an Independent Task Force, July 2003, www.cfr.org/pdf/public_diplomacy.pdf.

8. *Building Public Diplomacy through a Reformed Structure and Additional Resources*, report of the U.S. Advisory Commission on Public Diplomacy, 2002, www.state.gov/documents/organization/13622.pdf.

Changing Minds, Winning Peace: A New Strategic Direction for U.S. Public Diplomacy in the Arab & Muslim World, report of the Advisory Group on Public Diplomacy for the Arab and Muslim World, submitted to the Committee on Appropriations, U.S. House of Representatives, October 1, 2003, www.state.gov/documents/organization/24882.pdf.

Finding America's Voice: A Strategy for Reinvigorating U.S. Public Diplomacy, noted above.

How to Reinvigorate U.S. Public Diplomacy, Heritage Foundation, April 2003, www.heritage.org/Research/NationalSecurity/bg1645.cfm.

Managed Information Dissemination, report of a Defense Science Board Task Force sponsored by the Department of Defense and Department of State, September 2001, www.acq.osd.mil/dsb.

Public Diplomacy: A Strategy for Reform, report of an Independent Task Force sponsored by the Council on Foreign Relations, July 2002, http://www.cfr.org/publication.php?id=4754.xml.

Public Diplomacy for the 21st Century, report submitted by the Public Diplomacy Institute and Public Diplomacy Council in response to requests from staffs of the Committee on Foreign Relations, U.S. Senate, and Committee on International Relations, U.S. House of Representatives, May 31, 2002, http://pdi.gwu.edu.

Reclaiming America's Voice Overseas, Heritage Foundation, May 2003, www.heritage.org/Research/NationalSecurity/wm273.cfm.

The Need to Communicate: How to Improve U.S. Public Diplomacy with the Islamic World, Brookings Institution, Analysis Paper No. 6, January 2004, www.brookings.edu/fp/saban/analysis/amr20040101.htm.

The New Diplomacy: Utilizing Innovative Communication Concepts That Recognize Resource Constraints, report of the U.S. Advisory Commission on Public Diplomacy, 2003, www.state.gov/r/adcompd/rls/22818.htm.

Strengthening U.S.-Muslim Communications, report of the Center for the Study of the Presidency, July 2003, www.thepresidency.org/pubs/USMuslimCommunications.pdf.

The Rise of Netpolitik: How the Internet is Changing International Politics and Diplomacy, report of the Eleventh Annual Aspen Institute Roundtable on Information Technology, 2003, www.aspeninstitute.org/AspenInstitute/files/CCLIBRARY FILES/FILENAME/0000000077/netpolitik.pdf.

U.S. International Broadcasting: Enhanced Measure of Local Media Conditions Would Facilitate Decisions to Terminate Language Services, report of the U.S. General Accountability Office to the Committee on Foreign Relations, U.S. Senate, February 2004, www.gao.gao/cgi-bin/getrpt?GA0-04-374.

U.S. International Broadcasting: New Strategic Approach Focuses on Reaching Large Audiences but Lacks Measurable Program Objectives, report of the U.S. General Accountability Office to the Committee on International Relations, U.S. House of Representatives, July 2003, www.gao.gov/new.items/d03772.pdf.

U.S. Public Diplomacy: State Department and Broadcasting Board of Governors Expand Efforts in the Middle East but Face Significant Challenges, testimony of the U.S. General Accountability Office before the Subcommittee on National

Security, Emerging Threats, and International Relations, Committee on Government Reform, U.S. House of Representatives, February 10, 2004, www.gao.gov/cgl-bin/getrpt?GAO-04-435T.

U.S. Public Diplomacy: State Department Expands Efforts but Faces Significant Challenges, report of the U.S. General Accountability Office to the Committee on International Relations, U.S. House of Representatives, September 2003, www.gao.gov/new.items/d03951.pdf.

U.S. International Broadcasting: Challenges Facing the Broadcasting Board of Governors, testimony of the U.S. General Accountability Office before the Subcommittee on International Operations and Terrorism, Committee on Foreign Relations, U.S. Senate, April 29, 2004, www.gao.gov/new.items/d04627t.pdf.

9. *Report of the Defense Science Board Task Force on Strategic Communication*, Office of the Under Secretary of Defense for Acquisition, Technology, and Logistics, September 2004.

A Call for Action on Public Diplomacy, report of the Public Diplomacy Council, January 2005, www.pdi.gwu.edu.

U.S. Public Diplomacy: Interagency Coordination Effort Hampered by the Lack of a National Communication Strategy, report of the U.S. General Accountability Office to the Subcommittee on Science, State, Justice, and Commerce, and Related Agencies, Committee on Appropriations, House of Representatives, April 2005, www.gao.gov/cgi-bin/getrpt?GAO-05-323.

Cultural Diplomacy: The Linchpin of Public Diplomacy, report of the U.S. Advisory Commission on Public Diplomacy, September 2005.

10. *Report of the Defense Science Board Task Force on Strategic Communication*, 83.

11. *Report of the Defense Science Board Task Force on Strategic Communication*, 83.

12. *U.S. Public Diplomacy: Interagency Coordination Effort Hampered by the Lack of a National Communication Strategy*.

13. *A Call for Action on Public Diplomacy*.

14. *U.S. Public Diplomacy: State Department Efforts to Engage Muslim Audiences Lack Certain Communication Elements and Face Significant Challenges*, General Accounting Office, Report to the Chairman, Subcommittee on Science, the Departments of State, Justice, and Commerce, and Related Agencies, Committee on Appropriations, House of Representatives, May 2006, GAO-06-535, 41.

15. Col. Ralph O. Baker, U.S. Army, "The Decisive Weapon: A Brigade Combat Team Commander's Perspective on Information Operations," *Military Review*, May–June 2006, 12.

16. Baker, "The Decisive Weapon," 20.

17. Baker, "The Decisive Weapon," 20.

Chapter Seventeen

Misreading Machiavelli

A wise prince . . . should never be idle in times of peace, but should industriously lay up stores of which to avail himself in times of adversity. . . . [And], above all, should he always strive to avoid being hated.

—Niccolò Machiavelli

Typically, the term *Machiavellian* connotes a derogatory, even sinister intent. Webster's dictionary defines it as pertaining to "the political principles of craftiness and duplicity advocated by" the Renaissance Florentine, whose enormous contribution to modern political theory has been matched only by its consistent misunderstanding. Michael A. Ledeen, resident scholar at the American Enterprise Institute, offers a refreshing new look at the key ideas of the Italian genius whose frank assessment of human nature and its foibles could not be more relevant. This paraphrase of Machiavelli by Ledeen reads like a commentary on the current predicament of the United States: "Your troubles don't end when you make it to the top; indeed, they actually multiply. You will have to worry about your own enemies and those of your people, as well as about enemies and competitors."[1]

Machiavelli had warned against the illusion that success guarantees happiness—far from it. Once a desire is satisfied, man craves more. This truism applies even—indeed particularly—in the case of the best political system, namely, a republic: "For even if she does not molest others, others will molest her, and from being thus molested will spring the desire and the necessity of conquests, and even if she has not foreign foes, she will find domestic enemies amongst her own citizens."[2] As it happens, the United States has found plenty of both.

One would have expected Machiavelli to be read with great interest in this country; after all, he speaks plainly and directly. Americans like it when words are not minced. But this supremely cultured and talented man, admired by the most powerful leaders of sixteenth-century Europe, who negotiated treaties, organized and trained the militia, commanded them in battle, and also managed to write cleverly subversive comedies, was nothing if not sophisticated. His prose is deliberately shocking, its intent in fact complicated while deceptively blunt, oscillating between satire and directed candor. No wonder readers clashed over its meaning: British philosopher Sir Isaiah Berlin detected no fewer than twenty different interpretations of Machiavelli's political theory, covering the spectrum from sardonically satanic to anachronistically humanist.

The former has been rather more common, especially in the United States. It was evidently the choice of John Foster Dulles, for in his review of a celebrated book by Harold Laswell, *Propaganda Techniques in the World War*, which had evolved from Laswell's groundbreaking 1927 doctoral thesis, the young Dulles panned it as a "Machiavellian textbook which should promptly be destroyed!"[3] Describing this comment as an unfortunate underestimation of both Laswell's brilliant insights and the growing need for using mass media to affect public opinion is a monumental understatement. But in the process, he also revealed a deplorably myopic reading of a great political thinker, who not only deserved better, but whose wisdom Dulles would have been well advised to heed later on in his career, as President Dwight Eisenhower's secretary of state.

Disdain for the "sophisticated use of information and cultural resources to support national interest"[4]—in other words, ideological warfare, as defined by Wilson P. Dizard—has been difficult to overcome. The result has been an embarrassingly clumsy record of botched attempts at using ideas as weapons with only occasional brilliant exceptions. But ideological warfare, notes Dizard, first outlined by Machiavelli, who "codified its basic rules . . . in his advice to Renaissance princes [only] took on new importance during World War II and the Cold War." We were certainly slow to catch on.

John Foster Dulles's reaction was hardly unique; on the contrary, it represented a typical American distrust of "war by other means." Americans were straight shooters and proud of it. They detested Europe's sly ways and tended to distrust the subterfuge of diplomacy with its soft—why, even effeminate—power of deceit. The insight of University of Chicago professor Leo Strauss, whom the distinguished sociologist Seymour Martin Lipset (in stark contrast to professor Claes G. Ryn) considers "the major modern theorist of classical liberal politics," brilliantly and succinctly captures the nature and rationale of this mindset: "The United States of America may be said to be the only country in the world which was founded in explicit opposition to Machiavellian principles,"[5] to the power of the Prince. We thought ourselves above it all, unwilling to believe there was a price. We did so at our own peril.

Just as the first man's satanic enemy lay in wait for his—and his bold consort's—divinely fashioned birth, so did hostility to America precede its consolidation. Alongside those Europeans who believed the new continent might offer a chance to implement ideas the Old World found either too bold or unacceptable, the majority assumed the worst. Even highly educated people—notably the great German philosophers G. W. F. Hegel and Arthur Schopenhauer, along with their less well-known compatriot Friedrich von Schlegel—dismissed America for a variety of reasons. For example, the continent was either too cold and too new (and thus devoid of history) for civilization to flourish; the region lacked most of the noblest species of mammals, favoring the most unseemly and degenerate; but worst of all, Americans were ignorant, conceited, and vulgar, and exhibited an idiotic veneration of women.[6]

In their excellent history of anti-Americanism, Barry Rubin, director of the Global Research in International Affairs Center, and his wife, journalist Judith Colp Rubin, note that all these prejudices "drove Americans crazy," especially Benjamin Franklin and Thomas Jefferson, who both "felt angry and frustrated in trying to prove that their inevitable inferiority was a myth,"[7] particularly since they needed military and financial help to secure their nation's independence. Their instrument of choice was refuting prejudice with truth. Franklin, for example, published a brief work[8] showing that America's population was thriving, not decaying; and Jefferson's *Notes on Virginia* was written partly to disprove the degeneracy concept. But while the degeneracy theory itself declined through the nineteenth century and anti-Americanism entered a new phase, Europe continued to treat the newcomers across the Atlantic as uncivilized and degenerate. We didn't seem to care, but by now the Rubins throw in the towel, concluding that Americans "had no one to blame but themselves for this sorry state of affairs."[9]

Americans' resort to facts was perfectly sincere, reflecting the brand of unvarnished self-confidence that made settlement of the New World possible in the first place. Having inherited a healthy dose of it himself, President John Quincy Adams, at one memorable Independence Day celebration, confidently told an audience that included the European diplomatic corps that America was "destined to cover the surface of the globe. It demolished at a stroke the lawfulness of all governments founded upon conquest. It swept away all the rubbish of accumulated centuries of servitude."[10]

Overlooking the blatant presence of slavery, whose abolition would have to await the bloodiest war in American history, and the conquest of obstreperous natives before the former Europeans could declare their own national identity, was unlikely to be noticed by his foreign audience. But the otherwise cosmopolitan Quincy, whose extensive international experience and broad education seemed to have been amply trumped by his father's legendary bluntness, managed not merely to offend with his bravado but even to strike fear among those governments whose legitimacy he had so categorically and self-righteously rejected.

Little would change for over a century, until the start of the Second World War. Astonishingly enough, writes Wilson P. Dizard Jr., "the United States was the only major power that did not have a strategy, with a supporting bureaucracy, for carrying out ideological operations beyond its border."[11] It was no sooner than seven months after Pearl Harbor, in June 1942, that a White House executive order finally created the Office of War Information (OWI), whose double mandate was to carry out information programs both within the United States and overseas. Its beginnings were rocky at best. Not only did Republicans in Congress oppose the OWI because they saw it as Roosevelt's personal public relations operation, but its staff hadn't a clue how to sell foreign policies. Observes Dizard, "The OWI staff suffered in particular from general ignorance of the cultural barriers involved in reaching out to foreign audiences. Coming from a consumer-marketing background, they brought with them an insouciant belief that U.S. advertising techniques would work in the wider world: if you could sell it in Kalamazoo, you could sell it in Karachi, Kuala Lumpur, and Kyoto."[12]

But the ignorance went both ways, as indeed it continues to do. The author of several books on international communication in the aftermath of the explosive growth of electronic media, Dizard observes that "even now, despite the Internet and global television, it is probably still true that most of the world's population knows the United States primarily as the name of a large foreign country."[13] More precisely, the "don't knows" outnumber those who have a reasonably accurate view of American life—a hard thing to believe for the inhabitants of the self-described "shining city on a hill." Does everybody see only the shiny façade and assume it's all there is?

At midcentury, Americans were definitely not ready for public diplomacy. The very name—Office of *War* Information—revealed its temporal intent: after the end of the war, its mission would end. But it wasn't long before Harry Truman learned the import of Machiavelli's theorem that after war comes the harder work of peace. On January 30, 1948, Truman signed Public Law 402, which established the principle that "ideological operations" would become a permanent part of U.S. foreign policy. In April 1950, moreover, he proposed a "Campaign of Truth," committing the United States to coordinate its information activities with those of other free nations in what he called "a sustained, intensified program to promote the cause of freedom against the propaganda of slavery."[14] It sounded like a marvelous idea, and soon the Republican Party embraced the expansion of "psychological warfare" as a centerpiece issue in General Dwight Eisenhower's campaign for the presidency in 1952.

But before long, the Senate Government Operations Committee, under the leadership of the infamous Senator Joseph McCarthy, dealt it a severe blow. McCarthy, who, as mentioned earlier, had turned an entirely legitimate fear of Communist infiltration into so outlandish a caricature that the KGB itself would have shunned it, found an unlikely ally in the new secretary of state, John Foster Dulles, whose chronic diplomatic myopia should have disqualified him for that job. But if Dulles's plan to evict the international communication function from the State Department reflected his profound disdain for international public opinion as a factor in foreign policy,[15] he was by no means alone. Dulles, who did not believe that dealing with foreign opinion had anything to do with traditional diplomacy, was joined by others in the administration equally opposed to Eisenhower's wish to raise the profile of public diplomacy.

Over the ensuing forty-five years of its short life, the U.S. Information Agency struggled for identity, mostly without success. Like Rodney Dangerfield, embattled and underfunded, USIA could "get no respect." Criticized by the Left for using taxpayer funds to engage in jingoist propaganda, and by the Right for insufficiently muscular anti-Communism, the agency was quietly abolished by the Clinton administration in 1999 with the full acquiescence of its director at the time, Joseph Duffey. Although most of USIA's functions were nominally absorbed by the State Department, its status plummeted even further, as did its effectiveness, scope, claim to relative independence, and slice of the budgetary pie. The popular perception was that USIA, the rebaptized Office of [Cold] War Information, had completed its task once the war itself, however unorthodox its frigidity, had ended for good.

The same could not be said for History, much to the surprise of some new world neo-Hegelians who were already writing its obituary. USIA was thrown into the coffin, just for good measure and good riddance. Before the dust settled over the prematurely dug grave, history awoke with a vengeance. Among the vanquished was the hapless former agency, whose new reincarnation predictably led to its virtual demise. The overseas public diplomacy operations were placed under the control of the State Department's regional bureaus, where they sank to the bottom of the priority pile, slightly below PA (derisively known as "public affairs," long considered the foreign service equivalent of a dishonorable discharge). The State Department's Intelligence and Research Bureau would inherit what was left of the media reaction and public opinion research staffs, while the foreign press centers were transferred to the Bureau of Public Affairs whose domestic orientation seemed designed to underscore—certainly to ensure—their near irrelevance. William P. Kiehl, the diplomat in residence at the Center for Strategic Leadership at the U.S. Army War College and senior fellow of the U.S. Army Peacekeeping Institute, summarizes the situation succinctly: America's public affairs agency "was reduced to a shadow on the periphery of foreign policy."[16]

But wait, there's more. When America shoots itself in the foot, it does it with panache. The arguably most laughable, and certainly mind-boggling, self-inflicted piece of absurdity coming to us courtesy of the U.S. Congress is an infamous provision of the Smith-Mundt Act of 1948. While the bulk of the act has otherwise stood the test of time remarkably well, having provided the foundation for U.S. information and exchange programs, it also contains a clause that practically everyone agrees "hamstrings American public diplomacy unnecessarily," as Kiehl puts it politely. This provision prohibits the dissemination of American international informational material in the United States. Not only is this glaringly unnecessary and unenforceable in this age of global communication, but it is especially surreal for seeming to imply that it's all right to tell others what we must not tell one another.

Yes, you're reading this right: employees of overseas and cultural programs are forbidden from giving out the URL addresses of their websites to U.S. citizens, even though all of these websites remain easily accessible through Google and other Internet search engines.[17] In practice, this provision also makes it far more difficult for Americans to become informed about the activities of their own government, not only in international public diplomacy, but also in foreign assistance. Yet when recently several members of a congressional committee considered taking the matter up again and repealing the risibly anachronistic provision, after some deliberation it was decided not to take chances with giving the rival party an opportunity for posturing in righteous indignation. After all, it's easy to score political points when hardly any taxpayers have a clue about this provision or would give a hoot even if they did.

So alas, Machiavelli would be forgotten again, as information programs sank to the bottom of every politician's list of priorities, proof positive of Washington's glaring disregard, if not outright contempt, for the function and significance of these activities. It took the Bush administration no less than nine months following the 2000 election to appoint an undersecretary of state for public diplomacy and public affairs. When it finally did select someone, it was New York advertising executive Charlotte Beers. Ms. Beers accepted the position as if it were a plum new account: "I consider the marketing capacity of the United States to be our greatest unlisted asset."[18] Her new boss, Secretary of State Colin Powell, defended her before Congress, apparently with a straight face: "Guess what? She got *me* to buy Uncle Ben's rice. So there's nothing wrong with getting somebody who knows how to sell something."[19] Beers had gotten it exactly right: the United States had done precious little to exploit that asset. What she couldn't have understood, because neither did anyone else, was that America is not a product.

On the beautiful, sunny morning of September 11, 2001, Americans stood helplessly while airplanes hijacked by Arab terrorists were crashing into the body of our nation. Slowly, it dawned on them that they were not hallucinating or watching another budget-busting Hollywood science fiction production; they were witnessing another kind of Pearl Harbor. This time, the enemy who had outwitted us was a shadowy Saudi on the run, who operated outside the nation-state academic framework of realist political theorists. Dayton Accords architect and UN ambassador Richard Holbrooke asked a question that plagued everyone in the country: "How can a man in a cave outmaneuver the world's leading communications society?" At least part of the answer was obvious: the world's leading communications society hadn't a clue how to communicate—indeed, hadn't even understood that it had to communicate—with the rest of the world. Proudly prejudiced with self-confidence, the United States had manifestly done precious little over the course of its entire history to counter misconceptions, prejudices, and deliberately orchestrated disinformation that have consistently distorted—and continue to distort—the nature of its dynamic, vibrant society and its powerful, liberating ideals.

America's modern default communications strategy (or nonstrategy) had amounted to little more than a blissfully nonchalant, tacit endorsement of a general quasi-mythical image. As British journalist Malcolm Muggeridge reflected on a trip to the Midwest three decades ago, "Driving at night into the town of Athens, Ohio (pop. 450), bright colored lights stood out in the darkness: 'Gas.' 'Drugs.' 'Beauty.' 'Food.' Here, I thought is the ultimate, the logos of our time, presented in sublime simplicity. It was like a vision in which suddenly all the complexity of life is reduced to one single inescapable proposition."[20] *Sublime* is an ironic euphemism for *appalling* to capture its unflattering if not outright moronic, misleading simplicity.

Is the complexity of America similarly reduced by the ersatz stridency of our catchy logos? We don't mean to portray ourselves this way, of course; but then, we really don't mean not to, either. To most of the world, we are what we seem to be. It is hard to believe our luck; the United States has actually been remarkably popular considering how blatantly it has eschewed any kind of strategic communication. Observes Ambassador Kishore Mahbubani,

America had accumulated these reservoirs of goodwill almost absentmindedly, without intending to do so. Indeed, most Americans were probably unaware of these huge reservoirs of goodwill. Tragically, most Americans were also unaware when these reservoirs of goodwill began to be drained away over the past decade or so, to be replaced in recent times without Americans taking much notice.[21]

Americans are at last slowly beginning to notice. But the results reflect the legacy of self-righteousness that inhibit us from stooping to anything even slightly tinged by "Machiavellianism." So when the Defense Department engages in ominous-sounding "strategic communications," the alarms are sounded by the ever-vigilant media.

On April 10, 2006, for example, *Washington Post* reporter Thomas E. Ricks revealed the leaked contents the U.S. military secret campaign against Iraq's then–top terrorist, Musab al-Zarqawi. He reports that the Machiavellian "goal of the campaign was to drive a wedge into the insurgency by emphasizing Zarqawi's terrorist acts and foreign origin, said officers familiar with the program." How, exactly? It's right there, black on white, on the slides prepared for the top U.S. commander in Iraq, General George Casey. [Sound effects, please]: "Through aggressive Strategic Communications, Abu Musab al-Zarqawi now represents: Terrorism in Iraq; Foreign Fighters in Iraq; Suffering of Iraqi People (Infrastructure Attacks); Denial of Iraqi Aspirations (Disrupting Transfer of Sovereignty)." And if this doesn't seem Machiavellian enough, consider the deliberately intended effect of this tactic: "Eliminate popular support for a potentially sympathetic insurgency. Deny ability of insurgency to 'take root' among the people."[22] The prosecution rests, your Honors.

But it gets worse, at least according to Ricks. "The military's propaganda program largely has been aimed at Iraqis," but in clear violation of the Smith-Mundt Act, the military actually selected a journalist to impart this information, by the name of Dexter Filkins, a *New York Times* reporter based in Baghdad, who ran it on the *Times* front page on February 9, 2004. Well sure, "leaks to reporters from U.S. officials in Iraq are common, but official evidence of a propaganda operation using an American reporter is rare." It is not clear whether Ricks was irked mainly by the fact that a U.S. official was not leaking it on his own but was actually authorized to do so.

Perhaps he thought it especially outrageous that the Pentagon had selected the *Times* rather than the *Post*? In any event, look at this lame response: "'There was no attempt to manipulate the press,' Brigadier General Mark Kimmitt, the U.S. military's chief spokesman when the propaganda campaign began in 2004, said in an interview Friday. 'We trusted Dexter to write an accurate story, and we gave him a good scoop.'" Mindful of legal constraints, however, Army Colonel James A. Treadwell noted that U.S. military policy is not to aim any psychological operations (a fancy term for government-produced information designed for foreign publics) at Americans: "It is ingrained in U.S.: You don't psyop Americans. We just don't do it." He did admit, however, that an officer, speaking "on background because he is not supposed to speak to reporters," revealed the disturbing fact that the military's campaign "probably raised [Zarqawi's] profile in the American press's view." Scandalous on all counts. The prosecution rests again, your Honors, but is still fuming.

Please don't ask what the point of this article was, more than a year later and after thousands of murders attributable to the infamous Zarqawi, target of said Machiavellian "offensive strategic communication" operation whose now-revealed object was "fighting the negative insurgency." Never mind that the Pentagon is legally mandated to conduct "strategic communication" in a military context. Never mind that no harm has been done to anyone, so far as a reader can figure out. The fact is that, clearly, the whole operation was deemed highly offensive by Ricks and his editors. The innuendos do give the impression of impropriety. Now, your Honors, readers of the *Washington Post* wherever you may be, you be the judge.

Ambassador Kishore Mahbubani, for one, is confused: "Given the enormous contribution America has made towards decolonization and thereby to liberating billions of people, it is puzzling that American chattering classes are now fascinated with the idea of 'The Age of the American Empire.'" Rest assured, Mahbubani tells them; even if the United States wanted to become an empire—and it most emphatically does not—"the American political system is inherently incapable of running an empire."[23] Machiavelli couldn't agree more.

NOTES

1. Michael Ledeen, *Machiavelli on Modern Leadership: Why Machiavelli's Iron Rules Are as Timely and Important Today as Five Centuries Ago* (New York: St. Martin's Press, 1999), 67.

2. From Niccoló Machiavelli's *Discourses*, 2:9, cited in Ledeen, *Machiavelli on Modern Leadership*, 3.

3. Cited by Wilbur Schramm in *The Beginnings of Communications Study in America: A Personal Memoir*, ed. Stephen Chaffee and Everett M. Rogers (Thousand Oaks, CA: Sage Publications, 1997), 35.

4. Wilson P. Dizard Jr., *Inventing Public Diplomacy: The Story of the U.S. Information Agency* (Boulder, CO: Lynne Rienner Publishers, 2004), 1.

5. Leo Strauss, *Thoughts on Machiavelli* (Glencoe, IL: The Free Press, 1958), 13. For a useful new study of Leo Strauss' political philosophy, see Stephen Smith, *Reading Leo Strauss* (Chicago: University of Chicago Press, 2006).

6. See Antonello Gerbi, *The Dispute of the New World: The History of a Polemic, 1750–1900* (Pittsburgh, PA: University of Pittsburgh Press, 1973), esp. 457–59.

7. Barry Rubin and Judith Colp Rubin, *Hating America: A History* (Oxford: Oxford University Press, 2004), 13.

8. Benjamin Franklin, "Observations Concerning the Increase of Mankind, Peopling of Countries," http://bc.barnard.columbia.edu/~lgordis/earlyAC/documents/observations.html.

9. Rubin and Rubin, *Hating America*, 19.

10. Cited in Edward Tatum, *The United States and Europe 1815–1823* (Berkeley: University of California Press, 1936), 219.

11. Dizard, *Inventing Public Diplomacy*, 1–2. For an overview of the other major powers in the interwar years, see Philip M. Taylor, "Propaganda in International Politics, 1919–1939," in *Film and Radio Propaganda in World War II*, ed. K. R. M. Short (Knoxville: University of Tennessee Press, 1983), 7–25.

12. Dizard, *Inventing Public Diplomacy*, 19.

13. Dizard, *Inventing Public Diplomacy*, 22.

14. See "Going Forward with the Campaign of Truth," in Department of State Bulletin, September 2, 1950, 669 and passim.

15. See Dulles' conversation with Abbott Washburn and Henry Loomis shortly after he took office. Loomis interview, *Foreign Service Oral History Project*, February 25, 1989, 16.

16. William P. Kiehl, "Can Humpty Dumpty Be Saved?" *American Diplomacy* 8, no. 4 (November 13, 2003), www.unc.edu/depts/diplomat/archives_roll/2003)_10-12/kiehl_humpty/kiehl_humpty.html. See also the excellent panel discussion "Winning the War of Ideas," sponsored by the Heritage Foundation on May 8, 2006.

17. See www.ku.edu/carrie/specoll/AFS/library/5-AFXIX/laws/Congress1.html for the full text of the law; also Alvin Snyder's "Is the Domestic Dissemination Media Ban Obsolete?" in *U.S. Foreign Affairs in the New Information Age: Charting a Course for the 21st Century*; and "Smith Mundt Act" overview, at http://wiki.uscpublicdiplomacy.com/mediawiki/index.php/Smith_Mundt_Act.

18. "From Uncle Ben's to Uncle Sam," *The Economist* (London), February 23, 2002, 70.

19. "From Uncle Ben's to Uncle Sam," 70.

20. Malcolm Muggeridge, *Things Past* (London: Collins Publishers, 1978), 125.

21. Kishore Mahbubani, *Beyond the Age of Innocence: Rebuilding Trust between America and the World* (New York: Public Affairs, 2005), xvii.

22. "Military Plays up Role of Zarqawi," *Washington Post*, April 10, 2006, pp. A1 and A14.

23. Mahbubani, *Beyond the Age of Innocence*, 10.

Chapter Eighteen

Speakers in Chief
Define the New World

We must meet our duty and convince the world that we are just friends and brave enemies.

—Thomas Jefferson

When Louis XIV matter-of-factly proclaimed "*l'Etat c'est Moi*" ("the State is Myself"), he did not think himself unduly immodest. He was, in truth, merely stating the fact that as the divinely ordained father of the French nation, he was also the head of state—a twin function (absent celestial license) later assumed by republican presidents. Quite apart from the legal authority of the chief executive, which varies in different political systems and at different times, at issue is the actual power of his (or, far less frequently, her) pronouncements—a matter of ever greater significance in this century of rapid global communication. The impact of language as employed by the most visible official person, for good and ill, has become especially poignant with the advent of democratic elections that such a position increasingly presupposes.

The presidents of the United States have varied widely in oratorical talent, some excelling primarily in their writing, others in delivery, and others still in deficiency regarding either or both. A brief overview of some outstanding examples should serve to elucidate the special challenges faced by any incumbent whose difficult mission from now on is to have to please both the nation and the world, at a moment in history when business as usual is no longer an option: the rules of the international game have changed no less irrevocably in the military than in the cultural sphere. Besides "rogue" states, "failed" states, about-to-fail states, not-yet-failed ones, and for that matter unfailing— though hardly infallible—states, there are transnational actors and organizations whose capacity for destruction ranges from huge to devastating. Our multistriped enemies accuse us of evils various and sundry, but chief among them is the contention that we aim to rule the world. Hence, all our high-sounding rhetoric is little more than thinly disguised euphemisms, transparent to all but the terminally gullible.

The charge is not new, but its plausibility has increased exponentially with time. A reasonably objective assessment of the historic record should indicate that the first settlers did not set out to establish an empire. As to the authors of our institutions, whose minds had been nourished on Greek and Roman classics, they could be counted upon to assume their public duties mindful of the responsibilities owed to the city politic. Anyhow, most of them preferred the luxuries of private occupation. Talented, learned, uncommonly public spirited, the Founders accepted official duties for reasons mostly worthy. They defined who we are, to ourselves and to the world. America's image would be forever painted on their palette.

One is hard-pressed to find any historic figure to rival George Washington's grace in relinquishing power, the popular adoration he enjoyed during his lifetime and thereafter more amply justified perhaps than any other world leader before or after. His greatest merit was balancing an unflinching, loving commitment to his nation's ideals, tempered by a realistic assessment of its—as well as his own—limits. Admittedly, he was lucky to preside at a time that America's survival was still in question. America's eventually overwhelming strength and wealth were bound to exacerbate its unfortunate propensity to think itself exempt from the laws of nature and of human passions.

It behooves all subsequent commanders in chief to reflect upon and take to heart from the legacy bequeathed to them by the George who defeated his British namesake against all odds. If a divine right were required besides popular coronation by ballot, Washington was more clearly so graced than any fellow mortal distinguished by a mere jeweled crown. The great revolutionary first president, who mercifully would not be king, had been reluctant to take on the First Job in the first place, were it not for the universally acknowledged fact that the success of the American experiment so manifestly depended on him.

Having written his Farewell Address (with some help from James Madison) as far back as 1792 in anticipation of declining the First Job for a second term, he was eventually persuaded to stay, though another four years would prove more than sufficient. Calling upon then-treasury secretary Alexander Hamilton, his best speechwriter, to help update his parting message, in the end Washington put his final touches and had it printed in the *American Daily Advertiser* on September 19, 1796. While the idea to print rather than deliver the speech had originally been Madison's, it suited Washington perfectly. Everyone knew all too well that the decision of the self-taught stylist to decline personal delivery had no basis in any oratorical shortcomings on Washington's part. Rather, it graphically, and dramatically, deflected attention away from its protagonist and onto its seminal subject: the destiny of the American people. The audience of the Farewell Address—as both Madison and Hamilton explicitly acknowledged, and no one could fail to recognize— was nothing less than the American people, both present and future.[1]

Easily the most important presidential speech in American history, George Washington's Farewell "Address," as his letter is known, is a superb blend of noble humility and genuine devotion to the public good. It captures the very essence of democratic leadership as scrupulously obeying the people's will yet simultaneously transcending it so as to fulfill the highest ideals and interests of the commonwealth. Washington's eloquent silence underscored his determination to become an ordinary citizen at the earliest time. In the exquisitely penned letter, Washington assured his fellow Americans that his decision had been taken after serious deliberation "influenced by no diminution of zeal for [their] future interest, no deficiency of grateful respect for [their] past kindness."[2] He reminded them that he had been prepared to leave sooner, having embarked upon the second term only after "mature reflection on the then perplexed and critical posture of our affairs with foreign nations." Washington's stated conviction that now, at last, he could leave with a clear conscience, if not entirely candid, certainly underscored his hope that saying it might help make it so.

His parting message served to define for his own and future generations the meaning of a strong, emergent national character that can and must overcome all lesser, parochial identities: "The name American, which belongs to you, in your national capacity, must always exalt the just pride of more than any appellation derived from local discriminations." The new nation would be defined by a common cause, by an independence and liberty they earned by joint effort, common dangers, sufferings, and successes.[3] The explosive power of his withdrawal from the ship of state was equaled only by the eloquent silence of the undelivered address. Our first president's most important act of public diplomacy seemed designed to demonstrate that here was a nation whose grandeur would consist in minding its own business. America's reputation would grow as a result of what it would refrain from doing to others rather than what it would force others to do. This required leaders who would never seek their own aggrandizement at the expense of others. With majestic humility,[4] Washington made that statement tacitly. The resonance of its message was accordingly exponentially amplified: no wannabe kings need apply for America's top office.

An equal antipathy to the accoutrements of royalty was felt with no less fervor by Washington's two worthy successors in that exalted office, John

Adams and Thomas Jefferson. Considering the president's oral delivery of an annual report to Congress (known after 1935 as the "State of the Union Address") too monarchial, too reminiscent of the Queen's Speech, Washington's successor, Thomas Jefferson, in 1801 delivered the customary document to the legislature in writing, to be read by a clerk. More than a century would pass until Woodrow Wilson reestablished the practice of oral delivery in 1913, just prior to America's assumption of a radically new global posture.

Subsequent American presidents had to adapt to the seminal advances in communication technology: Calvin Coolidge's 1923 speech was the first to be broadcast on radio, while Harry S. Truman's in 1947 was the first to be broadcast on television. Lyndon Johnson's 1965 address was the first to be delivered in the evening, at prime viewing time. George W. Bush's, in 2002, was the first broadcast available live on the Internet.

The advantages and disadvantages of a far wider audience balance each other out, at best. An electronically wired, mainly videocentric, world community is bound to scrutinize any American president's dramatic performance, including semantic choices, body language, and charisma, more mercilessly than ever. An otherwise small faux pas, when magnified by instant messaging, remessaging, and—most precarious—repackaged messaging, can become egregiously expensive. But so it must be. However wistfully regretted by the nostalgic, the fact is that aloof "independence"—which some call "isolationism"—will never again be a plausible policy option for the United States. Its leaders have no choice but to learn how to speak and avoid being misunderstood.

Why marketing gurus Simon Anholt and Jeremy Hildreth believe that America had its "brand" figured out by 1776 is definitely a mystery. Alas, not so: America did not know from the start what it wanted to be when it grew up; or, to put it differently (and mildly), not all its people wanted it to grow up the same way. The policy divisions, real enough in themselves, were alternately smoothed over or exacerbated at various points in its history. The Declaration of Independence, hailed by Anholt and Hildreth as laying out to the world "the brand values of the nation," was surely an astute political instrument designed to target the British Parliament while attacking King George, but it deftly (ominously) glossed over the contentious problem of slavery.

The same was true of the Constitution, with lethal repercussions to follow. The Declaration's loftier national intent was dormant for over a century, when Lincoln finally had to fight half of his nation's states into submission. Its global reach would only be articulated still another half century later by a president who would repudiate his own electoral platform, which promised to keep the United States out of war.

Identifying Abraham Lincoln as merely the greatest American presidential orator of the nineteenth century risks understating his timeless grandeur, political acumen, and courage, his seminal impact equaled only by the Founding Brothers. Only the most sophisticated and humble understanding of tragedy could result in the world's most eloquent three-minute speech delivered softly, as before an altar, on November 19, 1863. Known forever after as the Gettysburg Address, Lincoln led the fifteen thousand or so family members of those recently laid to rest beside them, at Cemetery Hill, in what can best be described as a prayer, vowing "that this nation, under God, shall have a new birth of freedom; and that government of the people, by the people, for the people shall not perish from the earth."[5]

Just as the Declaration of Independence has spoken of "all men" having been "created equal," with no specific national pedigree by way of qualifier, so Lincoln was implicitly speaking at Cemetery Hill for all the world. Democratic government would evidently have to be instituted first upon the soil of the painfully re-United American States—whose common name would at last be referred to in the singular—but its span was meant universally, at least in metaphor. Absent electronic communication, virtually no one heard Lincoln's shot across the bow of history. It would be Woodrow Wilson who would not only render the international dimensions explicit but would decide, for better or worse, to back it with America's military might.

It has been argued persuasively that America's expansionist character may be best understood in terms of an original "frontier" mentality, a concept seminally elaborated by Frederick Jackson Turner at the dawn of the new century, which would be ominously inaugurated by the Great War, as World War I was then known. Turner saw the reason for America's involvement in that war as a way to ensure "that the history of the United States, filled with the promises of a better world, may not become the lost and tragic story of a futile dream."[6] Nothing captured better the hope for new beginnings; the courage required to make a home in the wilderness with little or no resources, confronting dangers both human and natural; and the feel of possibility than the seemingly endless frontier, its infinity as magical as it was illusory. Its lure lost nothing in appeal for being so demonstrably paradoxical—on the contrary, for it met the primary requirement of any miracle, of which America was paramount, with the possible exception of the Christian Mystery.

Turner saw the frontier as both a geographic and a spiritual reality, a metaphor whose emotional complexity would have to await the talent of Willa Cather. In *My Antonia* and other splendid novels, literary trailblazers themselves in both style and subject matter, Cather paints the complex canvas of that spirit with exquisite finesse. Her characters struggle to survive after reaching the bleak territory of Nebraska, their indomitable spirit no match for the daunting indifference of the seemingly interminable, stark land, especially ferocious in winter. That spirit of the Western frontier, sometimes ferocious and even destructive, but more often triumphant, was something truly new; it would define the American spirit and make possible the constant renewal of the American Dream of rebirth, promise, and hope.

NOTES

1. For a truly brilliant analysis of Washington's Farewell Address in all its splendid complexity, see Joseph Ellis, *Founding Brothers: The Revolutionary Generation* (New York: Vintage Books, Random House, 2002), chap. 4.

2. George Washington, "Farewell Address," *Writings of George Washington*, ed. Worthington Ford (New York: G. P. Putnam's Sons, 1889–1893), 13:277–325.

3. Washington, "Farewell Address," 13:277–325.

4. Humility apparently was harder for his vice president and later successor to the presidency, John Adams, as documented in David McCullough, who reports that Adams, writing in a diary he kept while studying at Harvard, chided himself, "Oh! That I could wear out of my mind every mean and base affectation, conquer my natural pride and conceit!" in *John Adams* (New York: Simon & Schuster, 2002), 41. Fellow Founder Benjamin Franklin's *Autobiography* testifies to a similar affliction, confessing to a battle lost—or at least, mostly lost. Franklin delightfully admitted that since he never succeeded "in acquiring the *Reality*" of the virtue of humility, he "had a good deal with regard to the *Appearance* of it." With equal candor, he confessed that he added this to the list of virtues belatedly, even reluctantly, recognizing its resilience. "In reality, there is perhaps no one of our natural passions so hard to subdue as pride. Disguise it, struggle with it, beat it down, stifle it, mortify it as much as one pleases, it is still alive, and will every now and then peep out and show itself." He adds, at most half in jest, though more likely in earnest, "For even if I could conceive that I had completely overcome it, I should probably be proud of my humility." Benjamin Franklin, *The Autobiography and Other Writings* (New York: Signet Classics, 1961), 104–5. For more on Franklin, see the brilliant book by Pulitzer Prize–winning professor Gordon Wood, *The Americanization of Benjamin Franklin* (New York: Penguin Press, 2004), esp. 207.

5. Abraham Lincoln, "The Gettysburg Address," in Annals of America, Vol. IX, *1858–1865: The Crisis of the Union*, 463.

6. Cited in Allan G. Bogue, *Frederick Jackson Turner: Strange Roads Going Down* (Norman: University of Oklahoma Press, 1998), 351. Bogue's study offers a readable, comprehensive, insightful analysis of Turner's ideas, life, and lasting influence.

Chapter Nineteen

Presidential Highlights from the Three World Wars

You have to take chances for peace, just as you must take chances in war. . . . The ability to get to the verge without getting into the war is the necessary art. If you cannot master it, you inevitably get into war.

—John Foster Dulles

Was it postfrontier malaise that accounted for Woodrow Wilson's eventual decision to venture beyond the shores of the North American boundaries? Once its frontier had closed at the end of the nineteenth century, so the argument goes, America's destiny was to look forward, to carry the spirit of expansion to other lands—all in the name of democracy. Wilson's sense of mission was especially acute with regard to countries that he considered to be suffering under despotic regimes. Convinced that his nation was destined to save the world's soul, Wilson chose the site of Independence Hall and the date of July 4, 1914, to reveal why American ships should pay tolls at the Panama Canal Zone: to do otherwise would diminish our standing in the world as the beacon for the principle of sovereignty, self-determination, and mutual respect. Orated Wilson, "A patriotic American is never so proud of the great flag under which he lives as when it comes to mean to other people as well as to himself a symbol of hope and liberty. . . . And so I say that it is patriotic sometimes to prefer the honor of the country to its material interest."[1] Alas, this pulpit-style rhetoric made for poor policy, divorced as it was from both military and political reality.

Admittedly, Wilson had as keen an appreciation for the importance of public diplomacy as any president. In an address before the American Bar Association on October 20, 1914, he recognized that "the opinion of the world is the mistress of the world; and the processes of international law are the slow processes by which opinion works its will."[2] (Unfortunately, Wilson did not always exhibit much patience for such "slow processes," with dire results for world peace and his own credibility.) He was deeply impressed by the radical changes caused by the speed of modern wireless communication. Not only did it enable conationals to become ever closer, but also people throughout the world, thereby creating a single community, where "every man can make every other man in the world and his neighbor speak to him upon the moment."[3]

In seeming deference to George Washington, Wilson acknowledged his oft-repeated admonition against foreign entanglements (a term actually coined by Thomas Jefferson to translate what Washington called America's "independence" in foreign policy), but he managed to stand it on its head. In a speech delivered in the frontier town of Omaha, Wilson offered his novel exegesis: "I understand him to mean avoid being entangled in the ambitions and the national purposes of other nations . . . and nothing that concerns the whole world can be indifferent to us."[4] No matter how liberally one interprets Washington's premonition, indeed expectation, that America would some day play a (even *the*) leading role on the world stage, suggesting that "*nothing* can be indifferent"—hence, ipso facto, that *everything* is of at least some interest—to the United States would have struck the solidly grounded general as sheer nonsense.

Wilson's record has been amply criticized by a plethora of historians on many grounds, both tactical and strategic. Among his many weaknesses, however, the most insidious may well have been a stunning inability to appreciate the complexity of geopolitics. Evidently inebriated by his own rhetoric, he bragged about the esteem in which the people of Europe held Americans, believing that the United States had single-handedly converted the war to "the cause of human rights and justice."[5] The felicitous effect of Wilson's internationalism was a vigorous expansion of intellectual communication between America and the rest of the world. This included educational exchanges, conferences, the creation of new organizations, and a boost to the study of non-Western cultures, even to the extent that some textbooks were rewritten to compensate for a rather pervasive, entrenched parochialism.[6]

But the negative fallout from America's newfound global reach was no less important. Wilson himself would recognize, far too late, that his "idealism" barely concealed a naïveté at best embarrassing. Speaking in Connecticut on January 8, 1920, a chastened Wilson recognized that "the world has been made safe for democracy, but democracy has not been finally vindicated. All sorts of crimes are being committed in its name, all sorts of preposterous perversions of its doctrines and practices are being attempted."[7] No kidding. One might say that Wilson fell victim to his own hype: the hypnotist inadvertently entrances himself.

Not to put too fine a point on it, Wilson made a mess of it. His own close friend and collaborator Walter Lippmann later asserted that Wilson himself recognized the impracticality of his own rhetoric, for he could not possibly have believed in the principle of self-determination at the time that he decided to break up the Austro-Hungarian Empire after the end of the Great War. "To invoke the general principle of self-determination, and to make it a supreme law of international life, is to invite sheer anarchy. For the principle can be used to promote the dismemberment of practically every organized state."[8] Boston University professor David Fromkin is hardly alone in accusing Wilson of having created a contradictory stance for the United States, which would have to contend thereafter with three different principles in international politics.[9]

Those principles were the following: the sanctity of existing states and frontiers, the legal protection of minorities (which Jimmy Carter later took on as his mission to champion "human rights"), and the right to engage in what today is called "regime change" in the name of self-determination. As these principles were in conflict, Fromkin notes that "resolving these inherent contradictions would not prove easy for future American leaders."[10] It would wreak havoc in public diplomacy, inevitably bringing America's intentions into question with renewed vigor before a world prepared to believe the worst of us, egged on by savvier adversaries far better versed in hardcore political warfare. The Cold War would eventually be won by the West, but it can also be argued that it was, instead, merely lost by Communism. That distinction is not without a difference; leave it to tone-deaf presidents to miss that point, fumbling the golden rhetorical opportunity of the century.

If Reagan was the master communicator in the age of television during the second half of the twentieth century, that title during the first half, the age of radio, clearly goes to Franklin Delano Roosevelt.[11] It was fortunate for the country and the world that no less talented a public speaker than FDR would be fated to join Winston Churchill in articulating the Anglo-American reasons for fighting the Second World War. The two men's special friendship[12] reflected not only a worldview that was similar in most respects, but also a shared oratorical prowess that was nothing short of extraordinary.

It is true that, in some ways Churchill did eclipse FDR on the world scene, not least because the awe-inspiring prime minister inveighed against Hitler with stentorian force as British troops were initially virtually alone in rebuffing German forces (with the notable exception of the stunningly valiant Poles, whose resistance continued long after the occupation of Warsaw). But mainly it would soon become obvious that Churchill had risen to the historic occasion with phrases of such Olympian majesty, and delivered with such earnest sincerity, as to preclude any supporting role from another mere mortal, even if he happened to represent the richest, most dynamic country on earth.

And finally, the course of war itself simplified FDR's task. For a while, it had seemed as if the president would have to use neo-Wilsonian arguments to persuade Americans to come to Europe's rescue, but Pearl Harbor spared him the trouble. After December 7, 1941, it would be crystal clear to the whole world that America was going to fight a war in self-defense, whatever additional benefits would ensue to the world community. The fact that, technically, it had been Japan and not Germany that had attacked our soil was more or less lost in the geopolitical shuffle as the two multinational coalitions faced one another on the battleground that encompassed well-nigh the entire planet.

Four short weeks later, on January 6, 1941, FDR delivered what may well have been the most significant speech of his presidency and one of the most influential of the century. Known as the "Four Freedoms Address," the speech described America's role in the world as leader of "a perpetual peaceful revolution" meant eventually to attain a world order secured by cooperation among free countries "working together in a friendly, civilized society." He went, however, one step further to name the specific object of that revolution. It was freedom, which to him meant "the supremacy of human rights everywhere." And in case the "peaceful" tactic may have appeared insufficiently potent, Roosevelt added, "Our support goes to those who struggle to gain those rights or keep them." Whether he knew it or not, he had thereby delivered a rationale for a later president—who specifically invoked FDR as his main inspiration—to provide indigenous freedom fighters with both military and tactical assistance. But FDR's midcentury manifesto declaring America's peaceful revolution resonated even sooner in decidedly more bellicose ways. In fact, it turned out to be a lot sooner.

Few would have expected the midwesterner who inherited FDR's oversized mantle—plainspoken, straight-shooting Harry Truman—to author a doctrine that defined America's strategy for most of the period now known as the Cold War. Spelled out in the famous speech defending his decision to aid Turkey and Greece, Truman declared that "it must be the policy of the United States to support free peoples who are resisting attempted subjugation by armed minorities or by outside pressures," adding however that this "support" would be "primarily through economic and financial aid," a caveat conveniently forgotten by those who consider this admittedly passionate speech as proof of American quasi-imperial designs.

Even so, it admittedly exceeded what either Congress or the public found comfortable. Writes historian Anne Pierce, "It seemed to jump too drastically away from the cautiousness of the isolationists at the same time that it seemed to violate the open spirit of the internationalists."[13] Yet Truman was not one to tone down his rhetoric for the sake of public opinion. In a wonderful letter to his daughter Margaret explaining why he had chosen to phrase the Truman Doctrine as he did, Truman stated bluntly that he had already realized at the fateful meeting in Potsdam that there was "no difference in police states," whatever they may have called themselves. If they succeeded in fooling "the American Crackpots Association," he, Truman, would have none of it. "Your Pop had to tell the world just that in polite language."[14] Polite it may have been, but also slightly misleading insofar as it implied that the United States would fight Communism everywhere, an interpretation for which the participants in the Hungarian uprising of 1956 could hardly be blamed.

Truman continued FDR's metaphor when he declared on July 19, 1949, that "this country has had a revolutionary effect in the world since it was founded."[15] It would take another four decades for the revolution that finally toppled the police state that posed the greatest danger to the world community to take place in virtually[16] bloodless fashion. The president who delivered the Evil Empire's last straw was the consummate communicator whose direct, simple language more than matched Truman's, except that Reagan's simplicity but lightly camouflaged the strategic genius of the man who had set out to win the Cold War. And in fact, after two terms, he did.[17] Reagan was without doubt the most-skilled messenger for America of the last half of the twentieth century. It is not too far-fetched to suggest that his rhetoric gave the Evil Empire its last push by calling it the name it truly deserved.

I was hardly alone to realize early on the providential role that Reagan was likely to play in changing the course of history. It was the final evening of the Republican National Convention. Kansas City was especially beautiful that warm July evening, its Romanesque fountains celebrating the triumph of democracy in America even as the more popular of the two Republican candidates had failed to win a majority. Without notes or teleprompter, Reagan spoke not only to the party faithful, not only to his countrymen, but to the world, deploring how "the great powers have poised and aimed at each other horrible missiles of destruction, nuclear weapons, that can in a matter of minutes arrive at each other's country and destroy virtually the [entire] civilized world we live in."[18] He told all of us listening to him, standing stunned as if in prayer, that whether Americans a hundred years hence will "have the freedoms that we have known up until now will depend on what we do here." He meant here in America. It was the message we all felt the moment he said it. If there was a dry eye in that audience, I didn't see it.

What Reagan conveyed, especially when you saw him in the flesh, was a disarming warmth and humility, a sunny optimism that reflected his belief in the fundamental goodness of ordinary men and women, in the eventual triumph of good so long as it was backed by the necessary tools for winning. He was the right man for the times, and he understood the power of the message.

To no one's surprise, the rhetorically challenged, even if remarkably decent, President Gerald Ford would lose to physicist-turned-peanut-farmer Jimmy Carter. Carter's toothy, cold smile and his "human rights" rhetoric did not quite manage to mask the arrogance he displayed in private. Natan Sharansky relates how he and other Soviet dissidents, who were otherwise ecstatic over the Ford-era 1975 Helsinki Accords—specifically Basket III, which required the Soviet Union to observe its commitments to respecting human rights—considered Carter's policy as hypocritical—chutzpah without teeth, or style without substance.[19] Writes Sharansky: Carter "was almost never willing to back his rhetoric on human rights with decisive action." Iranians evidently agreed as well, with disastrous consequences. As a humiliated America watched, helpless, its hostages being held in Tehran for hundreds of days, it defied the chattering pundits and went to the polls in November 1980 to elect Ronald Reagan by a landslide.

During the Carter years, the U.S. Information Agency coasted ineffectually in the penumbra to which it had been relegated under John Foster Dulles, Eisenhower's anti–public diplomacy Secretary of State, who has responsible for the bureaucratic split between information and cultural programs. "Bureaucratic legerdemain"[20] is how the eminent USIA historian Wilson Dizard describes the split, with "information" programs directed at international publics being exiled to the little-known agency, while the presumably more genteel "cultural" programs were permitted to languish inside the State Department. This arrangement would not end until 1979, the very end of Jimmy Carter's term. Dizard explains USIA's problems in that period by "the Carter White House's general disinterest in exploiting the agency's resources."[21]

After his election the following year, Ronald Reagan proceeded to appoint as director of the U.S. Information Agency his close friend, Charlie Wick, a member of the Reagan inner circle, who succeeded not only in revitalizing the agency, lifting its profile, and doubling its budget, but "melded the new Reagan policies into USIA operations in ways that were arguably the most successful coordination of White House and agency activities in the agency's history."[22] Reagan understood the power of people-to-people communication activities as no president did before or since. But more about such communications in a later chapter.

Presidential rhetoric is a complicated field all its own that deserves far more space than I plan to dedicate in this book. Professor Jean Bethke Elshtain is surely correct that presidential rhetoric is defined primarily as a relationship developed between "the foremost rhetor" (better known as the president) and America's "people, culture, and history,"[23] since it is U.S. citizens he must persuade to support him. Hence the president must speak first and foremost to his people. The obvious problem is that words resonate differently, even diametrically so, inside and outside the United States. It is the latter that concerns me primarily in the current discussion.

And it is the latter that must concern any president who takes seriously the proposition that American global leadership after the end of the Cold War is not a choice but a reality. Whether we prefer to describe ourselves as a "reluctant empire," an arrogant one, or no empire at all, the fact is that we are currently the only contenders to superpowerdom. Miscommunication, or dysfunctional communication, is not merely regrettable but dangerous. The price is paid not only in dollars—well, all right, megadollars—but in lives.

NOTES

1. Cited in Anne R. Pierce, *Woodrow Wilson and Harry Truman* (Westport, CT: Praeger Publishers, 2003), 13.

2. Pierce, *Woodrow Wilson and Harry Truman*, 22.

3. Pierce, *Woodrow Wilson and Harry Truman*, 22.

4. Pierce, *Woodrow Wilson and Harry Truman*, 35.

5. Pierce, *Woodrow Wilson and Harry Truman*, 114.

6. For an excellent account of these initiatives, see Akira Iriye, *Cultural Internationalism and World Order* (Baltimore, MD: Johns Hopkins University Press, 1997).

7. Woodrow Wilson, *Presidential Messages, Addresses, and Public Papers*, ed. Ray Stannard Baker and William E. Dodd (New York and London: Harper and Brothers, 1927).

8. Walter Lippmann, *U.S. War Aims* (Boston: Little, Brown, & Co., 1944); cited in David Fromkin, *Kosovo Crossing: American Ideals Meet Reality on the Balkan Battlefields* (New York: The Free Press, 1999), 130.

9. For a recent in-depth study whose rather exaggerated, if sincere, outrage spills over in its subtitle, see Jim Powell, *Wilson's War: How Woodrow Wilson's Great Blunder Led to Hitler, Lenin, Stalin & World War II* (New York: Random House, 2005).

10. Powell, *Wilson's War*, 131.

11. A common assessment, as reported by David Von Drehle, "Ronald Reagan Dies: 40th President Reshaped American Politics," *Washington Post*, June 6, 2004.

12. See John Meacham's *Franklin and Winston: An Intimate Portrait of an Epic Friendship* (New York: Random House, 2004).

13. Pierce, *Woodrow Wilson and Harry Truman*, 184.

14. Margaret S. Truman, *Harry Truman* (New York: Quill, 1972), 343.

15. Harry S. Truman, Public Papers of the Presidents (Washington, DC: US Government Printing Office, 1961–1966).

16. *Virtually* is a poor understatement for what amounted to billions of dollars in covert military assistance to the enormously dangerous *mujahadeen*.

17. For a fine, well-deserved, informative tribute to Reagan, see Lee Edwards, *The Essential Ronald Reagan* (Lanham, MD: Rowman & Littlefield, 2005).

18. Edmund Morris, *Dutch: A Memoir of Ronald Reagan* (New York: Random House, 1999), 402.

19. Natan Sharansky, with Ron Dermer, *The Case for Democracy: The Power of Freedom to Overcome Tyranny & Terror* (New York: Public Affairs, 2004), 131.

20. Wilson P. Dizard Jr., *Inventing Public Diplomacy: The Story of the U.S. Information Agency* (Boulder, CO: Lynne Rienner Publishers, 2004), 149.

21. Dizard, *Inventing Public Diplomacy*, 200. It so happens that among the hostages held by the takeover of the U.S. Embassy in Tehran in 1979 were four USIA employees.

22. Dizard, *Inventing Public Diplomacy*, 201.

23. Jean Bethke Elshtain, *Real Politics: At the Center of Everyday Life* (Baltimore, MD: Johns Hopkins University Press, 1998), 198.

Chapter Twenty

Post–Cold War Semantic Impasse

Peace and friendship with all mankind is our wisest policy, and I wish we may be permitted to pursue it.

—Thomas Jefferson

Strange that we should be defining the current state of affairs as coming *after* something. It's a bit like "postmodernism," which vaguely echoes "post-mortem," both somewhat metaphysical: since modernity is supposed to refer to the present, what comes "afterward" should belong to the same category as the afterlife. The current era is equally eerie, for, since the early 1990s, as Cold War rhetoric became obsolete, nothing emerged that could capture with similarly graphic, Manichean, dialectic simplicity the timeless struggle of good against evil. The end of that narrative, which had served so well to both mobilize American support for international actions and justify those actions abroad, caught Americans ideologically flat-footed when it came to making sense of world affairs. Elated by the anticlimactic rapidity of the Communist implosion, liberals and even conservatives nevertheless floundered, bemoaning—albeit for diametrically opposite reasons—the loss of the old "conceptual frameworks" to which they had become so comfortably accustomed. Everybody had snuggled into ideological grooves that they surprised themselves to be missing so keenly, having underestimated the intellectual laziness that had gradually crept up over the decades.

Even as they all sighed with relief at the startlingly uneventful end of the dreaded arms race between East and West, the search for "the vision thing" fell upon the hapless successor of the Great Communicator, the affable but incurably patrician George H. W. Bush, who wouldn't even try to fill the shoes of his former boss. The singularly nonpedigreed William Jefferson Clinton may not have shared that handicap (although he had plenty of his own), but he too was saddled with the reality that the country and the world were in need of leadership. It didn't help that Bill Clinton tended to take his policy cues from public opinion polls—a risky business when the public is even less coherent than the chattering classes when it comes to foreign affairs. Preoccupied by other affairs of his own, moreover, Clinton was ill-served by the foreign policy community itself, including those in the media and the academy, whose opinions about the Cold War and its legacy were muddled at best.

In the end, the elder Bush and Clinton administrations, while divergent in other respects, both found refuge in such rhetorical staples as America's "unique" role in the world as the champion of "freedom" and "democracy" (with greater emphasis on the former by Republicans and the latter by Democrats). The semantic poverty of presidential discourse evident throughout the nineties bears a large portion of the blame for the inability to explain clearly and persuasively America's multiple interventions in conflict areas where its territorial integrity was blatantly not threatened, notably in Somalia, Bosnia, Kuwait, Kosovo, and Serbia.

With self-defense unavailable as legitimate justification for military action, and all other arguments formerly adduced by America's commanders in chief equally inapplicable, the only way to prevent failure in the court of public opinion would have been to construct a paradigm that built upon America's moral preeminence. It was not only George "read my lips" Bush or Bill "depends what is is" Clinton who could never pull off such a feat; nor would Dubya, who had eventually found religion; perhaps no one could. Religious discourse wasn't much help; moral arguments, especially the more ostentatiously apocalyptic, are so similar on the two sides of the great divide as to defy easy refutation of the relativist's cynical claim that one man's terrorist is another's freedom fighter.

In a useful study entitled *American Exceptionalism and U.S. Foreign Policy: Public Diplomacy at the End of the Cold War*, using a narrow definition of "public diplomacy" to refer to official, mainly presidential, rhetoric, George Washington University professor Siobhan McEvoy-Levy describes sympathetically the predicament of post–Cold War American leadership. She takes it as given, as she well should, that words generate their own reality— or, as she puts it, "cumulative rhetoric creates a climate of belief."[1] Past pronouncements, entrenched national metaphors, cannot be obliterated, even as history changes, no matter how radically. Evidently, one of the main reasons for studying presidential rhetoric is to gain insight into "how U.S. elites wish the United States to be viewed either at home or abroad."[2] Ideally, both publics can be targeted effectively, but that is a very tall order. For one thing, it is far from clear that sufficient accurate information is available—let alone tapped—regarding either audience, though world opinion is obviously the most opaque and most complex by far.

The principal target is necessarily the home audience. McEvoy-Levy finds that for both presidents, Bush Senior and Bill Clinton, "American exceptionalism is more than a 'frame'"; it has the precarious "potential both to foster and prevent international peace and stability."[3] Such a double-edged sword, however, cannot be used cavalierly; the overconfident, underprepared swordsman will end up slicing off his own head. Or, more to the point, unless we find the real source of our heartbeat, we could risk stopping it altogether. While Americans like hearing themselves described as exceptional, the opposite is true of the rest of the world. Crusaders tend to be admired mainly, if not exclusively, by the home team.

In their highly acclaimed book *The Age of Sacred Terror*, Clinton advisors Daniel Benjamin and Steven Simon explain why this kind of warfare makes it especially difficult for America to explain its rationale for military intervention in the world disorder when lethal enemies are transnational actors. Since the rules of modern statecraft and warfare do not apply, neither do the old diplomatic protocols and the methods of public communication. President George W. Bush ran smack against this reality after his decision to "declare war" against terrorism in response to 9/11. The old semantics needed a makeover. He would soon come to learn the hard way just how radical.

Benjamin and Simon reveal that it should not have come as quite such a surprise that America was about to be forced into its hardest policy sell of its history. If the wake-up call for most Americans came on 9/11, many in the U.S. government heard it long before—to be exact, on August 7, 1998. The event was the almost simultaneous bombing of two American embassies in East Africa, in Kenya and Tanzania. But the really critical date came two weeks later, on August 20, when the United States struck Al-Qaeda targets in Afghanistan and Sudan, announcing that Osama bin Laden was behind the destruction of the two embassies.

Except that the evidence justifying that claim, and a great deal more intelligence painstakingly obtained over many years, as Benjamin and Simon amply demonstrate, were not (presumably because they could not be) revealed to the public. The decision was made problematic by the fact that withholding the highly sensitive information that led to the bombing of the Sudanese target ended up being further exacerbated by public diplomacy errors by senior officials in the Clinton administration, notably National Security Advisor Sandy Berger.[4] To be sure, Bill Clinton's personal scandal was no help, especially as it bore an uncanny resemblance to the movie *Wag the Dog*, released eight months earlier, starring Robert De Niro and Dustin Hoffman, whose plot revolved around a president's decision to attack Albania to deflect attention from a sex scandal.

The net effect was that in 1998 the media failed to appreciate the importance of the bombings, which obviously meant that the public would too. Write Benjamin and Simon, "The belief that the nation was genuinely threatened, and that the nature of the threat justified measures such as the bombing, was not getting through."[5] It had completely escaped even the nation's premier source of foreign news, the venerable *New York Times*, which ran a story on September 21, 1998, by Tim Weiner and James Risen accusing the president of having approved an act of war "on the basis of shards of evidence."[6]

Unfortunately, nothing could be further from the truth. Bill Clinton's otherwise impressive rhetorical skills were not to blame. Under the circumstances, they were completely irrelevant, not only as a result of lying about his sexual indiscretions but due to the very nature of the evidence against what was, after all, a massive, ongoing global terrorist threat. Benjamin and Simon are probably correct in speculating that even resorting to "much bolder rhetoric was not likely to have made a difference" in changing the complacent public perceptions.[7] People did not give up easily the comfort of knowing that the Cold War had ended with America essentially "in charge" as sole superpower. It would take more to awaken them from their blissfully ignorant slumber.

What it did take was nothing less than the heart-stopping shock of 9/11. George W. Bush's words immediately following the attack certainly managed to capture America's boundless outrage and determination to retaliate. Many people all over the world—though by no means everyone—understood that outrage. Even those who thought we "had it coming" could appreciate the impulse to fight back. The decision to kill Osama bin Laden, who boastfully took full responsibility for masterminding the attack, was eminently understandable. Rather less prudent was president George W. Bush's prediction that it would be done without fail, and soon.

The war against Saddam Hussein's Iraq launched in March 2003, however, was of a different order. Whatever its "real" rationale, the public justification for the war that the administration finally settled for involved twin claims of (a) an imminent threat to the United States coming from Saddam's alleged readiness to use weapons of mass destruction, together with (b) a connection between him and Osama bin Laden. Either of these might have sufficed to justify portraying America's aggressive action against Iraq as motivated primarily, even if not exclusively, by defensive security considerations. When both claims would turn out to have been based on flawed intelligence analysis, the job of selling the war to the American people proved dauntingly difficult. But harder by far was selling it to the world. Selling it to both audiences simultaneously was bound to be closer to impossible.

The president had no choice but to address his countrymen first and foremost, and so he did what would have been expected: he told them what they had been accustomed to hearing. But in the process, he further reinforced the prejudices against America. His choice of the "crusade" image could not have been less felicitous. The tone deafness of his advisors, unsurprisingly, reflected our inability to see ourselves as others see us. This does not mean tailoring who we are to please others; it merely implies that unless we make an effort to learn about our audience, our message will either be lost or, worse, misfire—which clearly it keeps doing.

NOTES

1. Siobhan McEvoy-Levy, *American Exceptionalism and U.S. Foreign Policy: Public Diplomacy at the End of the Cold War* (New York: Palgrave Macmillan, 2001), 3.

2. McEvoy-Levy, *American Exceptionalism and U.S. Foreign Policy*, 5.

3. McEvoy-Levy, *American Exceptionalism and U.S. Foreign Policy*, 5.

4. Sandy Berger and other senior officials, who had been referring to the al-Shifa plant in Sudan, which had been attacked by a U.S. missile, as a chemical weapons factory rather than merely a pharmaceutical plant, "were caught flat-footed when it became clear that the plant did produce medicines." Daniel Benjamin and Steven Simon, *The Age of Sacred Terror* (New York: Random House, 2002), 356.

5. Benjamin and Simon, *The Age of Sacred Terror*, 357.

6. Tim Weiner and James Risen, "Decision to Strike Factory in Sudan Based on Surmise Inferred from Evidence," *New York Times*, September 21, 1998.

7. Benjamin and Simon, *The Age of Sacred Terror*, 385. To be sure, some argue that, rhetoric aside, President Clinton might have undertaken bolder action. But that discussion is beyond the scope of this book.

Part V

OPTING FOR SENSE
AND SENSIBILITY

Chapter Twenty-One

Is the United States Really Such a "Hard Sell"?

America means freedom, opportunity, power.

—Ralph Waldo Emerson

Is there a certain headline value in throwing the worst light possible on America's international reputation, even within the United States itself? Speculation as to motives aside, the phenomenon is irksomely not uncommon. It includes even the most prestigious and widely cited polling data on worldwide attitudes regarding the United States, sponsored by the Pew Charitable Trusts. Robert Satloff, executive director of the Washington Near East Institute, for example, reveals in a previously unpublished essay, in his book *The Battle of Ideas in the War on Terror*, that a press release incorrectly, indeed misleadingly, summarized the results of a nine-nation survey conducted in February–March 2004 by Pew's Global Attitudes Project. The release ominously claimed that the survey "only showed a deepening divide between the United States and Arab and Muslim peoples."[1]

The widely respected Pew polls would seem to reinforce the results of Gallup, Zogby International, and other survey firms. Yet Satloff accuses the pollsters of bias or worse, claiming that they "seem to have *massaged* [emphasis added] the analytical findings to make them appear even more hysterically anti-American than the numbers suggested."[2] A more dispassionate and careful assessment reveals a much more complicated picture "of stunning contradiction, not a mind-numbing series of anti-American outbursts." No matter how "stunning," contradiction presumably makes for less dramatic headlines. Information provided by surveys tends to be wildly overrated by a public hungry for information "on the cheap"—the "wanna know what they think?—just ask" approach.

Survey results should never be expected to provide gospel truth. Where survey research can be of considerable value is in detecting the contradictions and erroneous information that form the basis of public opinion. *America Against the World* does a commendable job in that regard, and the results are in some ways rather encouraging. According to authors Andrew Kohut and Bruce Stokes, widespread impressions to the contrary notwithstanding, "a careful reading of the data suggests that the value gaps between Americans and non-Americans are not, in fact, so great—except in a few cases."[3] After all is said and done, "despite the current negative image of America, its people and policies, there is broad global acceptance of the fundamental economic and political values that the United States has long promoted." To put a finer point on it, "its free market model and democratic ideals are accepted in all corners of the world."[4]

Nevertheless, Kohut and Stokes concede that "nothing is more vexing to foreigners than the notion that Americans have an exalted view of their country," which indeed they do. The survey results confirm the fact that "average Americans are more likely to see their culture as superior to that of others and to express more patriotism."[5] But pay close attention to the rationale: although many Americans are distrustful of government, wary of the news media, and disinterested in politics, overwhelming majorities credited the Constitution, free elections, and free enterprise for the success of the United States. In brief, "there is little question that Americans take great pride in their 'system.'" What else does the immigrant experience teach if not the rational basis for American patriotism: most of the people who came here *chose* to do so.

By far the most counterintuitive of the findings summarized in the study based on the Pew Center surveys, however, is the startling realization that, "while U.S. citizens are alone in thinking it is a 'good thing' that American customs are spreading all around the world, they see people from other countries benefiting more from such Americanization than themselves."[6] Kohut and Stokes underscore, "These are hardly the sentiments of cultural imperialists, as Americans are so often portrayed." They are mostly concerned about preventing terrorism and the spread of weapons of mass destruction, and maintaining U.S. military power for essentially defensive purposes. Not to put too fine a point on it, "Having become the world's sole superpower at the end of the Cold War, the American people rejected the imperialist role that comes with such hegemony." Much has changed in the past fifteen years, but this attitude persists.

Based on their research, therefore, Kohut and Stokes find that "much of what fuels current anti-American sentiment around the world—perceptions of American nationalism and religiosity—is misinformed. A better understanding of the American people could change that."[7] This is just a different way of saying that we've been doing a miserable job of communicating with the rest of the world. Again, as my mother used to ask my father, "How can anybody so smart be so stupid?"

Evidently, the most virulent anti-Americanism is found in the most woefully underinformed and misinformed region, the Middle East, especially the predominantly Arab-populated areas. But even in these poor, knowledge-starved places, there is reason for hope. Thus Satloff is arguing for a more nuanced analysis of the surveys conducted in the Middle East. Admitting that "bouts of mass anti-Americanism are real [and] powerful" there, he insists that they are also "episodic" rather than inevitable. Although there is no doubt that Islamists do exploit the idiom of anti-Americanism to the hilt, a defeatist attitude, which considers the battle for the hearts and minds of the inhabitants of the Middle East to have already been irrevocably lost, is unwarranted and bound to become self-defeating.

"Why do they hate us?" is not, however, the only question, perhaps not even the main question. As Satloff intimates, it is by no means clear that "they" hate the United States so much as a twisted view of vulgar modernity, of which America is only the most convenient symbol. Having won the uncontested title "leader of globalization," it reaps not only the benefits but the blame for the worst effects of commercialism and secularism.

Robert W. Merry, publisher of the widely read *Congressional Quarterly*, cites Thomas Friedman and other students of globalization, who cannot help but note that nearly every country under its spell—which amounts to little less than the entire planet—has spawned at least one populist party or major political candidate bent on fighting the fallout from modernity. "And that's where America comes in," writes Merry. Both Friedman and Merry believe that "most peoples and nations around the globe"—backlash aside—"accept American might as the linchpin of world stability."[8] If this is true, it would seem to contradict survey data reporting an increase in anti-Americanism. But even if only partially correct, the claim points to an additional complication: one may recognize the indispensability of a force without welcoming it.

"Indispensability" would seem to imply a certain inevitability bordering on a determinist imperative. Whatever the merits of so strong a claim—hardly self-evident to its many opponents—it does not lead with syllogistic certainty to the additional belief, which Friedman shares with historian Ronald Steel, that Americans "are not content merely to subdue [other societies]: We insist that they be like us. And of course for their own good. . . . It must be tied into the subversive messages of the World Wide Web. No wonder many feel threatened by what we represent."[9] When we fear something, we are not likely to embrace it, even if we acknowledge its necessity.

Whether the Internet carries a "subversive message" is far more commonly accepted by members of the chattering and scribbling class—ironically the folks who tend to use it most. The motley crew of homegrown anti-Americanism, whose pedigree goes back to prerevolutionary times, has included over the years unregenerate Anglophile loyalists; Southern patriots, both prior to and following the Civil War, who considered the metamorphosis of the plural United States of [North] America into the singular nation of the "USA" as a repudiation of its original intent; Communist Party members, some of whom chose treason and became agents for the Soviet government,[10] and others who merely opted for open criticism; and leftists and assorted curmudgeons for whom hating America is what John Gibson has called "the new world sport," who see the United States as the missionary shark swallowing its lessers on the global food chain with all the oblivious zeal of a supreme, unchallenged predator.

Specifically, as professors Andrew and Kristin Ross observe in the introduction to their anthology *Anti-Americanism*, "leftists have been quick to point out that the Bush administration's recent season of militarism is not qualitatively different from Washington's long record of foreign intervention dating, in the postbellum era, from the 1893 coup that led to the annexation of Hawaii. . . . [While] left responses to the new American imperium draw on the traditions of neo-Marxist analysis that see imperialism as an intrinsic aspect of capitalist accumulation,"[11] not all forms of anti-Americanism are equally elaborate. In its most virulent form, however, it is invariably visceral. While criticism as an intrinsic aspect of pluralism is healthy, even necessary, anti-Americanism is corrosive, even dangerous. The former aims to improve, the latter to destroy.

Barry Rubin and Judith Colp Rubin ask, "What could be more ironic than the fact that a postmodernist America-faulting theory that the United States was taking over the world culturally and intellectually—invented mainly in France and the Middle East—gained hegemony among much of the American intelligentsia?"[12] Meanwhile, equally "ironically but inevitably, the ones born in other lands who best knew America and were most favorable toward that country were those who had chosen to immigrate to the United States."[13]

Blessed with the freest press in the world, Americans have naturally paraded their dirty laundry in public to fight their vicious factional battles. Political opponents resorted to vilifying one another with shocking epithets, half-truths, and outright lies, both big and small. Oblivious to our growing notoriety, with our economic, political, and military strength expanding at the same time as the technology of communication, we continued washing our laundry, dirty or not, in an increasingly global limelight. By the time we realized the colossal size of the audience, there was little we could do. America's scandals, real or imagined, true or manufactured, made headlines in all the languages, losing plenty in translation, deliberately and otherwise.

While the Rubins discuss anti-Americanism largely from a foreign perspective, Amherst professor Paul Hollander focuses primarily on the domestic scene, particularly its appeal to intellectuals, principally academics. He devotes most of his book, *Anti-Americanism: Rational and Irrational*, to symptomatic manifestations such as multiculturalism, political correctness, victim culture, and other forms of sacred cows that all boil down to a kind of self-absorbed whining. It would be merely embarrassing were it not for the plethora of material these prolific *kvetchers* provide to the deadlier enemies of this nation and civilization.

In a later anthology that expands the study to anti-Americanism abroad, Hollander notes at least one similarity between the two, which he attributes to "the psychodynamic of hate that springs from disappointment over unrealized and unrealistically high expectations originally directed at American society and its critics."[14] In a sense, it is precisely because America has been held to a higher standard than other nations that an overreaction was bound to follow.

Obviously, the disproportionate representation of anti-Americanism in the publishing, knowledge, and entertainment industries cannot fail to affect the perceived magnitude of this sentiment. Nevertheless, with apologies to the Irish bishop George Berkeley and his fellow empiricists in the seventeenth century and beyond, being perceived is not quite equivalent to being as such. *Esse es percipe* only up to a point; sometimes there are actual facts to which one may point.

For example, the impression that America is hostile not only to terrorists and Islamicists but to the Muslim population as such is reportedly widespread. Ambassador Kenton W. Keith finds that "the perception in the Arab world is that Americans are rigorously anti-Islam,"[15] which, according to professor Shibley Telhami of the University of Maryland, has been further confirmed by the Iraq war and "the war on terrorism that most people in Muslim countries see as a war intended to weaken Muslims."[16] When taking a closer look at some of the programs that are actually being conducted in places like Afghanistan and Iraq and the opinion of people in those countries, however, a different picture emerges.

For example, programs organized by the Center for International Private Enterprise (CIPE) since October 2003, when it opened offices in both countries, reached over 4,500 businessmen and women in Afghanistan alone, providing them grants, training, and materials; in collaboration with the Center for War and Peace Journalism and the World Bank, CIPE also trained 45 economic journalists in the principles of a market economy, trained more than 150 women entrepreneurs, and hosted the first annual Women's Leadership Conference in Kabul, spurring the creation of a mentorship program, the

Garvin School of International Management. In Iraq, CIPE introduced the concept of business talk television, provided over $1 million in small grants, engaged over thirty political parties in issues of economic reform, and built a nationwide virtual network of business associations and chambers of commerce, providing them with computer and Internet training.

The success of such programs was reflected in a survey conducted by Zogby International, targeting Iraqi business leaders, which was released in fall 2005. The respondents were not asked what they thought about the United States. Instead, the questions related to reality and their perceptions of that reality. It turns out that businesses have grown since the end of Saddam's regime: 43 percent say they have added employees, with 24 percent saying their staff had grown since the January 2005 elections alone. Almost half of Iraq's business leaders visit their American-organized chambers of commerce frequently or occasionally. Most importantly, the survey indicated that the percentage of business leaders who are optimistic about Iraq's future remained at the same high percentage as the previous year: 69 percent. In some areas such as Arbil, 99 percent expect positive future economic outcomes; in Basra, 92 percent. Even in troubled Kirkuk, where only 9 percent express optimism, only 19 percent are outright "pessimist," while 69 percent are neutral.

Objectively, at least, the American involvement appears to have done quite a bit to help many ordinary people in both Afghanistan and Iraq. The same may be said for a great variety of programs throughout the Muslim world, notably Indonesia, the fourth largest nation in the world, where a great variety of programs has resulted in better-informed citizens and considerably strengthened democratic institutions.[17]

Perhaps the first step in assessing the true nature of the danger posed by anti-Americanism is to recognize that, while certainly present, it is not in the least clear. It is, in fact, systematically ambiguous. The "America" that its enemies so love to hate consists of an inseparable duality: the nation-state on the one hand, and its idealized ideology on the other. It is indeed the case that for different audiences, "America" may connote any of the following, or a combination thereof: the people, the government, the culture, the business elite, or the nation's professed or inferred ideals. Advocates of the "it's not the people; it's the policies" thesis may defend some aspects but not others, some policies but not others, and some groups and individuals but not others. Such fine distinctions often elude opinion researchers, whose questions may contain systematic ambiguities, which render interpretation difficult. But it is not impossible, for this is still a sufficiently robust democracy, which promotes a high degree of interaction among various components of the broad civil society, including the sources of greatest commercial and cultural power, and government officials who wield political power. Accordingly, referring to

"America" as a whole, evaluating it without clearly discerning one component or another, retains an element of plausibility. The end result, however, is added confusion.

A serious appraisal of anti-Americanism cannot afford such conceptual imprecision. Whenever possible, the effort should be made to determine the target of any particular attitude with the greatest degree of precision as to its nature and its source. Even the most irrationally devout anti-American may be expected to draw distinctions and be open to at least some degree of dialogue. Conversely, criticisms of any human behavior are not only to be expected but should be welcomed when offered in a spirit of rational debate. "American" actions run the gamut from the most inspired and generous to the most foolish and even vile. No matter how high on the proverbial hill we may be perched, we simply cannot expect to shine at all times. Moreover, given that enviable—and amply envied—location, opprobrium and worse are par for the course.

When America's defenders overdo it by adopting the America-right-or-wrong tactic, they unnecessarily engage in a kind of reverse prejudice, which is bound to backfire. When Americanism is proclaimed as a fourth religion by its most ardently faithful believers, its "enemies" castigated for failing to appreciate its lofty spirituality, misunderstanding is inevitable. Religion takes us into a realm that transcends reason—hence its power to inspire, yet also to destroy.

Some in the Western media had a field day exposing the Islamicists' flawed sense of humor by publishing cartoons mocking Mohammed; now everybody knows that they can't take a joke. Now there's a surprise. The answer is obviously not only to stop ridiculing Muslims, while continuing to offend everybody else; political correctness of any stripe is lethal to civilization and education.[18] For starters, we might try being actually funny. (Though we must never forget that humor is always dangerous.) Next, we may leave the riskier forms of merriment making to insiders; haven't we learned anything from Richard Pryor, or for that matter, from the famous self-satirizing Jewish jokes? But when political action is suffused with religious righteousness, there is serious danger. One cannot underestimate the power of the supernatural to stop not only jokes but the very use of reason dead in its tracks.

This is one reason why Professor David Gelernter's argument put forth in his *Commentary* article "Americanism and Its Enemies," and in a more recent version at the Bradley Series Lecture held under the auspices of the American Enterprise Institute on February 13, 2006, is fraught with danger. While recognizing that "Americanism is notable . . . for its spectacular ability to arouse hate," he commends it for having "inspired remarkable feats of devotion."[19] He offers ample, entirely convincing evidence for "religious interpretations of American destiny," the subtitle of a 1971 anthology, *God's New Israel*, which shows how from the seventeenth century through John F. Kennedy and Martin Luther King, "Americans kept talking about their country as if it were the biblical Israel and they were the chosen people."

The metamorphosis of Puritanism into Americanism, which Gelernter calls "the end-stage of Puritanism," gives rise to the "American creed," which embraces "liberty, equality, and democracy." Abraham Lincoln profoundly understood this to apply to everyone: Gelernter points out that Lincoln's reference to "the great family of man"[20] revived an idea that had been articulated more than two and a half centuries earlier. In his *Good Newes from Virginia*, Alexander Whitaker had urged that Indians be well treated because "one God created us, they have reasonable soules and intellectuall faculties as well as wee; we all have Adam for our common parent: yea, by nature the condition of us both is all one."[21] Since Gelernter counts Judaic studies among his many specialties, he can point to the remarkable similarity between Whitaker, Lincoln, and a rabbinic midrash reflected in Genesis: "These are the archives of Adam's descendants," which implies that all men are equal before God insofar as all men are his creation. (As indeed are all women; Gelernter gallantly observers that one version of *Genesis* has Eve created simultaneously with Adam. It would take Americans a bit longer to digest that particular datum.)

One may approach "Americanism" as described by Gelernter in a slightly less messianic fashion if one wishes to avoid the idea of "American Zionism," a concept which, at this stage in the nefarious evolution of global political culture, is likely to do far more harm than good. Gelernter is absolutely correct in insisting that Americanism is not a secular concept. Calling it a "religion" is closer to the truth. And yet, what he tries hard to demonstrate is its incomparable universality, far greater even than the Old Testament's universality that so inspired Mohammed. The Abrahamic creed was surely meant to embrace monotheism as the spiritual source of world harmony. History, unfortunately, didn't quite live up to the ideals of its great prophets.

The United States seems to have failed in conveying the emphatically non-ideological nature of the creed that has inspired and continues to inspire the American spirit. This spirit, after all, is what accounts for the undeniable uniqueness of the American experiment. While obviously far from perfect, the United States has proven to be the most tolerant, most all-embracing, and most benevolent nation in the bloody story of our species.

It is not clear that America has quite grown up yet. Like Peter Pan, it had decided to move to a realm of dream where homeless boys may find a home and youth is a way of life. For a few centuries already, innocence has seemed worth the price: a puerile pride and barely conscious prejudice. We still hang on to it for dear life, as the world watches, frustrated that the richest and most powerful nation in the world should be so clueless. America must finally "get real," to use the apt vernacular.

We've been rather lucky so far. Whatever the verdict of alarmist survey results, almost despite ourselves, we can still count on the trust and affection of a great portion of mankind. In a remarkably astute personal chronicle, whose explicit purpose is to start "Rebuilding Trust between America and the World," former Ambassador Kishore Mahbubani observes that until quite recently America had accumulated "huge reservoirs of goodwill" among its six billion fellow earthlings. But it did so "almost absentmindedly, without intending to do so. Indeed, most Americans were probably unaware of these huge reservoirs of goodwill."[22] We didn't seek the world's approval, didn't cultivate it, and frankly didn't much care whether it existed. If we had stopped to think about it, we would have agreed that it was a good thing, though, in our innocence, we didn't realize what it was to be hated outright until 9/11.

Ambassador Mahbubani offers specific reasons for that goodwill by describing specifically how America has helped the world. "The single biggest gift that America has shared with the impoverished billions on our planet is hope."[23] In addition, it "also unselfishly shared its great universities with the best minds in the world"[24] and gave new confidence to all sorts of nationalities, religions, and other groups that often found themselves trapped in repressive, hierarchical regimes opposed to social, economic, and cultural mobility. When it reached beyond its borders, America meant to extend its democratic system, deemed superior to all others; accordingly, "this inherent American desire to liberate rather than subjugate explains why America has accumulated reservoirs of goodwill even in countries with which it has had painful experiences," most notably Japan.[25]

Married to an American woman himself, Ambassador Mahbubani is intimately acquainted with the people of the United States and has had ample opportunity to observe the depth and extent of their generosity and warmth, which he credits as the country's most valuable asset by far. "The real source of goodwill towards Americans," writes Mahbubani, "comes from daily interactions between ordinary people."[26] He does not hesitate to generalize: "Most Americans tend to be generous souls. They seem to have a natural instinct to help the underdog."[27] He offers by way of example the particularly striking case of Vietnam. At the nation-to-nation level the North Vietnamese government demonized the American government, but at the personal level, Vietnamese people encountered many friendly Americans. The people of Vietnam "could see clearly that most came with good intentions, to help and not to destroy Vietnam"; this undoubtedly played a critical factor in the country's decision to quietly assist America in Iraq. While that assistance is small, mainly in the form of shipments of rice, Ambassador Mahbubani finds it curious that few commentators have noticed it. "The contribution was clearly symbolic, but it was a very powerful symbol. The country that came to assist America in its new 'Vietnam' was Vietnam."[28]

NOTES

1. Robert Satloff, *The Battle of Ideas in the War on Terror: Essays on Public Diplomacy in the Middle East* (Washington, DC: Washington Institute for Near East Policy, 2004), 95.

2. Satloff, *The Battle of Ideas in the War on Terror*, 95.

3. Andrew Kohut and Bruce Stokes, *America against the World: How We Are Different and Why We Are Disliked* (New York: Times Books, 2006), 69.

4. Kohut and Stokes, *America against the World*, 71.

5. Kohut and Stokes, *America against the World*, 75.

6. Kohut and Stokes, *America against the World*, 76.

7. Kohut and Stokes, *America against the World*, 239.

8. Robert W. Merry, *Sands of Empire: Missionary Zeal, American Foreign Policy, and the Hazards of Global Ambition* (New York: Simon & Schuster, 2005), 52.

9. Cited in Merry, *Sands of Empire*, 55.

10. Herbert Romerstein and Eric Breindel write, "In 1946, however, the Republicans did not fully understand the nature and scope of Soviet espionage. They were concerned that Communists, who might be potential Soviet agents, were obtaining government employment. The reality was much worse—Communist Party members in government had been actively recruited by Soviet intelligence," in *The Venona Secrets: Exposing Soviet Espionage and America's Traitors* (Washington, DC: Regnery Publishing, Inc.), 53.

11. Andrew Ross and Kristin Ross, *Anti-Americanism* (New York: New York University Press, 2004), 9.

12. Barry Rubin and Judith Colp Rubin, *Hating America: A History* (Oxford: Oxford University Press, 2004), 236.

13. Rubin and Rubin, *Hating America*, 238.

14. Paul Hollander, ed., *Understanding Anti-Americanism: Its Origins and Impact at Home and Abroad* (Chicago: Ivan Dee, 2004), 7.

15. Kenton W. Keith, "'The Last Three Feet': Making the Personal Connection," in *Engaging the Arab & Islamic Worlds through Public Diplomacy: A Report and Action Recommendations*, ed. William A. Rugh (Washington, DC: Public Diplomacy Council, George Washington University, 2004), 20.

16. Shibley Telhami, "Reaching the Public in the Middle East," in *Engaging the Arab & Islamic Worlds through Public Diplomacy: A Report and Action Recommendations*, ed. William A. Rugh (Washington, DC: Public Diplomacy Council, George Washington University, 2004), 5.

17. See, for example, Hank Valentino, "People Power: Case Study—Indonesia," in *Every Vote Counts*, ed. Richard W. Soudriette and Juliana Geran Pilon (Lanham, MD: University Press of America, 2007).

18. See the excellent work of Diane Ravitch, notably *Language Policy: How Pressure Groups Restrict What Students Learn* (New York: Vintage, 2004).

19. See David Gelernter, "Americanism and Its Enemies," http://commentary magazine.com/article.asp?aid=11901043_1.

20. Gelernter, "Americanism."

21. Gelernter, "Americanism."

22. Kishore Mahbubani, *Beyond the Age of Innocence: Rebuilding Trust between America and the World* (New York: Public Affairs, 2005), xvii.

23. Mahbubani, *Beyond the Age of Innocence*, 1.

24. Mahbubani, *Beyond the Age of Innocence*, 2.

25. Mahbubani, *Beyond the Age of Innocence*, 11.

26. Mahbubani, *Beyond the Age of Innocence*, 24.

27. Mahbubani, *Beyond the Age of Innocence*, 25.

28. Mahbubani, *Beyond the Age of Innocence*, 26.

Chapter Twenty-Two

Global Strategic Outreach: Doing It Right

> Non-violence knows no defeat. It must, however, be true non-violence, not a make-believe.
>
> —Mohandas Gandhi

Journalist Edmund Taylor meant to convey the moral power of American cultural and informational activities conducted in the Soviet-occupied area of Germany immediately after the end of the Second World War when he chose to describe it as "the Gandhian strategy of constructive subversion, a technique against which the Communists seem to have no effective psychological defense."[1] He was referring to the Radio in the American Sector program known as "RIAS," originally set up temporarily to substitute for the Berlin radio stations closed down by the Allies until a denazified network would be established.

Denazification, which at times was also called "democratization," had been a consciously designed massive initiative to reeducate an entire population exposed to years of Nazi propaganda: it was never intended to combat Soviet active measures directed against Western nations in general, but especially the United States. The "constructive" element that gave it a Gandhian quality was, in a word, truth. American "propaganda," in that context, is in fact a misnomer, insofar as the word carries pejorative connotations.

The American approach to psy-op (short for "psychological operations") had always differentiated between, on the one hand, disinformation techniques for immediate, short-term use in active warfare and, on the other hand, the "campaigns for truth" of public diplomacy traditionally so called. The former, when used at all given Americans' traditional distrust of deception, fell under the province of the Defense Department or the CIA. The latter, America's truth-campaigning activities, had been conducted by USIA until it vanished inside the State Department in 1999.

Deception is often critical not only in peacetime but in warfare, especially when the object is to prevent or at least minimize the use of force. No one has put this better than Sun Tzu, who recognized that since all warfare is based on deception, refusing to engage in it is tantamount to conceding defeat. "Therefore, when capable, feign incapacity; when active, inactivity."[2] Is this not sheer common sense? The problem with engaging in disinformation is that it can sometimes sabotage peaceful, truthful, and benevolent activities whose purpose is entirely self-evident. This was the case, for example, of Radio Free Europe/Radio Liberty, as well as a variety of Cold War–era publications of the very highest quality, such as *Encounter*, *Minerva*, and *Survey*,[3] all of which were funded by the CIA, even though nothing remotely deceptive was being disseminated.

So, does this mean that the United States must not engage in any psy-op? That the Pentagon, the CIA, and even the State Department shouldn't even think of getting into the deception or "active measures" business? Hardly. But it does suggest keeping the two kinds of activities as separate as possible, even though coordination and synchronicity should be the rule. When Moroccan journalist and Carnegie Endowment visiting scholar Mustapha Khalfi reminds us that democracy promotion "is a good in itself and should not be put at the service of other goals, such as improving the U.S. image or gathering support for other U.S. policies,"[4] he is making a simple point: you can't have your altruistic cake and eat it too. In the same vein, if you are going to engage in deception operations, make sure there is a foolproof firewall separating those guys from all the folks who are in the business of telling the truth.

Any country worth its salt, especially a superpower, however, ought to be able to walk and chew gum at the same time. Tactics vary with circumstances: sometimes deception is called for, sometimes not. Guidance is provided by strategic planning, which serves the national interest. The value of a word such as *strategic* in the semantics of democratic—and specifically American—statecraft, unfortunately, has been greatly devalued by its deplorable history, including overuse and imprecision. Alexis de Tocqueville could have written these words at almost any time, including the present: in foreign policy, he laments, "a democracy can only with great difficulty regulate the details of an important undertaking, persevere in a fixed design, and work out its execution in spite of serious obstacles."[5] This is due to "the propensity that induces democracies to obey impulse rather than prudence, and to abandon a mature design for the gratification of a momentary passion,"[6] assuming that such a design can even emerge in the first place.

These prophetic words have been amply confirmed by experience. Americans have little patience with drawn-out strategies, and they do not seem to mind that every new administration starts out, if not from scratch, at least with insufficient regard for the experience of its predecessor. This is not to say, however, that we don't like the word itself: *strategic* has a nice, quasi-military ring to it. It seems to convey strong determination, organization and management, direction and purpose—in other words, all the things that public diplomacy lacks.

Which is why "strategic communication" is so apt. And just to prove its existence, strategic communication comes with its very own task force, a group that did what task forces do best: study the issue. In September 2004, a report was issued recommending, among other things, the creation of a nonpartisan Center for Strategic Communication to support the National Security Council and the departments and organizations currently represented on the Strategic Communications Committee.[7] The report concluded that unfortunately "United States strategic communication lacks sustained Presidential direction, effective interagency coordination, optimal private sector partnerships, and adequate resources," adding that "tactical message coordination does not equate with strategic planning and evaluation."

Similarly, the General Accountability Office found in its own report that the State Department, despite having nominally established a strategic framework for U.S. public diplomacy efforts in 2005, has failed to implement them, as "these early efforts lack guidance from Washington to the field on strategies and tactics." This is a polite way of saying that there really isn't a strategic communication plan; we are just pretending there is one, and nobody seems to be able to tell the difference between strategy and tactics.

According to that report, moreover, strategic communication describes a variety of instruments used by governments to understand global attitudes and cultures, engage in a dialogue of ideas, advise policy makers on the public opinion implications of policy choices, and influence public attitudes through communications strategies.[8] But it would seem that the report falls into the very trap it criticizes, for "a variety of instruments" is just what defines "tactics." Strategy, by contrast, involves setting goals, priorities, and direction. Understanding, dialogue, and influence are all significant tools to be used for strategic purposes. That should not surprise anyone, of course, for if nobody can distinguish strategy from tactics, why would the task force members?

The first step could be to define *strategy*. The word originates—as does democracy—in ancient Greece, where *strategos* meant simply "general." Like his modern-day contemporary, the general of that ancient world gave the orders, inspired the troops, and directed them bravely in battle. Unlike today, however, the generals of yore were expected to show wisdom in deciding not only how to fight, but when, where, and why. Independently of the Greeks, Sun Tzu also defined the principal quality of a general to be wisdom, followed by sincerity, humanity, courage, and strictness. "There is no general who has not heard of these five matters," declared Sun Tzu, adding, "Those who master them win; those who do not are defeated."[9]

Wisdom was clearly the most important, as it results in moral influence, which in turn is defined by Sun Tzu as "that which causes the people to be in harmony with their leaders, so that they will accompany them in life and unto death without fear of mortal peril." In other words, a general can never succeed unless he enjoys the absolute trust and allegiance of the people. But such devotion is only possible if the people understand the full import of his course of action. That involves a clear indication of what has to be done, and why—in other words, his strategy.

Since strategy requires vision, and vision often requires time—the one commodity that is notoriously scarce when the election cycle determines policy—it seems we're in a no-win situation. But the GAO report concludes with a surprisingly novel suggestion: in order "to increase the sophistication and effectiveness of outreach efforts, [the State Department must] develop written guidance detailing how [it] intends to implement its public diplomacy goals as they apply to the Muslim world and incorporate the strategic communications best practices"[10] by modeling and adapting private-sector approaches to suit its purposes.[11]

Increasing the sophistication and effectiveness of outreach efforts is exactly the purpose of a strategic plan for public diplomacy properly understood. Even "strategic communication" is inadequate; *outreach* is preferable to *communication* for a number of reasons. Not only is the primary meaning of *communicating* intransitive, indicating that something is imparted *to* someone, given *to* another, made known, revealed, or divulged; what is more, communication is often verbal, referring to intercourse by words, letters, or messages. In contrast, the Anglo-Saxon *outreach* connotes surpassing, extending, and expanding. When engaged in outreach, we seek to explore beyond, to take a chance, to emerge, perhaps to embrace—if nothing else, the unexpected.

One of the best documents outlining the purpose of U.S. public diplomacy is the National Security Decision Directive (NSDD) Number 77, now declassified. In his NSDD 77, entitled "Management of Public Diplomacy Relative to National Security," issued on January 14, 1983, President Ronald Reagan defined public diplomacy as "those actions of the U.S. Government designed to generate support for our national security objectives."[12] Reagan obviously had grasped that such actions must seek "to encourage the growth of democratic political institutions and practices," which in turn "will require close collaboration with other foreign policy efforts—diplomatic, economic, and military—as well as close relationship with those sectors of the American society—labor, business, universities, philanthropy, political parties, press—that are or could be more engaged in parallel efforts overseas."[13]

Public diplomacy expert William Kiehl has recently deplored the absence of any reference to public diplomacy in the latest National Security Strategy (NSS) released in March 2006. While technically correct, this criticism is not strictly accurate. Whether intentionally or not, the 2006 NSS echoes Reagan's objective, described nearly a quarter of a century earlier, to encourage the growth of democracy, in these words:

> It is the policy of the United States to seek and support democratic movements and institutions in every nation and culture, with the ultimate goal of ending tyranny in our world.

Which means—as it did for Reagan—that in order to provide enduring security for the United States, "it is the goal of our statecraft to help create a world of democratic, well-governed states that can meet the needs of their citizens and conduct themselves responsibly in the international arena."[14]

But to achieve that, we must engage in strategic outreach. Unlike the nonstrategic variety, whether recreational, self-promotional (especially appealing to celebrities), aesthetic, or the like, *strategic* outreach should strive to promote the strategic goals of the nation. In particular, it should aim "to seek and support democratic movements and institutions" wherever possible. But in order to do that, we must understand other nations and cultures, know how to promote democracy effectively, and make sure that our goal is not misunderstood by the very people we wish to help achieve the freedom that we believe is indispensable for security. Above all, therefore, the United States must try to convey the truth about its intentions and aspirations.

But what is "the truth" about America? Obviously, different views of America will result in radically different versions of "the" truth, if one can even speak of it in the singular. This enormously complex nation, an intricate amalgam of many cultural, social, and economic groupings, is bound to be perceived in conflicting, diametrically opposed ways by perfectly honest people with normal sensory functions. We can agree from the outset, moreover, that given the sheer quantity of information, though evidently preferable to scarcity, it is unwise to suspect an anti-American under every proverbial bed, and not only absurd but unnecessary to "combat" all or even most instances of anti-Americanism. How information is processed depends very much on what the information is and how it is understood. Does it offer a reasonably accurate description of reality? And if not, why not? Most distortions are the inevitable result of human frailty, bias, and historic context.

Outright disinformation designed to malign the United States is something else altogether. Surely the first step in countering a false image of the United States is to combat premeditated, consciously fabricated lies whose intent is to harm the reputation of our citizens and leadership. While tracking them all is obviously impossible, it would be useful to create an effective network to monitor disinformation, analyze it, and then take adequate, proportional measures to counter it when deemed sufficiently significant. Gandhi was surely right to insist that only truth is compatible with a peaceful, nonviolent world order. Deliberate, malicious falsehood is decidedly a form of violence, more vicious for being insidious. Americans must take the truth offensive seriously, particularly in the post-Internet world where anything is posted, with no benefit of editorial filter.

Even in the midst of military operations, in the final analysis, truth is what serves us best. Colonel Ralph O. Baker learned it on the battlefield in Iraq, where he "quickly discovered that IO [information operations] was going to be one of the two most vital tools (along with human intelligence) [he] would need to be successful in a counterinsurgency campaign."[15] What is more, he also learned that the traditional tools in his military kit bag were not only insufficient; they were marginal: nearly three-quarters of his time turned out to be spent managing information. He concluded, too, that among the most important targets were the Arab media, including Al Jazeera, since that is where most Iraqis received their information. Writes Baker, "We can, if we put enough effort into it, develop a good working relationship with almost any reporter as long as we are truthful and honest. They cannot help but respect us for that and, much of the time, respect is rewarded with fairer and more balanced news accounts because reporters know they can trust what we are saying."[16]

Part of the American truth offensive requires demonstrating what it is we do, and why. On a global scale, it involves promoting effective, as opposed to sham, illiberal, or pseudo-democracies. The National Security Strategy explains, "In effective democracies, freedom is indivisible. Political, religious, and economic liberty advance together and reinforce each other. Some regimes have opened their economies while trying to restrict political or religious freedoms. This will not work. Over time, as people gain control over their economic lives, they will insist on more control over their political and personal lives as well. Yet political progress can be jeopardized if economic progress does not keep pace."[17] This strategy dictates using a combination of tactics, which the NSS proceeds to enumerate:

> In the cause of ending tyranny and promoting effective democracy, we will employ the full array of political, economic, diplomatic, and other tools at our disposal, including:

- Speaking out against abuses of human rights;
- Supporting publicly democratic reformers in repressive nations, including by holding high-level meetings with them at the White House, Department of State, and U.S. Embassies;
- Using foreign assistance to support the development of free and fair elections, rule of law, civil society, human rights, women's rights, free media, and religious freedom;
- Tailoring assistance and training of military forces to support civilian control of the military and military respect for human rights in a democratic society;
- Applying sanctions that are designed to target those who rule oppressive regimes while sparing the people;
- Encouraging other nations not to support oppressive regimes;
- Partnering with other democratic nations to promote freedom, democracy, and human rights in specific countries and regions;
- Strengthening and building new initiatives such as the Broader Middle East and North Africa Initiative's Foundation for the Future, the Community of Democracies, and the United Nations Democracy Fund;
- Forming creative partnerships with nongovernmental organizations and other civil society voices to support and reinforce their work;
- Working with existing international institutions such as the United Nations and regional organizations such as the Organization for Security and Cooperation in Europe, the African Union (AU), and the Organization of American States (OAS) to help implement their democratic commitments, and helping establish democracy charters in regions that lack them.

Quite a menu to choose from, particularly given the fact that a vast majority of the foreign assistance budget is "prioritized" by congressional earmarks that have more to do with responding to constituencies than with national security. In addition, despite its higher profile, or perhaps because of it, foreign assistance funding, having seen the greatest increase in four decades, is plagued by "a proliferation of programs, policy incoherence, and organizational fragmentation."

This is the assessment of a comprehensive report of a task force on foreign aid, organized by the Brookings Institution and the Center for Strategic and International Studies, released in draft form in July 2006, entitled *Security by Other Means: Foreign Assistance, Global Poverty, and American Leadership.* Among the seven principles recommended by the task force deemed critical to successful reform is that "the United States must elevate development as an independent mission alongside defense and diplomacy in practice not just principle."[18] This impressive report is a long-overdue, impressively researched, well-thought-out, indispensable document for any serious discussion of foreign aid management, which has suffered too long from insufficient synchronization of effort, message, and strategy.

It is no easy task. The report's main editor, Brookings vice president Lael Brainard, recognizes that the two main professional communities engaged in aid policy making and analysis have diametrically different views of the enterprise: "National security professionals and political scientists tend to view foreign assistance as a 'soft power' tool designed to achieve diplomatic and strategic ends, often through an implicit bargain with the recipient government. In contrast, development practitioners and economic officials tend to view foreign assistance as a resource flow for poverty alleviation and development, implying that assistance should be allocated according to recipients' policy environment and needs."[19] The report proposes integrating these two perspectives as follows: potential recipients would be identified by their strategic position vis-à-vis U.S. national interests, while the amount and type of assistance, as well as who receives it and how it is distributed, would be determined by the development efficiency of the investment.

In essence, this means that national security trumps do-goodism. Brainard says it in so many words when she defines foreign assistance as "an instrument, not an end in itself. Foreign assistance variously serves to advance national security, national interests and national values."[20] This is true, though misleading. Dubbing it "an instrument" makes it look pragmatic. Advancing national security and national interests is one thing; advancing national values, however, requires a new paradigm for the very concept of "foreign assistance."

The mistake is to consider the two perspectives on foreign aid as being in conflict. Where some do-gooders sometimes go wrong is in thinking that generosity and dollar amounts are coextensive; where some hardheaded hawks go wrong is in thinking that strategic interests are best served by bargaining with governments, which are more often the problem than the solution. In a way, the do-gooders are closest to the truth, although they may not realize it. For among America's national values are not only philanthropy and compassion but also a desire to help others enjoy the same freedom we have secured over the years, within a classical liberal constitutional framework, respectful of tradition and common sense. Once its strategic significance is understood as fundamentally long term and symmetric, benefiting the putative recipient as well as the donor, "outreach" seems far more appropriate than the unnecessarily condescending "foreign assistance."[21] It's not just a matter of semantics, let alone political correctness, but of attitude, translated into policy. Reaching out is not only good politics; it is who we are. It is what America's feisty forefathers meant when, at the very outset, they took on the challenge of becoming a beacon unto the world.

NOTES

1. Edmund Taylor, "RIAS—The Voice East Germans Believe," *The Reporter*, October 10, 1953, 53.

2. Sun Tzu, *The Art of War* (London: Oxford University Press, 1982), 66 (1–19).

3. "These journals published scholarly and polemical articles that were devastatingly critical not only of communism and the Soviet Union but particularly of the 'useful idiots' in Europe and America who were ardently working, wittingly or unwittingly, on behalf of Soviet interests." Leonard Sussman, *Democracy's Advocate: The Story of Freedom House* (New York: Freedom House, 2002), 107.

4. Mustapha Khalfi, "Leaving Democracy Promotion Outside the State Department," *The Arab Reform Bulletin* 3, no. 9 (November 2005), www.CarnegieEndowment.org/ArabReform.

5. Alexis de Tocqueville, *Democracy in America* (New York: Vintage Books, 1945), 1:243.

6. Tocqueville, *Democracy in America*, 1:243, 244.

7. *Report of the Defense Science Board Task Force on Strategic Communication*, Office of the Under Secretary of Defense for Acquisition, Technology, and Logistics, September 2004.

8. "Strategic Communication: The Case for a New Vision," in *Report of the Defense Science Board Task Force on Strategic Communication*, September 2004, 11.

9. Sun Tzu, *The Art of War*.

10. GAO report, 41.

11. GAO-06-535, U.S. Public Diplomacy, 18 (emphasis added.)

12. www.fas.org/irp/offdocs/nsdd/23-1966t.gif.

13. www.fas.org/irp/offdocs/nsdd/23-1967t.gif.

14. www.whitehouse.gov/nsc/nss/2006/section1.html.

15. Col. Ralph O. Baker, U.S. Army, "The Decisive Weapon: A Brigade Combat Team Commander's Perspective on Information Operations," *Military Review*, May–June 2006, 13.

16. Baker, "The Decisive Weapon," 13.

17. www.whitehouse.gov/nsc/nss/2006.

18. http://www.brookings.edu/comm/news/20060622.htm.

19. Lael Brainard, ed., *Foreign Assistance, Global Poverty, and American Leadership* (Washington, DC: Brookings Institution Press and the Center for Strategic and International Studies, 2006), chapter 1, "A Unified Framework for U.S. Foreign Assistance in the 21st Century," www.brookings.edu/global/01brainard.pdf, page 5 of 24.

20. Brainard, "A Unified Framework," 2.

21. One notable exception is a recent study, entitled *Strategic Foreign Assistance: Civil Society in International Security*, by A. Lawrence Chickering, Isobel Coleman, P. Edward Haley, and Emily Vargas-Baron, which advocates "design[ing] a development policy that contributes strategically to U.S. and international security." (Stanford, CA: Hoover Institution Press, 2006), 11. Specifically, the authors propose that "funding ought to be allocated especially to strategic programs directed at priority countries, which would include weak and even hostile, undemocratic states" (11). Unfortunately, it is easier to decide which countries should be targeted than it is to figure out which programs are both strategic and successful.

Chapter Twenty-Three

False Sensibility vs. True Sense

When you say you are in love with humanity, you are satisfied with yourself.

—Luigi Pirandello

"They gave themselves up wholly to their sorrow, seeking increase of wretchedness in every reflection that could afford it, and resolved against ever admitting consolation in future." It is this exquisitely light touch that accounts for the delight with which *Sense and Sensibility* was greeted by audiences in 1811. Everyone was dying to know the identity of its obviously brilliant author, identified on the cover only as "J. Austen." Her readers were instantly amused by this altogether novel form of gentle ridicule, which targeted the risibly self-conscious sentimentality (or as it was derisively known in her time, "sensibility") of the disingenuous. Pathos, while hardly venal, is symptomatic of a deeper malady: the insidious pretense reflects the false values of a class society based on property, rank, and family, rather than personal merit.

The sin of fraudulent sentiment deserved little more than the merciless irony so deftly flowing from her charming pen. But Jane Austen was hardly a cynic. Her message was revolutionary, though not for exposing the vacuity behind the facade of respectability—others before her had excelled in the venerable art of social and political satire. Rather, Austen conveyed a profound understanding of man's (and even more, woman's) soul, providing the emotional, spiritual, and also, yes, intellectual underpinnings of a democratic society.

Like other British women writers at the time—notably Mary Wollstonecraft and her daughter, Mary Shelley—Jane Austen rejected the presumed superiority of mere logic, offering her own "critique of impure reason"

227

coincidentally soon after Immanuel Kant produced his parallel turgid tome. When tempered with "sense," sensibility is redeemed, just as its converse—cold sense mellowed by just a tad of sensibility—results in true felicity. In a word, there are here echoes of Aristotle: the individual is capable of reaching the ideal, golden mean, straddled between equally erring extremes.

It is useful to turn to Mary Wollstonecraft for context in order to properly understand Austen. In her undeservedly little-known short novel *Mary*, the heroine declares,

> Sensibility is the most exquisite feeling of which the human soul is susceptible: when it pervades us, we feel happy; and could it last unmixed, we might form some conjecture of the bliss of those paradisiacal days, when the obedient passions were under the dominion of reason, and the impulses of the heart did not need correction. It is this quickness, this delicacy of feeling, which enables us to relish the sublime touches of the poet, and the painter; it is this, which expands the soul, gives an enthusiastic greatness, mixed with tenderness, when we view the magnificent objects of nature; or hear of a good action. . . . Softened by tenderness, the soul is disposed to be virtuous. Is any sensual gratification to be compared to that of feeling the eyes moistened after having comforted the unfortunate? "Sensibility" is indeed the foundation of all our happiness; but these raptures are unknown to the depraved sensualist, who is only moved by what strikes his gross senses; the delicate embellishments of nature escape his notice; as do the gentle and interesting affections.—*But it is only to be felt; it escapes discussion.*[1]

No other passage captures as vividly the essence of the philosophy that underlies Jane Austen's timeless work. It is in this context that all her novels are to be understood. No mere rationalist, an avid student and advocate of the human heart, Jane Austen valued compassion along with its somewhat less reliable but far more powerful relative, romantic love, noting that, in its absence, "sense" simply cannot provide sufficient motivation for a happy life.

Wollstonecraft is far better known for her pioneer feminist treatise *The Vindication of the Rights of Woman*, published in 1792, consciously contrasted with Thomas Paine's *The Rights of Man*.[2] While failing to influence legislation on women's education being considered by the French Assembly at the time, the treatise succeeded in earning her the acclaim of her sisters for generations to come. Her feminism had been a product of many factors, but one she singled out was her erstwhile hero, Jean-Jacques Rousseau. The romantic advocate of a universal social contract had started his famous treatise as follows, "Man was born free, yet everywhere he is in chains." The phrase resonated with every woman who had applied the observation to herself—naively, as it turned out. In the educational novel *Emile*, the self-described lover of freedom displayed his true colors as he openly declared, much to the dismay of Mary Wollstonecraft, that women were little more than playthings for men.

Her hopes for French women would soon be similarly dashed, as the victorious revolutionaries echoed Rousseau (prerevolutionary intimations to the contrary notwithstanding) that only male citizens were to be considered equal. The former British colonies across the Atlantic followed suit, their lofty Declaration of Independence equally disingenuous in its use of the putatively androgynous "man." The theoretical basis for equality outlined by John Locke, most famously in his *Second Treatise on Government* published in 1688, had rested on the argument that insofar as all human beings possessed "reason," they were equally capable of grasping its law.

Locke's argument had been based on the assumption that the law of reason, being God's Law, could be discerned by everyone in possession of that faculty. And since everyone (with the exception of children and the feebleminded) had been born with reason, it followed that everyone could discern God's Law as well as anyone else. This fact by itself mandated equality: no one could claim special insights to the divine plan, which had been expressly designed by its Author for universal understanding. It is for this reason, therefore, that everyone must respect everyone else's right to manage his own life (or, more precisely, life, liberty, and property—all subsumed under one concept, "estate").

Accordingly, Mary Wollstonecraft, like all other political thinkers at the time, addressed directly the role of reason in deciding who is to wield power. But her principal concern—as Jane Austen's—was not merely that women could not vote. Even more tragically, their very souls had been imprisoned— to the point that they no longer even realized it—by lack of education, economic dependence, and lack of respect. Thus Wollstonecraft's answer took a form quite different from that later adopted by John Stuart Mill in his classic defense of feminism *The Subjection of Women*, published nearly a century later, in 1869.

Mill argued that no evidence existed to deny that women were equal to men in their capacity to reason, stating emphatically that "any of the mental differences supposed to exist between women and men are but the natural effect of the differences in their education and circumstances, and indicate no radical difference, far less radical inferiority, of nature."[3] His emphasis was on equality of rational ability, or, more precisely, on the presumption of equality absent evidence to the contrary.

While Mary Wollstonecraft did not disagree, she went one step further and defended the proposition that in fact women are superior, though not simply in their ratiocinative capacities. Instead, women were more likely than men to possess a faculty that was superior to "cold" reason, namely "sensibility," which she proceeded so eloquently to define and richly illustrate. It is that definition—and that philosophy—that Jane Austen fully embraced. But how would she address the dilemma at the core of this philosophy? For if it was true that such a feeling is indescribable, that "it is only to be felt" and hence "escapes discussion," what more is there to say? Jane Austen alone would possess the talent and acuity it took to illustrate the idea in the most ingenious and effective manner: through exquisitely crafted, brilliantly drawn fictional characters.

By the time Jane Austen came of age, the pendulum had already swung from the Age of [Mere] Reason to an extreme antinomy, an ostentatious sentimentality popularized by the popular novel. Written mainly by women, the precursors of the equally popular Harlequin romances glorified intense feelings. It was mainly to avoid being confused with the likes of Clara Reeve, Sophia Lee, and Charlotte Smith that Jane refrained from divulging her full name on the cover of her first novel, published at her own expense. The problem was not that women were being stereotyped exclusively or even primarily; perhaps the most famous of these novels, published in 1771, entitled *Man of Feeling*, describes a male hero identifying so completely with the sufferings of others that he spends his days weeping for them.

It is just this sort of maudlin hypocrisy, this self-conscious pathos, that Jane Austen found loathsome, yet also amusing enough to warrant mere dismissal by ridicule. In one of her earliest stories, entitled *Love and Freindship* (the misspelling having reportedly been preserved by subsequent editors in honor of the author's youth), the heroine proclaims that her only fault was a sensibility that trembled at every affliction of her friends. Trembling alone, however, produces only a sense of self-satisfaction in one's ability to empathize; it doesn't actually help anyone. In other words, it is little more than selfishness.

Professor Stephen Arkin astutely notes Jane Austen's similar treatment of the self-righteously passionate Marianne in *Sense and Sensibility*: Marianne's indulgence in the misery she feels when abandoned by her fickle lover blinds her in self-absorption, preventing her altogether from empathizing with her older sister Elinor's suffering that had been caused by a similar predicament. Professor Arkin captures perfectly the moral import of the book:

> It is clear then that in this novel sensibility is a road paved with selfish intentions. What is less clear (but equally important) is that sense, by contrast, isn't a monolithic virtue. Sense shows itself to be various and not all of its manifestations are admirable. Elinor is prudent about the realities of economic life, but the economic machinations of Lucy Steele and her sister as they make themselves agreeable to Lady Middleton do not make the kind of moral sense in fac-

ing the world that Elinor's choices make. The crucial issue is that Jane Austen does not set sensibility at a point diametrically opposed to sense. Rather, she asks us to see how much finer our discriminations must be, as we look at what a broad spectrum of behavior the two terms can encompass.[4]

We have, then, here too—as in *Pride and Prejudice*—a twin concept. Jane Austen's nineteenth-century fictional version of Aristotle's *Nicomachean Ethics* succeeds in illustrating the complex nature of this fascinating dialectic: straddled between the common sense of reason and the sensibility that inspires us to genuine generosity, human beings must resist succumbing both to soul-starving calculation and suffocating, indulgent sensuality. The answer is the sober form of "sensibility" that defines a life worth living—in dignity, with empathy tempered by sense. Such wisdom cannot be easily captured by mere philosophers; it takes an artist—preferably one in petticoats.

Jane Austen may have been surprised to find, little more than a century later, a kindred soul in the Indian sage who dared risk everything to prove the potency of true compassion wedded to intellect that he believed could save the world. Jane Austen—meet Mohandas Gandhi.

Never in her wildest dreams presuming to mobilize the multitudes, Austen had nevertheless conducted her own quiet, eminently civil disobedience. Her enemy had been the phony elite, whose claim to superiority, when based on empty titles and mere money rather than true sense and objective valor, was not merely laughable but vile. If Jane Austen, witty child of the Enlightenment, contributed to undermining the previously unquestioned supremacy of bogus caste by means of subtle humor, Gandhi sought to defeat it in his colonized country by fasting, faith, and fearless confrontation that defied the sword as it exulted the heart.

Both sense and sensibility are required to fight the twin infirmities of pride and prejudice. Having learned this lesson from Henry David Thoreau, who, in his essay on "Civil Disobedience," had explained why the evil of slavery was worth the price of incarceration, Gandhi transferred it to the world stage. But he never forgot his kinship with the American botanist. Both Gandhi and Thoreau had not hesitated to stand for principle, not in order to receive any prizes or any other form of secular recognition. These true aristocrats served a far higher master: the law of freedom and dignity.

Admittedly, Thoreau differed from Gandhi by not glorifying either humanity or altruism. The Concord resident generally preferred his own company and especially that of wordless creatures, the sounds of brooks or rain, and the calm of the elements. Like Jane Austen, Thoreau distrusted the ostentatiously altruistic. His words would have been music to her ears: "There is no odor so bad as that which arises from goodness tainted. . . . If I knew for a certainty that a man was coming to my house with the conscious design of doing me good, I should run for my life."[5] Genuine compassion is designed to help someone according to his real needs. Writes Thoreau, "Be sure that you give the poor the aid they most need, though it be your example which leaves them far behind. If you give money, spend yourself with it, and do not merely abandon it to them."[6] *Spending ourselves*: what a deliciously apt expression. It is the giving of ourselves—a very piece of our soul, offered wisely—that constitutes philanthropy in the best sense.

The true defenders of the rights of mankind, the enemies of prejudice, do not seek the false pride of self-righteousness; they need no one's accolades. What they revere is truth, love informed by knowledge, and the dictates of beauty which nature spells clearly to all who will read. But don't get too carried away. Jane Austen, Henry David Thoreau, and even Mohandas Gandhi would undoubtedly advise turning down the rhetorical thermostat, agreeing with Dostoyevsky, who wrote that "in abstract love of humanity one almost always only loves oneself."[7]

The so-called man of feeling egotistically basking in his own "sensibility," whom Jane Austen satirized and Thoreau fled for dear life, only escalates the problem. Unfortunately, this happens to be true for most handouts known as "foreign aid," the overwhelming bulk of which goes directly to governments that are themselves the main culprits. New York University economics professor William Easterly notes, "This is bad news for the poor."[8] The title of his newest book captures it very well indeed: *The White Man's Burden: Why the West's Efforts to Aid the Rest Have Done So Much Ill and So Little Good.*

Most of these countries happen to be in Africa.[9] African scholars from the Institute of Public Analysis in Nigeria offer ample evidence of graft and corruption. "Without domestic reform, African politicians will line their pockets, but Africa will remain desperately poor."[10] The West is equally culpable for not holding these kleptocrats accountable. After an internal evaluation of 107 health projects funded by the World Bank, for example, the analysts concluded that "the Bank does not adequately assess borrower capacity to implement planned project activities; notably lacking in most Bank analysis is an adequate assessment for health services; we know little about what the Bank has 'bought' with its investments." We know little and care less.

No one has said it quite as graphically and persuasively as Ugandan journalist Andrew Muenda with the *Daily Monitor*. A former World Bank consultant, Muenda writes, "Development aid equips African rulers with easily made money—from which stems their disrespect of their own people as well as their submission to the international money givers. Development aid undermines democracy. Over the past forty years, it has made Africa's thieving politicians rich and kept dictatorial regimes in power, while the continent became ever poorer."[11]

He does offer a solution: "What Africa needs from the West are the contributions not of the most generous, but of the most entrepreneurial. It needs not the most self-righteous, it needs the most highly self-interested." He implies, and perhaps should have said, that true self-interest is eminently altruistic and humble, but it would have diminished his rhetorical punch.

Which is why—thank heavens—we have Jane Austen, who reminds us to temper our narcissistic sensibility with seasoned experience and rational sense.

NOTES

1. Mary Wollstonecraft and Mary Shelley, *Mary and Maria; Matilda*, ed. Janet Todd (London, New York: Penguin Books, 1991), 43.

2. Throughout Paine's writings, only one passage deals with the plight of women—namely, "An Occasional Letter on the Female Sex," published in 1775—whom he describes as being "robbed of freedom and will by the laws; slaves of opinion which rules them with absolute sway and construes the slightest appearances into guilt; surrounded on all sides by judges who are at once tyrants and their seducers." http://www.thomas paine.org/Archives/occ.html.

3. John Stuart Mill, "The Subjection of Women," in *The Basic Writings of John Stuart Mill* (New York: The Modern Library, 2002), 178.

4. Jane Austen, *Sense and Sensibility*, introduction and notes by Stephen Arkin (Hertfordshire, England: Wordsworth Editions, 2000), viii–ix.

5. Henry David Thoreau, *The Selected Works of Thoreau* (Boston, MA: Houghton Mifflin Company, 1975), 293.

6. Thoreau, *The Selected Works*, 294.

7. Fyodor Dostoyevsky, *The Idiot*, trans. Alan Myers (Oxford: Oxford University Press, 1992), chap. 3.

8. William Easterly, "Planners vs. Searchers in Foreign Aid," presented at the Asian Development Bank Distinguished Speakers Program, January 18, 2006. This is one reason that the Millennium Challenge Corporation (MCC) was recently established at the initiative of President George W. Bush, predicated on the idea that countries should demonstrate some progress in alleviating poverty before good money continues to be thrown after bad dictators. Here is obviously not the place to assess the impact of the MCC, if only because it is far too soon.

9. The amounts are staggering. In a report released by the Joint Economic Committee of the U.S. Congress, Carnegie Mellon economist Adam Lerrick states that "the stolen dollars stashed away in off-shore banks are estimated at $95 billion. . . . Others estimate the level in excess of $500 billion." Adam Lerrick, "Aid to Africa at Risk: Covering up Corruption," *International Economics Report*, December 2005, 3.

10. Thomas Ayodele et al., "African Perspectives on Aid: Foreign Assistance Will Not Pull Africa out of Poverty," *Cato Institute Economic Development Bulletin*, September 14, 2005.

11. Andrew Muenda, "Das Mittlied Des Westens," *Der Spiegel: Jahres-Chronik, 2005*, 160–62.

Chapter Twenty-Four

The Five (or Six) Basic Rules
of Global Strategic Outreach

Always listen to experts. They'll tell you what can't be done and why. Then do it.

—Robert A. Heinlein

The lesson I remember most vividly, after some three decades in the outreach business, is that every new challenge is in critical ways unlike every previous one, yet past experience imperceptibly equips you with skills you never knew you were acquiring. The most appropriate analogy may be skiing: no two moguls are exactly alike, but a well-trained skier will navigate a bumpy terrain with seemingly effortless elegance. The key here is responsiveness to the challenge on the ground. The bumps are there; it then becomes your job to turn flaws on the earth's crust into assets. In keeping with the reciprocal logic of "outreach," the interaction between skier and mountain is a partnership, as each contributes to the total beauty and harmony. But where the analogy fails is in the dynamic asymmetry of the intercourse: mountains are merely worn down by human traffic, gaining nothing from the athletic assault. By contrast, genuine outreach changes both partners, sometimes quite radically, each emerging richer for having touched another, helping them both reach a higher potential.

If the rules outlined in this chapter sound too much like, let's say, so many steps to a slimmer self, that similarity is deceptive. These rules won't teach anyone how to "do" outreach; on the other hand, they should help prevent some deadly conceptual errors that are all too common among those who have either never engaged in it or have done so without the requisite strategic vision.

FIRST RULE: DO NOT OVERPROMISE

Promises are a politician's trademark: it's not only what he does best; it's what gets him elected. We like to feel good about the future, we like to hear what we want to hear, we like it simple and easy, and we want quick solutions to difficult problems. So let's not just dump on our leaders; remember who put them there: it's "youse guys," or rather, us guys. We like our public diplomacy well done, with plenty of Texas hot sauce, and we think that our foreign assistance is as big as our hearts. President Bush received thunderous applause to these words, spoken soon after the demise of the Saddam regime, when euphoria at home ran high: "These goals—advancing against disease, hunger and poverty . . . [define] . . . the moral purpose of American influence. . . . President Woodrow Wilson said, 'America has a spiritual energy in her which no other nation can contribute to the liberation of mankind.' In this century, we must apply that energy to the good of people everywhere."[1]

However well this may play back home, the high doesn't necessarily last long. Heartburn sets in, if not the morning after, then after reality kicks in, as it did in the case of the war that was supposed to have ended all wars and ushered in democracy. Wilson lived long enough to concede that "the world has been made safe for democracy, but democracy has not been finally vindicated."[2] He could have spoken those words today—or, for that matter, at any moment in history. Not only "democracy" but just about every other lofty abstract concept has been used to justify the most heinous crimes. It's not about abstractions; it's about ending crime. Indeed, the loftier the abstraction, the louder it seems to backfire.

Colonel Ralph O. Baker bluntly explains one of the biggest hurdles he faced in Iraq in his effort to communicate with the local population: "One of the more difficult credibility challenges we encountered among the Iraqis was a consequence of the initial mismanagement of Iraqi expectations before we ever crossed the berm [frontier] into Iraq. As a result, we were met with enormously unrealistic expectations . . . [which] grew out of Coalition pronouncements before Soldiers [*sic*] arrived that extolled how much better off the average Iraqi citizen's life was going to be when Saddam and his regime were gone."[3]

Colonel Baker generously believes that we meant well, yet he concedes that it "proved to be a terrible cultural misperception on our part because we, the liberators, equated better with not being ruled by a brutal dictator. In contrast, a better life for Iraqis implied consistent, reliable electricity; food"[4] and such. Others insist that it was not misperception but miscalculation: the United States really did imagine that all would go well, and soon, which turned out to be just plain wrong. Either way, we certainly led folks to believe they would soon be counting their blessings. Overpromising is just something we are prone to do, perhaps due to overconfidence in our power and good intentions. Unfortunately, it's not just rhetoric for public consumption—which would be bad enough when it fails—what is worse, we often end up believing it ourselves.

When the outcome does not live up to the promise, disappointment necessarily follows, and with it frustration, cynicism, and the inevitable accusations of devious hypocrisy and cheap politicking. Overpromising is worse than overspending; creditors simply want their money back, sparing those who happen to be cash challenged. In sum, be wary of what you lead others to believe; it may boomerang. Keep it humble; it will save your pride.

SECOND RULE: KNOW YOUR AUDIENCE

> Goodness must be joined with knowledge. Mere goodness is not of much use, as I have found in life.
>
> —Mohandas Gandhi

Hardly anyone save the blank-brained comes to a conversation with a fully open mind. We all carry around factoids whose share of truth ranges from outright falsehood, the product of either lies or just plain reality deficit, to least inaccurate. We cannot hope to engage in productive dialogue without having any awareness of this "baggage," both our own and our interlocutors'. And as it happens, one of the most effective methods of inquiry is also the most accessible, if seldom practiced: good old listening. Asking questions and waiting for the answers—sounds simple? It isn't.

Listening is not only a challenge for the respective inhabitants of the sexually divergent planets of "Mars" and "Venus," but for everyone. What may play well in Kalamazoo is very likely to require major translation before it gets shipped over to Kuala Lumpur. All types of expertise should be consulted, and none dismissed out of hand. No mirror imaging and half-baked preconceived notions should be allowed to cloud the evidence. Personal experiences count, as do carefully crafted opinion surveys, academic scholarship, and intelligence capabilities.

Intelligence is vitally important, in war as in marriage, and the United States may be proud of its achievements, but recent failures have spectacularly underscored its limits. The current National Intelligence Strategy, released in October 2005, urges much greater interplay not only among the alphabet soup of

intelligence agencies, notably the Defense Intelligence Agency (DIA), the
Central Intelligence Agency (CIA), and the Federal Bureau of Investigation
(FBI); but it also mandates "making the best use of all-source intelligence, including from open sources," and "improving human intelligence." Information
that is not available to those who need it, or cannot be accessed because the
wrong questions are being asked at the wrong time, is tantamount to no information at all. Before addressing any particular audience, assuming that all relevant information is at hand, the next important question is deciding whom to
tell what, when, and how. Some audiences are not worth engaging at all, if they
seem to be beyond reach; in most cases, choices must be made in light of such
variables as time, available resources, and means of communication.

There are many ways to tackle all of these critical questions, and today's
communications technology offers more options than ever before. Both what
people say and what they do are relevant; neither is a substitute for the other.
Beliefs are often changing or outright contradictory. Even more often, ostensibly held—or at least parroted—statements are belied by behavior. But this
only underscores the importance of assessment, evaluation, and context, best
appreciated by deep immersion in the respective culture.

The May 2006 General Accounting Office (GAO) report on U.S. Public
Diplomacy finds that "private sector best practices suggest that analyzing target markets in depth and segmenting these markets are critical to developing
effective information campaigns," yet American embassies "had not used
these practices to help them refine and focus their communication efforts."[5]
The GAO recommends targeting what it calls "key influencers," to be pre-
ceded by analyses of who such "influencers" actually are. Neither did the
posts visited by the GAO team reportedly focus on important subcategories
such as urban versus rural, men versus women, or intensity of opposition to
the United States. It wasn't for lack of responsiveness from headquarters;
rather, according to senior officials in Washington, only about half of the
posts worldwide even bothered to submit requests for such analysis.

Could it have been preemptive self-censorship, in light of the well-known
paucity of resources devoted by the Department of State to this sort of research? While the Intelligence and Research Division has conducted a number of well-regarded opinion polls, including both national surveys and focus
groups, this hardly qualifies as sufficient. Commercially commissioned surveys are harder to access, but some incentive should be provided to make at
least some portions more widely available. In the private sector, marketing research is done routinely before introducing a product. One would think the
same would be true of the U.S. government.

It is not, mainly because bureaucrats are paid to disburse funds allocated by
Congress, often specifically earmarked for political reasons; so why bother with

the research? Fortunately, contractors and grantees, who not only tend to care more about the people they seek to help but are also protective of their own reputations, have a strong incentive to figure out what is needed before running into brick walls. Writes professor Easterly, "Planners at the top lack knowledge of the bottom; Searchers find out what the reality is at the bottom."[6] But "Searchers know if something works only if the people at the bottom can give feedback."[7] Easterly recognizes, too, that "the working-level people in aid agencies or nongovernmental organizations (NGOs) are more likely to be Searchers than Planners."[8] So it's up to the Searchers to find out what the people need.

This was just the situation faced by the International Foundation for Election Systems (IFES) in Kazakhstan around 1996, as we began to realize that the electoral process that we had been seeking to assist was slowly but pretty surely headed toward a brick wall. We were not sure how to move to the next stage in the democratization process. We needed to do some research, a word not ordinarily in the vocabulary of USAID. It so happens that IFES was blessed at the time with unusually farsighted USAID staff, including an especially astute DG (Democracy and Governance) program officer, Mitch Benedict, whose previous business experience complemented a fine liberal arts education and native common sense—a rare combination indeed. Suffice it to say that USAID supported with alacrity an IFES proposal to conduct a series of comprehensive national surveys throughout Central Asia, Kazakhstan in particular, which provided fascinating insights into the mindset of the populations of this critical region—which at the time was still underappreciated by most so-called foreign policy experts.

The surveys revealed that an overwhelming 88 percent of Kazakhstan's people were displeased with their social welfare system, nearly as many with the fight against crime, and 69 percent with governmental protection of freedom. The majority, 58 percent, rejected the proposition that "in order to establish order and discipline it is necessary to limit the political and civil rights of the people." The majority also thought their economic reforms had been too slow. Especially heartening, in response to an open-ended question, was the revelation that the Kazakhstani people's favored political model turned out to be none other than the United States.[9]

It seemed to us that such a political culture would respond well to a civic education program. At first, we tried to interest the Chairman of the Central Election Commission, Mrs. Zagipa Balieva, who happened to be a very close friend of President Nursultan Nazarbayev. She seemed amenable to the idea, and it did make a lot of sense. We decided to target the voters of tomorrow— or at least the next election. High school seniors, age seventeen, would be eligible to vote in a year, soon after graduation. It was a pretty realistic timetable for IFES; we just needed to figure out how to approach them.

We were hardly alone in seeking to introduce civic education to Kazakhstan; a whole slew of organizations were busy meeting and talking about what might work. The Soros Foundation's Open Society Institute had commissioned something. We tried to find out more about those activities, but at the same time, we sent out an education specialist of our own, Dorrit Marks, to do some background research on what Kazakhstani students were actually learning. We wanted to make sure we were connecting with them; we didn't want to parachute ideas as if from another planet.

Dorrit duly delivered a huge box of materials, which awaited perusal. It sat in my office reproachfully, as week after week I looked forward to the day I would be able to mine its riches. One long weekend devoted to something apt, like Labor Day, I skipped the barbecue and dug in. Most of the Xeroxed material was predictably irrelevant, except for one three-paged item: it was a series of some forty questions that students were expected to answer. They ranged from types of political systems, international law, and economic regulation, to different branches of government and foreign policy. I had my answer: I was going to put together a textbook that answered these questions.

Evidently, USAID was not going to take a chance by funding me to do such a project, and I didn't even bother to ask. If I were in their shoes, I would have done the same; I didn't know myself if I would be able to do it. But I was certainly going to try; my main problem was when. The answer came in a flash of nothing short of genius: I decided, for the first time since my son was born a dozen years earlier, that I would take advantage of my long-accumulated vacation time that year. Instead, I would use the time to write.

To make a long story short, I emerged about two months later with a manuscript I entitled "Civic Education: A Primer," consisting of comparative and historic information on such topics as the family, property and economic laws, political society and civil society organizations, different electoral systems, media and interest groups, international law, and a few others. The only problem was that my son became convinced that he had been adopted: seeing his mother spending her vacation time "doing homework" provided irrefutable proof that he and I shared no genetic material.

Through circumstances that could only be called serendipitous, after I casually mentioned my little project to Penn Kemble, then acting head of USIA, he sent a note to Judy Siegel—in charge of civic education for USIA at the time—who proceeded to share it with her husband, Mark Siegel. Mark, it turns out, was representing Nazarbayev (for a hefty fee, I trust) and offered to show my primer to the big boss. Next we all knew, President Nazarbayev announced in his annual address to the nation later that March that Kazakhstan was going to work with IFES on a new civic education program . . . starting that fall! Mark urged me to go to Astana (Kazakhstan's capital) to "close the deal." I protested that we had no funds for the trip; Mark promised to pick up the tab.

The tab never did get picked up by Mark, but that's OK—the civic education program got off the ground, somehow. I went to Kazakhstan to meet with some of the relevant high officials. One of them, who looked like he could silence a Doberman, staring as if to say that my diminutive size wasn't about to fool him, asked ominously, "So what do you mean by 'civic education'?" I answered him with a calm amply justified by the navy blue passport and an English translation of Nazarbayev's State of the Union in my briefcase: "Mr. Secretary, the question actually is what you mean by it. Because, you see, our textbook is designed to be a cooperative venture." I added, just to be safe, "This is undoubtedly why President Nazarbayev proposed it to the nation." I could hear him snarling behind his nervous nod.

But I was not putting him on: the primer that I produced, using sources documenting international practices in addition to American, was deliberately incomplete; it had to be supplemented by local information. Teachers and scholars had to add the relevant material about Kazakhstan. The text had to place their nation on the map, both literally and figuratively. And also—most important—we had to make sure that the ideas were understood.

Everything had happened far too quickly for USAID's funding cycle. There was no money for printing all the textbooks needed even for the three dozen "pilot" schools the government agreed for us to start the rather prematurely advertised experiment. Fast-forwarding to the following summer, IFES organized an essay contest, which they called "an olympiad," for the students who had used the textbook—my poorly translated primer. Their topic: the state of civil society in their country.

The finalists traveled to Almaty, where the prizes would be announced and awarded. The U.S. ambassador who met with them was delighted, even stunned—and for good reason—as the top winner, a blond young woman who spoke confidently and without fear, assessed that civil society in Kazakhstan was virtually nonexistent. However, she went on, as young people like herself learn more about it, someday they will make huge changes. "We are the future leaders," she stated matter-of-factly. There wasn't any doubt in her mind; there could not be in ours.

There were still many hurdles. From pilot programs to universal adoption was a very steep road. For one thing, Nazarbayev finally decided that Mark Siegel had not delivered enough, though heaven knows he had tried. About a year later, Mark called me to ask whether IFES might be able to offer the president some kind of award, preferably a plaque, thanking him for his role in promoting democracy. We said we certainly could not do that. But we might consider spending forty dollars on a plaque that commended him for promoting our civic education program. Mark said OK, that would be close enough. So we agreed to hand President Nazarbayev a plaque that commended him for promoting democracy *through* our civic education program. The ceremony was at Blair House, on a Sunday afternoon, both literally and figuratively chilly.

We thought we were pretty smart. Instead, we completely underestimated how the media can distort a story—and the Kazakhstani media especially. When he discovered it more than a year later, January 24, 2001, Michael Dobbs reported in the *Washington Post*: "Siegel scored a public relations coup for Nazarbayev in December 1999 when he arranged for the president to receive a plaque from the Washington-based International Foundation for Election Systems for his 'outstanding contribution' to civic education and democratic development in Kazakhstan. The event was filmed by Kazakhstani television and used back home to suggest a Western seal of approval for the election process." Dobbs did say "suggest"; but then he added, "Foundation officials now say that their praise of Nazarbayev was limited to his backing the use of a certain civics textbook in Kazakhstani secondary schools."[10]

Oh dear; "now" we say it. Well, fair enough. Would we do it again? Please do not be quite so quick to blurt out "I should say not!" There is one more fact that I need to point out: the day following the blasted award ceremony, Kazakhstan's minister of education finally signed off, after many months, on a request to have the "certain civics textbook," which Michael Dobbs had a little too contemptuously dismissed as a pretty poor excuse for a public diplomacy faux pas, approved for use in every Kazakhstani high school. The latest draft had been built on my primer all right, but was virtually unrecognizable. It was accompanied first of all by a superb teachers' manual prepared by the unequaled New Zealander Simon Jenkins, helping the dedicated, underpaid (sometimes altogether unpaid for months at a time) teachers, who were untrained due to lack of resources, in how to use the new text, which also contained his ingenious, indispensable "practical exercises." The book, however, was not parachuted: it contained materials prepared by Kazakhstani scholars and teachers, exactly as originally planned, and as I had promised the poker-faced minister curious what I meant by "civic education." Those materials had gone through many drafts, back and forth between the affable teachers and our headquarters in Washington. We still did not have enough money from USAID to print the textbooks, so we had to find outside donors. Citibank chipped in, as did ExxonMobil, Motorola, and other companies.

Eventually, a similar textbook—following a similar methodology—was introduced in Kyrgyzstan, where fortunately we didn't have to give anyone an ill-starred plaque for the book to be adopted by the Ministry of Education. Next, Tajikistan was the easiest politically; the ministry there embraced it enthusiastically. But we rewrote it to reach girls in the eighth grade. That is the last grade that most of them will ever attend school, at least for now. Someday, perhaps they too will have a chance to be seniors in high school, and even college. I would love to be there to see it.

I will stop here, but not without noting the title of Michael Dobbs' article. He called it "Investment in Freedom Is Flush with Peril." I wholeheartedly agree; that it certainly is. But the title of the longer story, in my humble opinion, should be, rather, "Investment in Freedom Is Worth the Gamble."

All right, so maybe not a plaque.

THIRD RULE: PROMOTE TRUTH AND FIGHT HARMFUL DISINFORMATION

Half the truth is often a great lie.

—Benjamin Franklin

If only it were as simple as addressing those risible public proclamations by the likes of Iran's president, who charged that the Holocaust was a hoax, which don't even deserve an answer. Or do they? Given the systematic outpouring of bald-faced lies about Jews and Israel to which millions of Muslim children are routinely exposed on a daily basis, this may be a tougher question to answer than some may imagine. In fact, a good deal of toxic disinformation is manufactured and distributed right inside our own society, inside the United States. A recent study conducted by the Center for Religious Freedom of Freedom House, under the able leadership of longtime human rights activist Nina Shea, reveals a plethora of hate-filled absurdities, such as the allegation that Jews guided and controlled the industrial-capitalist movement in Europe, destroying the family as "they lured women to go to work in the factories" and causing a proliferation of groups "like the hippies, punks, and others,"[11] for good measure. According to the Freedom House report, "at times, the Saudi publications read like old Soviet propaganda tracts."[12] One Saudi author, for example, accuses the leading financial establishments, the "houses of capital," of controlling the largest American newspapers, which are in turn imitated by the smaller ones—a standard line with an impressive track record.

Which brings us to our old enemy, Russia, who, despite consistent, mollifying praise from consecutive U.S. presidents, is still at its favorite game: America bashing. While no one has yet surpassed the Soviet Union's skill in conducting "active measures," the competition is heating up. But the U.S. government does not seem to be terribly concerned about disinformation. Otherwise, one would expect the office charged with identifying "misinformation" (diplomatic euphemism for the real thing) to have more than one single solitary employee.

Admittedly, that overworked incumbent, Todd Leventhal, happens to be an eminently qualified political scientist whose apprenticeship with Herb Romerstein, head of the Office to Counter Soviet Disinformation at USIA during most of the 1980s, provided the best possible training. But he is still only one person. That is no typo; writes William Weir in *The Hartford Courant*: "He's the U.S. State Department's sole counter-misinformation officer. As such, he tracks conspiracy theories and urban legends, dissecting the inaccuracies and identifying the origins of the questionable information that reflects poorly on the nation and its government."[13] To be sure, Leventhal is unable to do more than skim the surface of disinformation—which, in the age of the Internet, is exponentially more difficult than it used to be, on grounds of sheer volume. Far from an argument for giving up altogether, however, this only underscores the importance of doing it right. Needless to say, rubbish proliferates in cyberspace like mosquitoes in swamps, and it would be futile—actually, insane—to refute it all. But some lies are obviously more dangerous than others.

You may wish to get a flavor by just taking a look at the website produced by Todd Leventhal. Relying almost exclusively on the few sources conveyed to him by U.S. embassies when there is some incident requiring a response or reaction, here is a list of juicy tidbits:

- The United States "created" Osama bin Laden—he doesn't really exist.
- AIDS is a bioweapon.
- 9/11 was actually the product of an Israeli-American conspiracy.
- The tsunami was the product of an American conspiracy.
- The United States is planning to invade Venezuela—it's allegedly called "Plan Balboa."
- John Perkins' *Confessions of an Economic Hit Man* claims that the U.S. National Security Agency recruited him to be an "economic hit man" to deliberately entrap foreign countries in unmanageable amounts of debt so they would be beholden to the United States.
- A secret network allegedly set up by Greece with CIA assistance committed acts of terrorism during the Cold War.

You will also find organ-trafficking myths, military disinformation (notably involving alleged depleted uranium), and state-sponsored disinformation such as—predictably—North Korea. And so on.

Do check out http://unsinfo.state.gov/media/misinformation.html. The site has a nifty section on "How to Identify Misinformation." I should add that, courtesy of a crucial portion of the Smith-Mundt legislation mentioned earlier, which prohibits disseminating inside the United States information designed for overseas, the site cannot be reached directly from www.state.gov, the official website of the State Department where the one-cubicle one-man office is located. The right hand pretends it doesn't know what the left hand is doing, and before you know it, the right hand—or is it the left hand?—forgets that it's attached to anything in the first place.

Fortunately, on occasion we are lucky to have others tell our story on our behalf. Saudi journalist Fawaz Turki, for example, informs us that "it is regarded as an example of reportorial acumen to write on the op-ed pages of prominent Arab journals about how the September 11, 2001, attacks were the work of Israeli agents, "how Monica Lewinsky was an agent-in-place, put in the White House by the 'Jewish lobby'—and so on with other infantile whimsies."[14]

Infantile would certainly seem to be the word that best describes the claim made by a cultural advisor to the Iranian Education Ministry on Iranian TV that Tom and Jerry is actually "a Jewish conspiracy to improve the image of mice, because Jews were termed 'dirty mice' in Europe."[15] One may find this information on the website of the Middle East Media Research Institute (MEMRI), which has provided timely translations of Arabic, Persian, and Turkish media since its founding in 1998. Independent, nonpartisan, and nonprofit, MEMRI also provides original analysis of political, ideological, intellectual, social, cultural, and religious trends in the Middle East, presented with little or no editorial comment. Headquartered in Washington, MEMRI has branch offices in Berlin, London, Tokyo, and Jerusalem. Besides English, the material is also translated into German, Hebrew, Italian, French, Spanish, and Japanese.

As a result, not only has MEMRI become a gold mine of information, but it "has earned widespread respect for its world-class translations," according to Institute of World Politics professor J. Michael Waller.[16] In addition to its use in the United States, the global reach of this material renders it invaluable as an outreach tool. Unfortunately, most of the information on its website is not quite as jejune as the allegations about the funny little rodents.

The communication explosion makes such resources available in ways never dreamt before. But in addition to the benefits, the Internet is also the source of many problems. Without doubt, one of the major challenges presented by the Internet is the proliferation of wrong information, whether maliciously inspired or not. To counter it, there are no easy options. Such measures as Wikipedia's "warning" signs, which accompany links that the popular web-based encyclopedia does not deem objective, are not exactly a viable option. Since no one likes reading errata, refuting disinformation might be approached with a touch of humor, which can do double duty by ridiculing the perpetrator. But the best solution by far is having local partners—trusted individuals whose motives are beyond doubt in their communities—refute information that is inaccurate and malicious. Such partners exist and may be tapped, but a bit of ingenuity is required, as well as the immeasurable instrument known as friendship and partnership. Just ask anyone who has engaged in so-called "democracy building"; they will tell you what it's all about.[17]

Here, Colonel Baker once again demonstrates how it can be done when the stakes are really high, as is the case with Iraq today, where lives are on the line on a daily basis. First, he and his colleagues in the field identified the key leaders who wielded the greatest influence with the local population: these included clerics (Sunni and Shiite imams, as well as Christian priests); sheiks and tribal leaders; staff and faculty at the universities; local government officials, who were actually being mentored; and select Arab media correspondents. The next step was to meet with each of these groups with rigid regularity, and listen.

It wasn't always fun, but it did offer these folks a forum to communicate the rumors they had heard through the grapevine. "In turn," reports Baker, "this gave us a platform to counter rumors or accusations and, using the detailed information we had collected, to invalidate untrue or unsubstantiated rumors or allegations. After fostering relationships with the leaders from our target audiences over a period of time, we were able to refute anti-Coalition rumors and allegations with some degree of success."[18]

Nor are the allegations simply a matter of factual observations, such as how many people were killed when and by whom. One of the most fascinating stories he tells involves an accusation, made by one of the sheiks in the audience at such a gathering to the effect that Americans were intentionally insulting Arab men when conducting raids. He specifically referred to the technique of placing a sandbag over the head of a suspect after apprehending him. The explanation given to the sheik was that the procedure had always been part of routine training, probably to prevent prisoners from knowing where they were being held captive. He didn't buy it, retorting that everybody knew where the prisoners were being taken, and it was humiliating for an Iraqi man to be taken captive in his own home with "that bag" on his head, especially in front of his family. "The sheik's point was that by following our standard operating procedure to secure prisoners, we were creating conditions that could potentially contribute to the insurgency,"[19] writes Baker.

As a result, after discussing the pros and cons of continuing this practice, Baker and his colleagues decided against it. The result evidently pleased the Iraqis; "the change played well with the target audience because it was a clear example that we valued the people's opinions and would correct a problem if we knew about it."[20] How to measure that kind of success? As they say in the MasterCard commercial, "Priceless."

FOURTH RULE: REWARD SUCCESS, NOT FAILURE, AND NEVER MIND WHO GETS THE CREDIT

Something must be done; anything must be done, whether it works or not.

—Bob Geldof, Live 8 concert organizer, on aid for Africa

All of us in the development community have learned the truth expressed by professor William Easterly that "the prevalence of ineffective plans is the result of Western assistance happening out of view of the Western public"[21]—indeed, out of view, period. Once money has been appropriated, it's in the minister's collection box, so to speak, the proverbial "white man's burden" thus lightened. Except that success takes more work than signing a check; the proof is in the pudding, assuming one ever gets around to being baked. So even the best-sounding recipe, with the most expensive ingredients, can only be deemed satisfactory by those who end up eating it. Being more open in the conduct of foreign aid is not so much to receive credit as to gather feedback, to see if we've got it right.

Ordinary Americans are generally quite good about letting others get the credit. In his book *Imperial Grunts*, Robert D. Kaplan describes a medical facility (MEDCAP) in the village of La Paz, set up by the United States by using a Taiwan-based, Buddhist NGO (nongovernmental organization). Lieutenant Colonel Dennis Downey, a Green Beret posted in the Philippines, explains, "The idea is for us to be in the background, so as to build up the credibility of the national government and the national army in outlying villages like this one. Besides, all of these people here know that without the security provided by United States Marines, none of this would be happening. The NGO and civilian doctors would have been afraid to show up, for fear of Abu Sayyaf." Adds Kaplan, "The MEDCAPS drove a wedge between the people and the insurgents."[22]

Kaplan found that the same attitude applied in Afghanistan. As Major Kevin Holiday put it, "Everything we do is 'by,' 'through,' 'with,' the *indigs* [short for locals, or indigenous forces]," and make sure to give them "the credit, put them forward in the eyes of the locals." To which he added a personal corollary, "The best kind of moral leader is one who is invisible."[23]

At IFES, we all learned the importance of staying in the background and allowing election commissions to take the credit for the poll worker training manuals, for clarifying the administrative implications of ambiguous electoral laws, and for setting up media centers to help inform people about the progress of the elections. It was one of the main reasons for IFES's credibility and its success in helping train the commissioners and the electoral staff. I especially recall the reluctance of the Russian Central Election Commission

(CEC) to accept advice from Americans. It took several months until our top election law expert Bob Dahl, whom we had sent to Moscow right after Yeltsin announced the country's first competitive elections in seven and a half decades, was finally allowed the privilege of advising the haughty CEC. It was only after we agreed to provide them several computers that they finally conceded to let us help them.

At all times, the IFES staff remembered that we were in the business of enhancing the ability of others to run better elections and strengthen the democratic process. So it was ultimately the people we were helping who had to get the credit for improving their country's performance. Those of us in Washington who managed the staff in the field had to depend on their information, and their judgments. In turn, they took very seriously the advice of their *indigs*. Many of these local advisors would gradually acquire the necessary administrative, leadership, and other technical skills as we groomed them to become executive directors of NGOs that would continue to carry on election-related activities after our departure.

The problem is, certainly in cases where the assistance is funded by the taxpayers, that despite good reasons for not worrying about "who gets the credit," few people know about the work and, as a result, well-deserved acknowledgment of American assistance all too often goes unrewarded. Not that it is always a good idea to plaster the USAID label on products funded by that agency if, for example, the products thereby become vulnerable to malicious tampering. But sometimes I have felt that Americans' hesitance to take credit for their generosity went too far. Robert Kaplan shares that impression, writing in Afghanistan: "I worried that the Americans were being too altruistic; nobody aside from the people actually helped would know about such programs, even as high profile projects with political payoffs, like rebuilding the ring road connecting the major cities, were behind schedule."[24] The same was true of many IFES programs—and in fact most activities that fall under the category of "humanitarian assistance," particularly so-called democracy-building projects. In fact, many philanthropic activities, especially those conducted through the private sector, are practically impossible to document.[25]

Another important corollary of this rule must be noted: we must not worry about America's standing in global popularity contests of the kind monitored by, say, World Public Opinion, or the Nation "Branding" survey conducted by Steve Anholz. When the one-party dictatorship known as the People's Republic of China "wins" the former,[26] and charming but altogether laid-back Australia "wins" the latter, it should be obvious that something is amiss in the evaluation—or, rather, that we are playing a different game.

Consider this entry posted on the USAID website, which recently has been updated in a most ingenious fashion to include little stories from the field.

Next to a picture of a turbaned man whose weathered face bespeaks decades of disappointment, identified merely as an Afghan shopkeeper from the Shahidan Market in Bamiyan Province, are his words: "Those of us who had to run are coming back, and we see this new market you have helped us start and we feel hopeful. As long as America is with us, we will start our new lives."[27] Now *that* is real credit.

Philanthropy carries its own reward, to be sure, as do learning and generosity. Yet appreciation for building bridges, for strengthening ties across borders, and for contributing to better understanding to replace prejudice and hatred should play a much more important role than it currently does. We don't do enough to honor those who do us honor. We seem to forget how little it takes to say "thank you."

And do tell others' stories, when they are worth telling. For example, when visitors come to us, local newspapers usually like to know. Sometimes it offers a glimpse into a whole new world, beauties heretofore undiscovered, and a chance to broaden our horizons while celebrating our guests. Americans who venture abroad and seek to help or engage others, whether out of a sense of responsibility, compassion, adventure, self-validation, or most commonly a combination of motivations, conscious and otherwise, bask in the satisfaction to which they feel privileged to contribute. Some work for companies, others for nonprofits, and still others are Peace Corps volunteers. The list of such organizations is mind-boggling in both variety and size. In most cases, our friends like to have their story told. The benefits need not always be quantifiable to be little short of earthshaking. Indirectly, moreover, by telling someone else's story, your own also emerges—and also, even more important, the spirit that makes it all possible, the spirit of the American Dream.[28]

Even more important, however, is the day-to-day encouragement that comes with cooperation—the heart of outreach. Too often we take others for granted—individuals as well as cultures. The greatest tribute we can pay is caring and respect. When abroad, visit the local museums—you will be amazed at the world-class quality of the indigenous art; read books, preferably in the original, but at least in translation, particularly the folk literature, and best-loved poets and novelists; listen to the music played on the street; and do let local folks order your food—the best meals I ever had were a complete mystery, since the hosts did not know the English translations of the ingredients. Someday, you might even get their jokes (and, if you're lucky, you won't be their object).

During the past year, the Legislative and Public Affairs Bureau at the U.S. Agency for International Development has made a concerted effort to publicize activities in the field. Starting in 2004, USAID launched a new Development Outreach and Communications Global Training Initiative to broaden understanding of U.S. development aid worldwide. The bureau's head, Assistant Administrator J. Edward Fox, with the invaluable help of his deputy and former fellow Hill staffer Jeffrey J. Grieco, decided to integrate an entire cadre of trained professionals into each of its missions worldwide, expressly in order "to support strategic and tactical communication efforts."[29] The training has paid off in spades, prompting State Department public affairs staff to request being included as well. In the process, successful USAID activities earned the praise they had long deserved but hardly ever received.

To be sure, practically nothing goes exactly as planned—a truism particularly applicable to so enormous and complex an enterprise as, say, a war to be waged right in the midst of arguably the world's worst ethno-religious hornet's nest. And since it could be easily predicted that such an action would necessarily evolve in a number of different ways that could have been preconsidered, it follows that a public diplomacy strategy worthy of a serious, grown-up nation would include more than one possible future scenario cavalierly described as a "cakewalk."

It surely isn't rocket science. Given that each of several possible outcomes can reasonably be expected to be misinterpreted by enough people across the globe, sheer prudence would suggest being ready with potential explanations on hand, just in case the best of all possible outcomes fails to materialize. Or, in any case, just in case it doesn't fall into place in quite the neat, slam-dunk fashion that some at the highest levels of the government—and hence with the least proximity to the raw data—might wishfully expect. If anyone in the administration of George W. Bush was ever in this kind of proactive mode, there seem to be no fingerprints.

One of the main differences between selling anything, whether a product or a policy, and being engaged in strategic outreach is that the former has a specific timeline with an endpoint, namely, the sale. To be sure, outreach too, involves distinct "peaks" or specific events that must be either communicated or, conversely, investigated—the reciprocal nature of outreach demands the concomitant pursuit of both. Such peaks include not only wars, and similarly drastic political actions, but rocket launchings, the discovery of a vaccine, an earthquake or tsunami, a terrorist attack, or a global conference. It is useful to think of these events by analogy with a concert or perhaps a marathon, whose success depends on constant, consistent, relentless, tireless, long-term practice and fine-tuning. But the simile is flawed in one crucial respect: both concerts and marathons depend only on the skill of the performer, the audience having been self-selected and disposed—indeed, expecting—to be entertained. Such is not the case in most of the strategic outreach examined in this book. The audience often needs to be convinced to listen to its own music. This is no mere crusade but a kind of physical therapy: we learned that prisoners who had been interred in small spaces for many years nearly lost the ability to walk. Worse, they may also lose the desire.

Moreover, marathons, if perhaps not concerts, may take place without an audience; by contrast, outreach cannot be a solo performance if it is to succeed. The only way to find out is by evaluating the results. No less important than correcting mistakes, evaluations provide proof that something has worked well and should be repeated, mindful of inevitably different circumstances. Private organizations, as well as USAID and other government agencies, do occasionally sponsor a variety of evaluation exercises.[30] But internal evaluation exercises are only useful if they are performed honestly and in a constructive spirit, which is hardly the rule. An overview of the challenges presented by evaluations designed to estimate the impact of democracy assistance on political change is demonstrated by a recent study conducted by Vanderbilt University, the University of Virginia, and the University of Pittsburgh, under the auspices of USAID.[31] That study, however, focuses on measuring the impact of programs on political change—which is altogether different from evaluations of effectiveness regarding specific, immediate goals of a particular project designed to improve the lot of its recipients.

The Vanderbilt study estimated the overall impact of U.S. democracy assistance by the United States government from the end of the Cold War in 1990 until 2003 in quantitative terms. The analysts' conclusion was that such assistance did indeed have a measurable effect, which they take as ample justification to continue funding. By using sophisticated methods (i.e., don't even bother reading unless you took advanced statistics), the study found that, while the total portfolio of democracy assistance "remains a relatively small proportion of total U.S. development assistance," it has "helped to increase democracy above the levels that would have been achieved based on all other factors that could reasonably have mattered" by some specific number, evidently meaningful to nonlaymen.[32] What the study did not do was take a look at the specifics of what works and how, in order to provide the best possible assistance. Most important in that endeavor is to share results and work collegially with others engaged in similar work.

One reason many organizations shy away from conducting evaluations, at least beyond what is required by their funders, is a fear of not meeting what are often seen as unrealistically high expectations. The two party institutes, the National Democratic Institute (NDI) and the International Republican Institute (IRI), for example, have always balked at having to show "impact": they argue, and not without reason, that democracy-building activities are not easily measurable, certainly not in the short run. One of the principal problems is that results have a completely different meaning if what is being built is a school or an attitude, if the end product is voter turnout or how the voter turns out. Both require outreach, but the latter is one gift that should go on giving.

Some evaluations, even in the more amorphous area of democracy building, are stark enough to be heeded or ignored at our peril. An astute recent analysis entitled "Is Civil Society the Answer?" by Middle East expert Amy Hawthorne explains why so much international, and especially U.S., assistance to so-called civil society NGOs was misguided and useless, or worse. She warns against comfortable myths that turn out to be baseless; against assisting the "usual suspects"—NGOs that learn how to talk the talk of donor foundations; about avoiding "cookie-cutter" programs; and about involving civil society organizations more extensively in needs assessments, program design, and—you guessed it—evaluation.[33]

Evaluations are not designed to assign blame; ideally, they serve as learning mechanisms. Some organizations have adapted better than others to evolving circumstances, and have learned their lessons. The Center for International Private Enterprise, which has recently expanded its programs promoting small business leadership and training to foster free market initiatives, is among the most successful.

The CIPE study, entitled "CIPE 15 Year Evaluation: Impact and Results, 1984–1999," by Geoffrey Geurtz, Steven Rogers, and John D. Sullivan, is among the most comprehensive of its kind produced by any nonprofit organization. Among its findings, it lists the evidently useful requirement that all CIPE grantees commit their own financial resources—matching funds—to each project. Those projects are conceived and shaped by the grantees within the context of their own strategic objectives. Midcourse monitoring allows grantees to make any necessary corrections—without doubt the most important element of ongoing evaluation. Financial and project management controls are designed not only to strengthen the organization by holding them accountable for expenditures but for tracking impact and results.[34]

FIFTH RULE: HAVE A SENSE OF HUMOR

The Six Commandments of a writer in a communist country:

1. Don't think.
2. If you do think, don't talk.
3. If you do talk, don't write it down.
4. If you do write it, don't publish it.
5. If you do publish it, don't sign it.
6. If you do sign it, write a denial.

—From C. Bank and Allan Dundes, *You Call this Living?*

Where would we be without a sense of humor? The Jews happened to have made it an intrinsic part of their culture. (An old joke is that God Himself had to have one: what else would explain His creating such a world) Most human societies have a penchant for humor (as in fact, I am increasingly convinced, do other species, but we'll let that pass). No one needs to be reminded of the unequaled power of ridicule: consider Charlie Chaplin's *The Dictator*; the Three Stooges' take on Hitler, Mussolini, and Goehring; John Cleese and company's rendering of the Crusades in *Monty Python and the Holy Grail*; and certainly Mikhail Bulgakov's *The Master and Margarita*. The use of ridicule as a tool of public diplomacy, although admittedly dangerous and re-quiring considerable finesse, is certainly underappreciated and underuti-lized.[35] There are good reasons for hesitancy; hardcore, one-hundred-proof, heavy-duty humor is not for the fainthearted or the culturally tone-deaf. But then, neither is strategic outreach—at least not when it's done right.

The possibilities for humor are limitless. For example, the use of amusing voter education television ads and brochures has proved remarkably success-ful, especially in post-Communist regimes where the former regime's prac-tice of noncontested, uniparty pseudoelections had left a sour aftertaste of deeply entrenched cynicism. But when it comes to humor, it is especially crit-ical to make use of local talent. No one can possibly hope to match the cred-ibility and the deep insights of natives; only they truly know what is funny, and—even more important—only they can deliver the message without seeming condescending or mocking. No one does self-deprecation as well as, well, oneself. Take a look at this *Jewish* joke: "Two Jews are walking in a tough neighborhood when they spot two burly gentiles coming toward them. 'Uh-oh,' one Jew says to the other. 'We better make a run for it. There are two of them, and we're alone.'"[36]

Quite aside from self-deprecating self-reference, which obviously requires self-delivery (non-Poles should never tell Polish jokes), humor in general is highly culture specific, in fact subculture specific. A voter education spot that worked very well in one country, for example, flopped completely in another despite common historical experiences and even the same language. Here goes. A telephone is heard ringing while the camera closes in on a lone tree in the desert. The ring gets louder as the camera gets closer, when a mongol-featured nomad is seen picking up an old-fashioned telephone receiver. After a few mo-ments, he responds, impatiently, "Of course I know that May 3rd [or whatever] is election day!" You got it, right? Tree in the desert? Phone in a tree? Nomad picks up phone? Funny, right? WRONG. The Kazakhstanis watching this clip poker-faced were silent for a while and then protested, "We can't give people all around the world the impression that we don't know you cannot put tele-phones in the desert." Maybe they were thinking that President Nazarbayev

would not be amused; who knows? In any event, the Kazakhstani voter education ads ended up not being very funny. As it happened, neither did the elections.

SIXTH "RULE": FORGET RULES—THINK OUT OF THE BOX

> [W]hen I have won a victory I do not repeat my tactics but respond to cir-
> cumstances in an infinite variety of ways. . . . Thus, one able to gain the
> victory by modifying his tactics in accordance with the enemy situation
> may be said to be divine.
>
> —Sun Tzu

Actually, it takes more than just *thinking* out of the box; it usually requires
getting out of the box altogether—especially when there are a lot of boxes,
some of them more stultifying than others. Take for instance the deceptively
straightforward expression "foreign aid." Many of these activities fall under
the purview of the State Department, notably the Bureau of Educational and
Cultural Affairs, which oversees exchanges, but at least a dozen agencies engage in some form of outreach to foreign nations. It would be a very good
idea to conduct a thorough inventory of taxpayer-funded activities of this
kind: here's a worthy project for the General Accountability Office, to be re-
quested by a congressional member who cares enough to find out.

But the master list should definitely not fail to include projects funded by
state and local government, such as the State Partnership Program (SPP).
Started by George H. W. Bush as a joint experiment by the Pentagon and the
State Department to accelerate the integration of former East European countries into NATO, it has since expanded to the former Soviet Central Asia,
Latin America, and Southeast Asia. The program is funded by the participat-
ing states. Bill Owens, governor of Colorado and vice chairman of the Republican Governors Association, and his aide Troy A. Eid write that "the
SPP's quiet achievements during the past decade have gone largely unnoticed
by many foreign policy specialists in Washington"[37]—never mind anyone
else. Owens and Eid underscore the fact that this was no mere humanitarian
program; while certainly conceived as a way to help reform the armed forces
of former East Bloc nations, it was also meant to strengthen the effectiveness
of state National Guard organizations through professional contacts and exchanges. Eventually, it extended to a variety of military as well as political relationships between states and their partner nations. In other words, the SPP
became a quintessential form of outreach.

Each of the fifty states has a strategic partner: Oklahoma is paired with Azerbaijan (clearly oil), Nevada with Turkmenistan (definitely not the gambling), Georgia with . . . Georgia? (Too cute, but true.)[38] Owens and Eid cite scholars such as Earl Fry "who have long contended that state-level international contacts are increasingly important because they help moderate excessive partisanship and parochialism, particularly in the formulation of U.S. foreign policy by Congress." These analysts point to the North American Free Trade Agreement (NAFTA), which, originally opposed by Congress, later gained support and was finally passed "after a successful lobbying campaign by the nation's governors and state legislators."[39] This is an obvious way to strengthen grassroots support for democracy building.

Another example that comes to mind took place in the summer of 1997, during a meeting that took place at the Department of State, where I was briefing several officials on my recent trip to Albania. The government of President Berisha had just collapsed in disgrace over a corruption scheme, and the Organization for Security and Cooperation in Europe (OSCE) was getting ready to administer elections in just a couple of weeks. IFES had sent me to Tirana frankly to assess whether such a feat was possible, given that the OSCE was actually subcontracting us to do it. Since most of the election experts in the OSCE team were IFES consultants, our reputation was on the line, even though we were perfectly happy to let the OSCE take the credit for running the election. Credit is one thing, blame another.

It did not bode well when, on the first day after our arrival, the Bulgarian head of the OSCE delegation quit, citing personal reasons, but the IFES team pulled together, and within a few days they had the place organized, feeling confident that the election would go smoothly, which I duly reported to the Department of State after assuring myself as best I could that it was probably a gamble worth taking. I had not anticipated that by way of gratitude, the State Department officials would ask me, point blank, whether IFES would organize the official U.S. observation team, which of course would have to consist of at least a hundred observers, maybe two. The European Council was sending its own team, but the United States wanted very much to do the same, to help the new government gain some legitimacy after its disastrous meltdown.

With visions of the entire organization coming to a complete halt in order to mobilize a team of such magnitude, I used every argument at my disposal. I pointed out that IFES does not do election observations in cases where it also assists with the election administration. The answer came back that the OSCE seems not to be hampered by the same, and anyway at this late stage, the State Department itself simply doesn't have the resources to do such a thing quickly. I then noted that we specialized in technical observation, and we absolutely could not and would not lower our standards. That went over even less well; was it necessary to remind anyone in the room about "electoral tourism," one of the less well-known types of junket available to the administration?

As my children will testify, saying no is not my strongest suit, so I did what any vice president does best: I called my boss, the president of IFES, Richard Soudriette. I could hear him smile on the phone; "I have an idea," he said impishly. "Paul De Gregorio [at the time, an election official in St. Louis, currently one of the four members of the Congressional Election Reform Commission] is just about to address the members of the IACREOT [the International Association of Clerks, Recorders, Election Officials, and Treasurers] in Atlanta. I'll call him right away and ask him to ask for a show of hands."

To make a long story short, this is exactly what he did. And instantly, almost every hand went up. Nearly two hundred members of his audience volunteered with alacrity. As I anticipated—and rightly feared—IFES fax machines overheated as resumes came in. A few of the eager volunteers had never left the shores of the United States, but some had actually had international experience. Every one of the applicants was incredibly enthusiastic. The observation went off smoothly; the State Department agreed it had been a complete success. Several went on to other electoral projects, most with IFES, some with other organizations such as the OSCE and the UN. But everyone caught the bug; they fell in love with Albania, and with the idea of helping another country run elections.

"Think out of the box" is not the public diplomacy equivalent of winging it. It requires imagination, innovation, creativity, and flexibility. And it certainly requires quite a bit of research, in order to explore what path to take beyond the box in a judicious, wise, and effective manner. Pilot projects intended to test hypotheses, cooperative enterprises to spread responsibility, and carefully designed feedback mechanisms can each contribute to render the box-exiting enterprise more deliberate and prudent.

A more complicated "box" that governments, nonprofits, and international organizations try, quite deliberately though not always successfully, to circumvent is the age-old prohibition against interference in another country's affairs. This is especially critical for strategic outreach aimed at radical change, or even fairly innocuous "democracy building," which can so easily be interpreted as (since it quite often is) thinly disguised subversion of existing regimes.

Never mind that such targeted U.S. aid—particularly in the area of political party assistance—is either too little, too late, or inappropriately based on the American experience. It is difficult to disagree with Thomas Carothers of the Carnegie Endowment, who writes in a recent issue of *Foreign Affairs*, "Many people around the world—not just autocrats feeling the heat—view external democracy assistance skeptically. They assume that if the United States decides to shape political outcomes in relatively weak countries, it can do so. In many places, the current wave of assertive democracy aid conjures up memories of covert U.S. actions during the Cold War," to say nothing of not-so-covert more recent U.S. actions. It certainly does not help, laments Carothers, that "some Western NGOs, whether propelled by hubris or the desire to convince funders of their importance, have a tendency to claim substantial credit for political events in which they played only a very minor role."[40] Amen.

William Easterly puts it with characteristic bluntness: "All the hoopla about having the right plan is itself a symptom of the misdirected approach to foreign aid taken by so many in the past and so many still today. The right plan is to have no plan."[41] The point is not to opt for anarchy; what he categorically rejects is the illusion that a plan is tantamount to a solution. This is no ideological divide, pitting Right against Left, both of which have supported the "Big Plan" approach, albeit for different reasons: the Left likes the idea of government-led poverty alleviation, while the Right likes imposing capitalism without always paying sufficient attention to the tactics. What they both share is what Easterly refers to as that wretched "White Man's Burden mentality, which emerged from the West's self-pleasing fantasy that 'we' were the chosen ones to save the Rest."[42] The more hardheaded new perspective, articulated by Lael Brainard, is that the main objective behind foreign aid is actually the pursuit of national security: hence what you get is intellectual dissonance caused by contradictory messages, a strong element of self-deception, and the ensuing perception of hypocrisy.

At this point, it may be worth revisiting Rudyard Kipling's famous lines, written just prior to the dawn of the twentieth century, in 1899:

> Take up the White Man's burden—
> In patience to abide,
> To veil the threat of terror
> And check the show of pride;
> By open speech and simple,
> An hundred times made plain,
> To seek another's profit
> And work another's gain.[43]

So much of this resonates with us today. We too have to cope with "the threat of terror," though we must do far more than "veil" it: we have to fight it, intelligently and effectively, with all the means at our disposal. We certainly have to "check the show of pride," and one of the most effective methods is to use "open speech and simple," though ensuring that it is "an hundred times made plain" is no easy task, particularly when what may be "plain" to us is utterly opaque to others. Where Kipling steers wrong, however, is in suggesting that we should "seek another's profit and work another's gain." It is only when others learn how to work for their own gain, when they learn to build their own institutions and protect their own freedom, tending their own gardens, that we can finally declare the "burden" to have been lifted. Except that it's no burden, or should not be seen as such. It is the result of outreach, which should provide joy to those who are lifted from the throes of poverty and tyranny no less than to those of us who enjoy, and enjoy sharing, the fruits of liberty.

Worse even than condescending arrogance is the raw prejudice implicit in the racist juxtaposition of "the white man" as against all "nonwhites." All too thinly camouflaged as "the West versus the rest," which imperceptibly becomes "America against the World," the neocolonialist dialectic must cease as must the patronizing attitude toward the hapless *recipients* of foreign aid, who are in fact our *partners* in outreach. Instead of needing to be treated like children, the poor, the downtrodden, and the long oppressed often know much better than we do what they need and when. They also generally prefer a friendly hand to a handout.

Conversely, the best public diplomacy is not patronizing but collaborative, a dialogue rather than a sermon, particularly when the pews are ideologically stacked against the pulpit. We've been cooped up inside the wrong semantic box far too long. We've been trying to win hearts and minds by branding ourselves as the Dream Goddess that bears the torch of all good things. It's time for a brandnew box. But please don't expect Jack to jump out of it; it will take a great deal of time, patience, and genuine education.

Exactly: just what America has in shortest supply.

NOTES

1. Speech to the Coast Guard Academy commencement, May 21, 2003.
2. Speech at a Jackson Day celebration in Connecticut on January 8, 1920. Woodrow Wilson, *Presidential Messages, Addresses and Public Papers*, 4:456.
3. Col. Ralph O. Baker, U.S. Army, "The Decisive Weapon: A Brigade Combat Team Commander's Perspective on Information Operations," *Military Review*, May–June 2006, 19.
4. Baker, "The Decisive Weapon," 19.
5. GAO-060535, *U.S. Public Diplomacy*, 21.
6. William Easterly, *The White Man's Burden* (New York: Penguin Press, 2006), 6.
7. Easterly, *The White Man's Burden*, 15.

8. Easterly, *The White Man's Burden*, 18.

9. For an overview of the context, methodology, and use of the Central Asian surveys, see my "Democratic Transition in Central Asia: An Assessment," in *SAIS Review*, Summer–Fall 1998, 89–103.

10. http://washingtonpost.com/ac2/wp-dyn?pagename=article&node=&contentId=A1404-2001Jan24notfound=true.

11. *Saudi Publications on Hate Ideology Invade American Mosques* (Washington, DC: Freedom House, 2005), 30.

12. *Saudi Publications on Hate Ideology Invade American Mosques*, 40.

13. See "Damage Control: State Department Officer Works to Dispel Lies, Conspiracy Theories and Urban Legends That Harm U.S. Image," by William Weir, *Hartford Courant*, Oct. 16, 2006.

14. Fawaz Turki, "How to Lose Your Job at a Saudi Newspaper," *Washington Post*, April 15, 2006, A15.

15. www.memri.org/antisemitism.html, Special Dispatch Series No. 1101, February 24, 2006.

16. J. Michael Waller, "Arab Press Fans the Flames of Hate," *Insight*, June 24–July 7, 2003, 22.

17. One organization is particularly worth mentioning: Internews, founded in 1982 primarily to foster independent media in emerging, then fledgling, democracies, later broadening to promote diverse mass media as an essential cornerstone of a free and open society. For nearly a quarter century, Internews has nurtured and developed an entire network of communicators, principally journalists, who stay in touch with the Washington headquarters and with one another: the Global Forum for Media Development was inaugurated in Jordan last October, 2005.

18. Baker, "The Decisive Weapon," 25.

19. Baker, "The Decisive Weapon," 25.

20. Baker, "The Decisive Weapon," 25.

21. Easterly, *The White Man's Burden*, 18.

22. Robert D. Kaplan, *Imperial Grunts: The American Military on the Ground* (New York: Random House, 2005), 154.

23. Kaplan, *Imperial Grunts*, 209.

24. Kaplan, *Imperial Grunts*, 218.

25. Carol Adelman, "Methodology," in *The Index of Global Philanthropy 2006*, 71–81.

26. www.worldpublicopinion.org. According to the results, released on April 17, 2006, 20 percent of countries had a "positive" view of China, while only half as many, 10 percent, had a "positive" view of the United States.

27. www.usaid.gov/stories/afghanistan/fp_afghan_shopkeeper.html.

28. An excellent example is the two-part documentary series *A Force More Powerful*, released on PBS in 2000, based on the book by Peter Ackerman and Jack Duvall. The series documents, using original footage, some of the 20th century's most important yet least-known stories, such as the efforts by Mkhuseli Jack and other South Africans to organize the black community in peaceful resistance against the apartheid

regime; the work by deft and courageous Solidarity leaders who succeeded in mobilizing the Polish people and eventually precipitating the collapse of the Soviet Empire; and the astonishing, coordinated resistance by the Danish people against the Nazi regime.

29. *USAID Primer: What We Do and How We Do It* (Washington, DC: USAID, rev. January 2006), 28.

30. An excellent "lessons learned" analysis of private democratization assistance is the analysis by Kevin F. F. Quigley, *For Democracy's Sake: Foundations and Democracy Assistance in Central Europe* (Washington, DC: Woodrow Wilson Center Press, 1997).

31. Steven E. Finkel, Anibal Perez-Linan, and Mitchell A. Seligson, "The Challenge of Studying the Impact of Democracy Assistance," in final report, *Effects of U.S. Foreign Assistance on Democracy Building: Results of a Cross-National Quantitative Study*, January 12, 2006, 6–12.

32. Steven E. Finkel, Anibal Perez-Linan, and Mitchell A. Seligson, "Conclusions," in final report, *Effects of U.S. Foreign Assistance on Democracy Building: Results of a Cross-National Quantitative Study*, January 12, 2006, 82–87.

33. Amy Hawthorne, "Is Civil Society the Answer?" *Uncharted Journey: Promoting Democracy in the Middle East*, ed. Thomas Carothers and Marina Ottaway (Washington, DC: Carnegie Endowment for International Peace, 2005), 81–113.

34. Geoffrey Geurtz, Steven Rogers, and John D. Sullivan, "CIPE 15 Year Evaluation: Impact and Results, 1984–1999" (Washington, DC: CIPE, 2001), 3.

35. Michael Waller, "Larry, Curly, and Osama: Ridiculing Terrorists as a Weapon of War," *Los Angeles Times*, May 21, 2006.

36. Rabbi Joseph Telushkin, *Jewish Humor: What the Best Jewish Jokes Say about the Jews* (New York: William Morrow, 1992), 77. This is a terrific book about the relationship between jokes and Jewish culture.

37. Bill Owens and Troy A. Eid, "Strategic Democracy Building: How U.S. States Can Help," in *The Battle for Hearts and Minds: Using Soft Power to Undermine Terrorist Networks*, ed. Alexander T. J. Lennon (Cambridge, MA: MIT Press, 2003), 131.

38. www.ngb.dtic.mil/staff/ia/spp_info_paper.shtml.

39. Earl H. Fry, *The Expanding Role of State and Local Governments in U.S. Foreign Affairs* (New York: Council on Foreign Relations Press, 1998), 5.

40. Thomas Carothers, "The Backlash against Democracy Promotion," *Foreign Affairs* 85, no. 2 (March–April 2006), 63. I would argue that another factor motivating my fellow do-gooders is the assumption that our most cherished assumptions are—or should be—shared by all. This was vividly illustrated on May 24, 2006, when David Yang, senior advisor with the UN Development Programme, organized a fascinating roundtable on the topic of "Aiding Political Parties: The Question of Impartiality." Representatives of the International Republican Institute (IRI), the National Democratic Institute (NDI), and the deputy assistant administrator of USAID, Paul Bonicelli, in charge of the Bureau for Democracy, Conflict and Humanitarian Assistance, defended in earnest the proposition that political party assistance can be nonpartisan, and that every possible technique is being used to ensure that democracy and

only democracy is being encouraged. Training, assistance, and general advice are doled out to all who favor a multiparty political dialogue. "Democracy" was being contrasted with "authoritarianism," "one-partyism," and "tyranny," echoing the antinomies heard from the presidential pulpit. Unfortunately, not everyone translates them uniformly. Nor does reality fall into quite such neat boxes.

41. Easterly, *The White Man's Burden*, 5.

42. Easterly, *The White Man's Burden*, 23.

43. http://www.wsu.edu:8080/~wldciv/world_civ_reader/world_civ_reader_2/kipling.html.

Conclusion

Not for Sale

What we in Iran had in common with Fitzgerald was this dream that became our obsession and took over our reality, this terrible, beautiful dream,
impossible in its actualization, for which any amount of violence might be
justified or forgiven. This was what we had in common, although we were
not aware of it then.

—Azar Nafisi

While teaching *The Great Gatsby* in Tehran, before emigrating to the United
States in 1997, Azar Nafisi reports gradually coming to the realization that the
fate of Iranians had become increasingly similar to that of Fitzgerald's tragic
hero: "He wanted to fulfill his dream by repeating the past, and in the end he
discovered that the past was dead, the present a sham, and there was no future."[1] But this is hardly the image of the stereotypical American, who tends
to exude an apocalyptic confidence in the future, more often defying the past
than craving its return. Eminently cognizant of the debt due to the great minds
of ancient civilizations, the Founders neither repudiated the past altogether
nor wished to relive it; they did seek to learn from it, to avoid repeating previous mistakes. A human vessel that looks only to the past for a rudder is
bound to capsize. Yet so is the present, without some map of the future, however approximate, a sorry floundering. Solid grounding requires a small space
in both temporal directions, no more; the center has to hold now.

While obsession with the past is pathological and paralyzing, seeking to
fulfill a dream of nebulous unreality based on metaphysical abstractions can
be even more dangerous. In many ways, of course, there is nothing wrong
with realizing dreams; on the contrary, they guide and energize us all. But
searching to recreate an imagined Golden Age, retrieving a preapocalyptic

purity, is fraught with peril. The genuinely American Dream requires no pre-
historic blueprint; rather, it is predicated on the future infusing the present.

Most commonly, this much-abused expression, "the American Dream,"
refers to upward mobility and personal fulfillment as potentially within anyone's reach. The "American system," which made such a dream possible, was
aptly defined in the nineteenth century by Orestes Brownson as "the abolition
of distinctions founded on birth or any other accident." Implicit in this system
was the right of "every man to stand on his own two feet, for precisely what
God and nature have made him."[2] The unmistakably universal ring of "God
and nature" (God qua nature?), as the divine authority behind this system,
was deliberate: its promise messianic, yet explicitly ecumenical.

Herman Melville spelled it out most boldly in *White-Jacket*: "We Americans are the peculiar, chosen people—the Israel of our time; we bear the ark
of the Liberties of the world."[3] Melville, bard of the sea, may well have been
referring to Noah's Ark when he selected the ark to symbolize America's
promise; he implied that the nation, precariously navigating in the midst of
murderous thunder and lightning, had been predestined to survive. In effect,
nature's God would see to it that the brave vessel carrying "the Liberties of
the world" would sail to safety.

In some ways, America has always had an easier job persuading itself—if
not, perhaps, quite everyone else—that it embodied a dream divine, especially when faced with obstacles, the bigger the better. Abraham Lincoln,
whose piety was notably nonsectarian, confessed, "If ever I feel the soul
within me elevate and expand to those dimensions not entirely unworthy of
its Almighty Architect, it is when I contemplate the cause of my country, de-
serted by all the world beside, and I standing boldly alone and hurling defiance at her victorious oppressors."[4] Far from feeling discouraged when their
ship of state sailed solitary, Americans have tended to believe even more fervently that "the Almighty Architect" would stand by them, steering them to
safety, their hope never more unquestioned than in the thick of the storm.

In essence, it is hope that constitutes the greatest inspiration of the American
Dream—hope for some kind of salvation. Not only does the servant anticipate
that he might someday change places with his master, but, even more radically,
he expects the very relationship to be redefined so as to underscore the common
venture. Put differently, America had not only stated that everyone had been created equal, that we were all brothers (and, eventually, also sisters) who should
stand on our own two feet without anyone arbitrarily preventing us, it has actually come close, certainly closer than any other nation in the history of the world,
to realizing that promise on a large scale. What is more, many Americans feel it
in their souls that they have been chosen to defend the fulfillment of that lofty
promise, on behalf of the Divine Architect, even beyond their nation's shores.

The "Liberties of the world," which Melville proclaimed fated to be rescued by America's ark, implied no preconceived homogeneity: the plural conveys potentially infinite diversity. The American Dream celebrates that diversity, the autonomy of each person's idiosyncratic vision, which has to guide the individual in search of a special place in that world before God. Harvard professor Andrew Delbanco's description of Abraham Lincoln's lifelong "passion to secure justice by erasing the line that divides those with hope from those without hope"[5] happens to capture perfectly the essence of the American Dream.

Azar Nafisi echoes the same idea, in nearly the same terms, although she uses *dream* as a synonym for *hope*. To dream is to imagine, to desire, and to choose what one wishes, without coercion. While agreeing with conventional interpretations of *The Great Gatsby* as the story of an American Dreamer who dreamed too much, who paradoxically sacrificed his life at the altar of his "reinvented" self, she boldly refuses to stop there. Yes, it is true that Gatsby dies.

> The dream, however, remains incorruptible and it extends beyond Gatsby and his personal life. It exists in a broader sense in the city; in New York itself, and the East, the harbor that once became the dream of hundreds of thousands of immigrants and is now the mecca of Midwesterners, who came to it in search of a new life and thrills. . . . The city is the link between Gatsby's dream and the American dream. The dream is not about money but what he imagines he can become. It is not a comment on America as a materialistic country but as an *idealistic* one, one that has turned money into a means of retrieving a dream.[6]

There is nothing crass about this, concludes Nafisi, because it is all about imagination. Without imagination, there is no hope. Hoping, like dreaming, is an emotionally and intellectually nourishing, creative enterprise; it sustains one's very soul. It is the fruit of vitality, the euphoria of promise—which is why some find it so dangerous. It is no accident that Tantalus, who had dared taste of the divine food, was punished by the furious gods with eternal hunger and thirst while the richest food was just out of his reach (yes, "tantalizing"). The fate of every mortal who sought to partake of the ambrosia that nourished the immortal inhabitants of Mount Olympus was equally doomed. Yet hopes and dreams offer just such spiritual sustenance, which is precisely why their pursuit is risky. But it is worth taking a chance, for without imagination, without hope, life is less than worthless.

Admittedly, imagination may well be vacuous, ambiguous, and confusing. It does matter *what* is being imagined; the content, the *object* of one's dreams, may be unmaterial, but is hardly immaterial. There is danger in inferring that tolerance is equivalent to a lack of standards, an "anything goes" mentality.

The late Professor Alan Bloom was right to ring the alarm against a positivist, value-phobic interpretation of America's pursuit of self-defined happiness. In his best-selling *The Closing of the American Mind*, Bloom insists that, on the contrary, "historicism and cultural relativism actually are a means of avoiding testing our own prejudices" by opening everything to doubt, including the right to freedom itself. It thus becomes an open question "whether men are really equal or whether that opinion is merely a democratic prejudice."[7] In brief, intolerance is no less respectable a moral alternative than is nihilistic absolutism. We may all exercise our nocturnal neurological faculties as we wish, but some dreams are surely better described as nightmares.

How men use their freedom, what they do with their political equality, is a separate question from the right to freedom and the assumption of human equality. Bloom defends the latter—democratic—"prejudice" as categorically distinct from its special application, which each person chooses for himself or herself. In other words, we may each decide to play different instruments, but every one of us has the right to select our own. To continue that analogy, one can love music in general yet prefer a particular genre and be especially partial to the fiddle. That is to say, religious tolerance does not have to be incompatible with holding a particular religious belief. Were it so defined, the idea would become meaningless, even outright incoherent. It should be possible to imagine that other religions can be entirely genuine and deserving of respect, even if their theology is essentially inscrutable to outsiders. The inscrutability merely acknowledges the idea of separateness, individuality, and freedom. It implies neither agnostic relativism nor impossibility of dialogue, let alone a "clash of civilizations" predicated on the puzzling assumption that a religious marketplace is necessarily a zero-sum game.

The American vision of tolerance does not require painting one specific idol on the wall of the spiritual cave. But this is unacceptable to someone whose cult is militantly exclusivist. Islamist fanatics who accuse America, as Karl Marx had done nearly two centuries earlier, targeting his fellow Jews, of worshipping at the altar of Mammon cannot be assumed to be entirely disingenuous. Materialism is alive and well in the United States, as indeed everywhere else in the world. Conversely, defenders of America's sectarian religiosity, and yes, it is true that Americans are, or seem to be, more pious than any other modern nation, are also missing an important point, for at issue is not church attendance but the staunch defense of spirituality as an entirely personal affair. The atheist, the agnostic, and the pantheist should be no less capable than a Catholic, Jew, Buddhist, or Muslim of appreciating the value of faith as such, the value of being left free to ponder the meaning of one's existence.

In a marvelous, quintessentially American vein, Oliver Wendell Holmes declared, "Faith, as an intellectual state, is self-reliance."[8] Ever the satirist, H. L. Mencken submitted that "faith may be defined briefly as an illogical belief in the occurrence of the improbable."[9] What both self-reliance and stubborn conviction in the triumph of improbability clearly share is the right of an individual to his own path according to the logic of his own convictions. Others may deem it illogical and may wish to persuade him to take another, in their view, wiser path, and they are welcome to try. They may or may not succeed, but in the final analysis, faith is up to each of us. Those among us whose hearts are "fresh and simple" may yet know "faith in God and nature," while the more jaded will not be as lucky. Cynicism may have its price, but everyone should be allowed to pay it. More likely, it is really out of our hands: a matter of Grace.

In brief, the true humility of the American Dream lies in its absolute, unquestioned universality: everyone should—which is to say, everyone in principle has the right to—pursue his own road to salvation. King and pauper are both entitled to dream, and let no one presume the king to be standing closer to heaven than his financially challenged brethren simply for wearing a crown or its politically correct equivalent. But dreams can only inspire if they represent a genuine possibility—provided, of course, that the dreamer understands everyone else's right to dream along. While much fine academic ink has been spilled defining this latter caveat, Rabbi Hillel in the first century stated it succinctly: "What is hateful unto you, don't do unto your neighbor. The rest is commentary; now go and study."

Expressed in more positive terms, a world where fewer people will do unto others what is hateful to them cannot fail to be better than the present. Fortunately, every day countless people are reaching out to others and sharing of themselves in ways that benefit both sides. Thus everyone wins, including people who aren't in the least aware of it. The American people have the means to be more generous, more philanthropic, than others, but generosity is only one form of outreach, not necessarily the most effective. At least as significant are creativity, energy, and optimism, all found in great supply in the United States.

So how can we make a better case for our nation? A report by the Center for International Private Enterprise, evaluating the organization's work for the past fifteen years, tucks this in toward the very end, in an appendix, in the following words: "In conclusion, CIPE's least tangible but very important contribution has been enhancing the good image of the United States, of its generous aid programs, and of the American way of doing things. The latter include organizing free and open debates, tolerance for different points of view, a 'can do' attitude, and the importance of cooperation and teamwork. In the process, it demonstrated that individuals can make a difference in society, and that they should insist upon exercising that right."[10] Simply put, this is, at bottom, strategic outreach. What a shame so few hear it.

No, America is hardly perfect, and patriotism does not oblige anyone to pretend otherwise. "My country right or wrong," wrote C. K. Chesterton, is like saying, "my mother, drunk or sober."[11] We have made lots of mistakes, and will obviously continue to make more. But far from proving us demonic, our fallibility merely reminds us and the rest of the world that we are human. Yes, we are now perched up on a shining hill, higher than ever: the world's most powerful nation, expected by too many to save humanity from itself. It is no longer a question of wanting to become an empire, of acting as if we are one, or of being one without knowing it. The fact is that we now have a golden opportunity to let the world know who we are. We can at last try to get the message out that the United States was founded on the promise of self-reliance and freedom. Its dream would extend that possibility to everyone, no matter how humble.

Exactly one quarter of a century ago, I picked up a book whose title I found most intriguing: *American Dream, Global Nightmare*. Its young writer, Sandy Vogelgesang, a State Department policy planner and foreign service officer, agonized over the dilemmas raised by President Jimmy Carter's 1977 pronouncements on human rights, troubled by what she called "the gap between expectation and reality." Believing that human rights should not be understood "narrowly" but had to include social and economic dimensions—what Isaiah Berlin called "positive freedoms," sometimes also known as entitlements—she asked of the American people, "Are they ready—faced by the global nightmare of human-rights violations—to give full credence to the American Dream?"[12] There is only one answer to the question as she framed it, and that is, "If that is what you mean by 'the American Dream,' such a task is impossible."

The problem is not merely that America does not have enough resources to address what Vogelgesang correctly identified as "the global nightmare" of repression and misery, but that no one should define our dream in so utterly unrealistic a manner. If our ideal is to right all wrongs, end poverty, and spread the bounty of America across the planet, there is no way to avoid charges of double standards and worse. Sweeping promises that the United States will spread democracy and well-being throughout the world make for uplifting speechifying but can only backfire in the long run. It is not merely a question of humility—although it certainly is that—but of conceptual and, indeed, historical accuracy. America's Dream was defined by self-reliance, or "the pursuit of happiness." It was never intended to secure happiness and well-being to everyone, not even within the borders of the United States. This is not to say that only presidents—and not just Jimmy Carter—have often overpromised. Despite the harm caused by their rhetoric, the justified accusations of hypocrisy and even cynicism, our leaders will undoubtedly continue indulging in their favorite pastime. Overpromising, after all, is just what politicians do for a living.

Not surprisingly, the American promise can only be fulfilled if it embraces human fallibility rather than deny it. As long as any nation considers itself omnipotent, omniscient, all wise, and all good, it is bound to fail. America has risen to greatness partly for valuing the ordinary pleasures of privacy—family, poetry, love, and nature—rather than conquest and power. Equally important has been a strongly held conviction that hard work was needed to attain true glory. It doesn't do any good to pretend that we don't have a long way to go to improve our style of communication. We gotta learn some manners, folks.

Few have articulated this better than our second president, the brilliant, if sometimes impetuous, great patriot John Adams: "My countrymen want art and address," he admitted, meaning that both qualities were *lacking* rather than desired. "They want knowledge of the world. They want the exterior and superficial accomplishments of gentlemen upon which the world has foolishly set so high a value. However, in solid abilities and real virtues they vastly excel in general any people upon this continent."[13] (He might have added, since he believed it, "or any other.") Then, referring to what later would be known as public diplomacy, he observed, "They have not the faculty of showing themselves to best advantage, nor the act of concealment of this faculty," which he attributes partly to his fellow countrymen's "inexperience in the world." Adams draws the inescapable conclusion: "These imperfections must be remedied, for New England must produce the heroes, the statesmen, the philosophers, or America will be no great figure for some time."

John Adams was not merely suggesting that Americans learn how to "show themselves" but that they achieve something worthwhile to show: outright accomplishments, along with the virtues that inspire their proper end, which is the betterment of mankind. To be sure, it wouldn't hurt if Americans also cultivated the faculty of "showing themselves to advantage" in a subtle, truthful, and sincere fashion. But at least they could work on the next best thing—the art of "concealment of this faculty"—for when in excess, a propensity for showing oneself to advantage achieves its opposite. Nothing sabotages even the loftiest actions quite as effectively as brash, clumsy, hard-hitting, insensitive, uninformed arrogance. The most insidious cancer ultimately originates inside the soul, in pride exacerbated by prejudice.

America has since become the great figure that Adams and his fellow Founders had ardently hoped and confidently expected that it would. Its greatness extends beyond her shores to every corner of the world where its ideals are properly appreciated. In America, imperfections that result from circumstance, whether birth, geography, or status, may be conquered with courage and patience—both attributes predicated on humility (in addition to industry and, yes, luck). Should the day come when this simple proposition is both understood and embraced universally, America may claim to have finally fulfilled its Dream.

I am not sure whether we will succeed in conveying this dream to others who have never visited our shores or, if they have, did not feel its true pulse, which lies beyond the glossy surface, the noise, and the anesthetic of consumerism that masks our true nature even (especially?) from ourselves. But I wholeheartedly share the confidence in our nation expressed by the great writer John Steinbeck in his splendid book *America and Americans*, written exactly three decades ago:

> How will Americans act and react to a new set of circumstances for which new rules must be made? We know from our past some things we will do. We will make many mistakes; we always have. We are in the perplexing period of change. We seem to be running in all directions at once—but we are running. And I believe that our history, our experience in America, has endowed us for the change that is coming. We have never sat still for long; we have never been content with a place, a building—or with ourselves.[14]

The book ends on no less humble a note, but his faith is magnificently unflinching:

> We have failed sometimes, taken wrong paths, paused for renewal, filled our bellies and licked our wounds; but we have never slipped back—never.[15]

That is no ordinary pride; it is the flame that lives inside the torch held by Lady Liberty, to light our way in the darkest night.

NOTES

1. Azar Nafisi, *Reading Lolita in Tehran: A Memoir in Books* (New York: Random House, 2003), 144.
2. Cited in Andrew Delbanco, *The Real American Dream: A Meditation on Hope* (Cambridge, MA: Harvard University Press, 1999), 59.
3. Delbanco, *The Real American Dream*, 57.
4. Delbanco, *The Real American Dream*, 59.
5. Delbanco, *The Real American Dream*, 74.
6. Nafisi, *Reading Lolita in Tehran*, 142 (italics in the original).

7. Alan Bloom, *The Closing of the American Mind: How Higher Education Has Failed Democracy and Impoverished the Souls of Today's Students* (New York: Simon & Schuster, 1987), 40.

8. Oliver Wendell Holmes, *The Autocrat of the Breakfast Table* (Reprint Services Corporation, Library Binding 1857), chap. 4.

9. H. L. Mencken, *Prejudices*, Third Series (New York: Octagon Books, 1976), 267.

10. Geoffrey Geurtz, Steven Rogers, and John D. Sullivan, "CIPE 15 Year Evaluation: Impact and Results, 1984–1999" (Washington, DC: CIPE, 2001), 139–40.

11. http://www.dur.ac.uk/martin.ward/gkc/books/The_Defendant.html#A_DEFENCE_OF_PATRIOTISM.

12. Sandy Vogelgesang, *American Dream/Global Nightmare: The Dilemma of U.S. Human Rights Policy* (New York: W. W. Norton & Company, 1980), 28.

13. Cited in the incomparable book by David McCullough, *John Adams* (New York: Simon & Schuster, 2001), 149. McCullough's portrait of Adams captures the quintessential American patriot, whose allegiance to freedom was excelled by none of the other Founders—with the possible exception of his wife, Abigail. But then, she was not a Founding Father but a Mother. (As my mother would say, "So, nuh?")

14. John Steinbeck, *America and Americans* (New York: Viking Press, 1966), 178.

15. Steinbeck, *America and Americans*, 221.

Index

About the Author

Juliana Geran Pilon teaches politics and culture at the Institute of World Politics in Washington, D.C. The author of *The Bloody Flag: Post-Communist Nationalism in Eastern Europe—Spotlight on Romania* and *Notes From the Other Side of Night,* her writings have appeared in the *Wall Street Journal, The American Spectator, The National Interest, The Freeman, Humanitas,* and many other publications both in the United States and abroad. Born in Romania, she received her PhD in philosophy from the University of Chicago, then held postdoctoral fellowships in international affairs at Stanford University's Hoover Institution on War, Revolution, and Peace, and the Institute of Humane Studies. During the 1990s she was Vice President of Programs at IFES (International Foundation for Election Systems) and is a member of the Council on Foreign Relations.